D0256529

ST GEORGE

UNIVERSITY OF WALES, NEWPORT
LIBRARY AND INFORMATION SERVICES
CAERLEON

To the memory of my grandparents
and the mixed heritage they bequeathed me:
English, Scottish, Irish, Romany, Scandinavian, Norman
and who knows what else

ST GEORGE

HERO, MARTYR AND MYTH

SAMANTHA RICHES

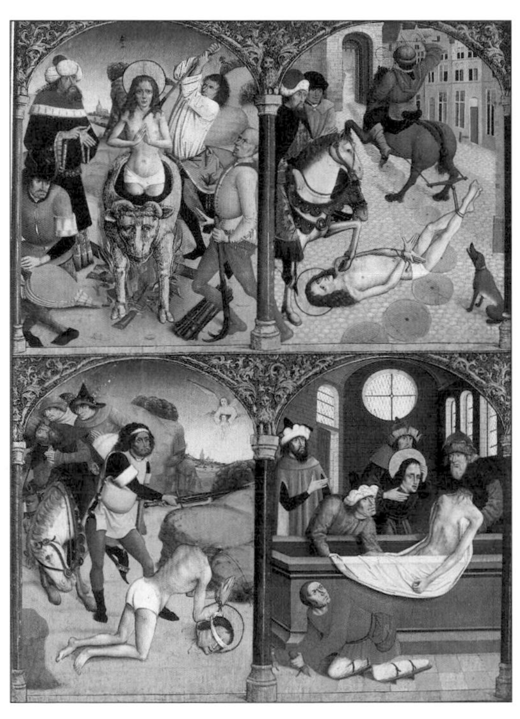

SUTTON PUBLISHING

First published in 2000 by
Sutton Publishing Limited · Phoenix Mill
Thrupp · Stroud · Gloucestershire · GL5 2BU

British Library Cataloguing in Publication Data
A catalogue record for this book is available from the British Library

ISBN 0 7509 3767 X

This paperback edition first published in 2005

Typeset in 11/14 pt Sabon
Typesetting and origination by
Sutton Publishing Limited.
Printed and bound in England by
J.H. Haynes & Co Ltd, Sparkford.

Enfors we us with all our might
To love Seint George, our Lady['s] knight

From a mid-fifteenth-century carol of St George,
BM MS Egerton 3307, fol. 63b

CONTENTS

ACKNOWLEDGEMENTS

Many people have contributed to the completion of this project, some through sharing with me their knowledge of the cult of St George and its associated traditions, others through practical help. My thanks go out to them all; any errors of fact or interpretation are, of course, my own.

Much of the research for this book was carried out during the preparation of my PhD thesis, 'The La Selle Retable: an English alabaster altarpiece in Normandy' at the Department of History of Art of the University of Leicester, and my first debt of gratitude must go to my supervisor, Dr Phillip Lindley. He gave freely of his time, advice and enthusiasm, and I have been very lucky to have benefited from his support and experience. I was also fortunate to receive financial assistance for my research from several organisations, particularly the British Academy, the Research Committee of the Arts Faculty Budget Centre at the University of Leicester, and the Richard III and Yorkist History Trust. Intellectual stimulation has been provided by many friends and colleagues at Leicester, most notably Professor Charles Phythian-Adams and Professor Greg Walker; particular thanks are due to Dr Graham Jones whose perceptive comments on an earlier draft of the text have been extremely helpful. I am also indebted to the University of Leicester Library, especially the Inter-Library Loans Department.

I have received valuable assistance from staff at several other libraries and research facilities: the British Library, the Bibliothèque Nationale, the Society of Antiquaries, the Library and Photographic Collection of the Warburg Institute, the Index of Christian Art at Princeton and the Wiltshire Archaeological Society at Devizes. Many other people have also contributed to this project, too many to name individually, but I am pleased to acknowledge the particular help of Professor Colin Richmond, Dr Eileen Scarff, Dr Sarah Salih, Dr Duncan Givans, Dr Wendy Larson, Philip Lankester, Dr Jenny Alexander, Dr Nigel Ramsay, Professor Pamela Sheingorn, Janet Backhouse, Professor Richard Marks, and Hr Palle, the parish priest of Borbjerg, Denmark. Alison Balaam, language assistant in the Department of Classics at Warwick University, provided very generous assistance with translations from Latin. I would like to express special gratitude to Dr Miriam Gill, who has given unsparingly of her time, knowledge and enthusiasm, and whose bibliographical suggestions have proved invaluable. In France I am indebted to Christine Jablonski-Chauveau, Conservator of Antiquities and Objets d'Art of the Eure *département*, Annick Gosse-Kischinewski and the staff of the Departmental Archives of the Eure at Evreux, and the mayor and community of Juignettes and La Selle.

Practical support was also offered by many friends in the form of hospitality during research trips and the provision of obscure books and other material: Cath Ranzetta and Roger Llewellyn, Annick Toujani, and Brian and Mary Goddard were especially helpful. In many ways the most essential support has been the provision of the childcare which allowed me to carry out my work, and I would like to acknowledge the contribution of Alex Davies in particular.

My editors, Christopher Feeney and Clare Bishop, have been very supportive throughout the process of transforming an academic thesis into a work of more popular history. I have also profited from the assistance of several other individuals and organisations during the additional research undertaken for this book, most notably the Guild of St George, the Royal Commission on the Historic Monuments of England, Dr Julian Eve, Georgia Wilder, and Steve Bell. I am very grateful to correspondents who have contacted me with suggestions for revisions since the publication of the first edition, notably Christopher Stace, Jeremy Harte, Claude Blair and Dr David Woods.

My greatest debt of gratitude is, however, to my long-suffering family. My son Kishon McGuire has accepted changes of home, school and carers with equanimity during my studies, and followed me around the churches, museums and galleries of England and France in search of saints and dragons with (usually) remarkable good humour, throughout the period of my PhD studies and the subsequent writing of this book. My parents, John and Olivia Riches, have offered emotional financial and practical support in many ways, and my former partner, Tom McGuire, similarly contributed to the successful completion of this work. I sincerely hope that all four of them are satisfied that their investment in me, in all its forms, is finally bearing fruit.

PREFACE

St George is the archetype of a figure who is instantly recognisable but little understood. At the beginning of the twenty-first century his image and emblem are all around us, everyday sights whose true meanings are rarely considered and, when they are, may often seem elusive. He is now invariably shown in combat with a dragon, a motif that frequently appears on items such as coinage and commercial insignia, while his flag, the red cross on a white ground, flutters on church towers and is painted on the faces of soccer fans. He is invoked by English nationalists, even claimed as a native of this country on occasion, and his encounter with the dragon is commonly used as a paradigm of the eternal struggle of good against evil, doubtless in the hope that the saint's victory indicates that good will eventually prove triumphant. English people are all familiar with the idea of him as their patron saint, their emblematic special protector, but few have any real idea of how and why he came to hold this position in English consciousness.

This book sets out to examine not only the 'truth' about St George – who he was, when he lived and what happened to him – but also when and why he came to be recognised as England's patron saint. Furthermore, it examines the wide range of meanings associated with him during the late medieval period, the time when his role in England's conception of itself was consolidated. The focus is primarily on the period between 1300 and 1550, a time of huge social, political and religious change across Europe which witnessed events such as the Black Death, a pandemic of the plague that killed between a third and a half of the population of Europe and reached England in 1348, and the Reformation, the theological quarrel sparked off by Martin Luther's 'Ninety-Five Theses' of 1517. These events had far-reaching social, political, religious, economic and psychological consequences, which included such fundamental issues as the end of feudalism and the rise of the middle classes towards one end of our time-frame, and, at the other, the break-up of the established Roman Church and the radical reappraisal of many social mores, such as the importance of marriage and family life. This book obviously does not aim to offer an analysis of these hugely important events, or to present an overview of the changing dynamics of English society and religious beliefs during these years. However, it must be recognised that the cult of St George did not develop, and could not, have developed inside a vacuum. Individuals' devotion to this saint was undoubtedly affected by these far-reaching historical changes: part of the function of a saint is surely to act as a steadfast figure of refuge, offering the hope of intervention or succour during the trials of human existence. Thus large-scale events such as wars, outbreaks of disease, the deaths of monarchs and religious and social changes form a kind of backdrop – seldom referred to yet present none the less – to the much smaller-scale narrative played out in these pages.

Some developments do play a more important role, however, and of these we should perhaps make special note of the rise of lay literacy, which is now recognised as an important aspect of the later Middle Ages. To a great extent this phenomenon seems to have been a concomitant of the development of an educated, and relatively affluent, middle class who were able to indulge both their pieties and their ostentation through the purchase, display and use of Books of Hours and other devotional manuscripts. An ability to read (although not necessarily also to write) opened up a whole world of religious possibilities to the devout lay man or woman, since reverence of God, in all his forms, the Virgin Mary and the saints no longer needed to be mediated through a priest. Rather, we encounter for the first time a clear desire of people outside the cloister to form a personal relationship with the objects of their veneration as well as the increasing availability of means by which this could be achieved.

In the early medieval period God had often seemed to be a remote and rather threatening figure of majesty and wrath, but as the later Middle Ages developed it is clear that new forms of devotion were arising within the Roman Church which encouraged a view of Christ as truly human as well as truly divine. Perhaps the most significant aspect of this trend was the movement now known as 'mariolatry', a cult that identified the Virgin Mary as a figure of importance in her own right, rather than simply as a convenient functionary of God the Father. By identifying the Virgin as a human being, albeit a perfect one conceived – according to the doctrine of the Immaculate Conception – without the stain of Original Sin, late medieval people were able to approach their God in the knowledge that this human intercessor would help their case if only they called on her with sufficient fervour and proved their devotion through prayers, pilgrimages, the veneration of her images and the giving of alms in her name. Saints could also be called upon to aid their human devotees, particularly when an individual saint was identified as being powerful healer in cases of a specific disease, for example. The possibility of visiting conveniently-located relics would undoubtedly have encouraged the cults of particular saints, but it will become clear that other factors seem to have been at work as well.

Another important development in late medieval society which should also be borne in mind is the rise of the guilds – groupings of lay people, sometimes retaining their own priest – which originally were purely religious in nature but soon came to be important in the control of both trade and civic government. The guilds were often, but not always, associated with a patron saint: as we shall see, the role of St George guilds seems to have been crucial in the urban social scene.

The conclusions suggested by this survey of St George's appearances in late medieval literature, historical sources and the visual arts are often surprising and sometimes unsettling, with apparently conflicting readings occurring with disconcerting regularity. We can perhaps view the cult of St George as indicative of late medieval society as a whole: many-layered and multifaceted, with an ability to give easy credence to apparently contradictory ideas. In the manner of Lewis Carroll's White Queen, believing six impossible things before breakfast was perhaps less of a challenge to the fifteenth-century English man or woman than it would be to a modern person, especially when those beliefs appear to be set up in opposition to each other. Hence St George will be considered in these pages as symbolic of both fertility and chastity; as a tortured martyr oppressed by a heathen ruler as well as a figure of noble authority; as a symbol of English nationhood in general but also a representative of quite discrete parts of English society. Even his very identification as the patron saint of this country is questioned, with an examination of his special relationship with several other countries and peoples.

The book opens with an examination of the earliest sources on St George and an overview of the ways that his legend and cult develop throughout the medieval period. This is followed by a detailed appraisal of those aspects of the saint's life and legend which seem to have been most salient to late medieval people, and we end with a review of post-medieval developments in the cult of St George in England and beyond. The ultimate aim is to facilitate a deeper understanding of this saint's position in the English psyche, while also uncovering some of the ways in which late medieval societies seem to have used religious figures as a vehicle for exploring aspects of their own lives and belief systems. We should, however, venture at the outset of this study to ask a few questions about the very nature of such an inquiry, and to define our terms of reference.

The study of sainthood is a field beset with difficulties. No aspect of it is without controversy, particularly when the modern-day writer seeks to reconstruct the mind-set of long-dead individuals and communities by utilising what may seem to amount to little more than a few oblique references in obscure texts or artworks. Even the very nature of what may and may not be discussed is open to debate: is hagiography, the writing and rewriting of a saint's life and supposed miracles, something that says more about the concerns of the individual writer and his or her community than about the 'facts' of a saint's existence? Is the search for the original, or *ur*, text the only worthwhile task, or are the later variations, subtractions and additions of equal, or even greater, value? Should hagiology, the study of saints and their cults, necessarily include or exclude less tangible evidence, such as slight references to images or practices long since destroyed or forgotten? For instance, a particular altar, image or votive light of a saint may be mentioned in only one will, made by an otherwise obscure benefactor. One such example is John Sayntmaur (or 'de St Maur'), who bequeathed a cow, valued at 10*s*., in his will of 1485, the profit of which (probably derived from the sale of the animal and subsequent investment of the proceeds) was to fund a wax taper to be burnt on Sundays and feast days before an image of St George in his local parish church of Rode (Somerset). Is it really desirable to cite this reference as evidence of a local cult of St George when we have no idea how large or valuable the image was, how many other people expressed their devotion to the saint through recourse to it, or even for how many years it was the object of individuals' interest?

How, indeed, should a saint cult be defined? One interpretation would suggest that a cult is something which is purely liturgical, based around the practices of the established Church where a clerical process was able to establish who was entitled to be called a saint and how they should be revered and invoked, but an alternative view would suggest that this 'imposed' religiosity was actually less important than the 'sainthood by acclamation' model, where popular movements were able to propel individuals to the official, or unofficial, status of saint. This current study tries to straddle both definitions, allowing that while the veneration of St George was officially encouraged the cult was also the product of genuine interest from ordinary people. Devotion to this saint was by no means the preserve of one specific group within late medieval society, but different manifestations of it were particularly important to some discrete groupings: the cult evidently fulfilled many different needs.

One particular problem faced by historians working in the pre-modern period is the undoubted loss of so much potentially significant evidence. In relation to saint cults, we can see that manuscripts and books containing legends, miracles or the scripts of dramatic presentations about saints may have been discarded, burnt, whether accidentally or deliberately, or allowed to be irreparably damaged by poor storage conditions. Paintings and sculptures of saints may have suffered the same fate, or have been deliberately defaced by iconoclasts, while many churches and other buildings that may have been connected with a saint cult have been demolished or refurbished, with consequent losses of wall paintings, stained glass windows, sculpted decorations, and so forth.

The evidence that would have been provided by these lost items is unquantifiable and irretrievable, but perhaps of even greater significance is evidence for a devotion to a saint which was never recorded in any tangible form. The extent to which late medieval England was an illiterate society is open to question, but it seems fair to say that, despite the rise of a literate middle class, a considerable part of the populace would have been largely illiterate and hence would have had little access to, or use for, written accounts of a saint's life and deeds, unless they were able to listen to someone else reading these works aloud. Furthermore, impoverished peasants would only rarely have had either the opportunity or the means to purchase even relatively cheap devotional objects, such as pilgrim badges or small images made from plaster or tin, even though their personal attachment to the saint may have been every bit as strong as the devotion of a much richer person who could afford to commission a magnificent image or even endow a chapel in the saint's honour. We know from the evidence of late medieval wills that many people chose to show their veneration of a saint by bequeathing money to buy wax to be burnt on an altar dedicated to that saint – this kind of activity was open to anyone with the means to buy or make a candle – but unless the person was wealthy enough to need to make a will (a group that excludes virtually all women, except widows of some property) there would be no tangible evidence for later historians to uncover. Likewise, many people will have undertaken pilgrimage to a particular shrine or image associated with a saint, and the vast majority of these pilgrimages will not have been recorded in any way.

In the light of these problems it may seem tempting to restrict an inquiry such as this current study to incontrovertible evidence, to consider only well-attested aspects of the cult of St George, such as chivalric orders, royal foundations and artistic achievements commissioned by named individuals. Yet such a survey, while relatively simple to research and write, would do a real disservice to our forebears, for it would omit any sense of the reverence felt for St George by the community at large during the late medieval period. A study of a saint cult, particularly one that seems to have been so widespread and so long-lasting, demands an inclusive approach despite the difficulties associated with reconstructing the concerns, loyalties, aspirations and mores of long-dead people who have left few traces of their lives. To privilege the accessible, easily quantified evidence left to us, which largely originates from one small section of society – the educated, the literate and the wealthy – over the concerns of the main body of the population is both undesirable and indefensible, and it is with this in mind that we should approach the texts, objects and records discussed in this book. For the most part we will be looking at accidents of survival, and we should always remember that, while these items may not have been truly representative of the actuality of the late medieval cult, they are important clues to reconstructing the society that created them. In default of direct evidence about their creation and use it is impossible to make definitive statements about these items; we can, however, suggest possible readings, and it is in this spirit that this book is conceived.

The types of evidence for the cult of St George considered in this book fall into three main categories, and for ease of reference I have endeavoured to maintain consistency in my use of language. Firstly, there is literary evidence, such as prose, poetry, drama and allusions within other texts. A major part of this literary evidence consists of retellings of the legend of St George, and within this book a literary retelling is referred to as a *life*. (Full details of the lives referred to appear in the bibliography.) Secondly, there is visual evidence, which takes the form of single images or groups of images; where a group of images forms a narrative it is referred to as a *cycle*. Finally, there are historical records. This evidence is derived from primary textual sources such as wills, invocations, civic ordinances and the records of guilds and other organisations.

Whilst these designations of literary, art historical and historical forms are largely discrete, there are some types of evidence that cannot be categorised so easily. For example, a literary text may be illustrated with images, for instance, in Alexander Barclay's *Life of St George* (1515), which is decorated with a cycle of woodcuts (see illustration 5.30). Again, we know that a St George play was held at Lydd (Kent) at least twice during the second half of the fifteenth century; no evidence survives about the text performed, the staging, or even whether the 'script' was varied between performances, so what we have, in effect, is a brief historical record of a literary event. This kind of cross-category evidence can be difficult to interpret accurately as we are invariably confronted with the product of several individuals' work that may not have been coordinated. For example, the woodcuts used in Barclay's *Life of St George* may well have been created with no reference at all to the specific narrative that the author was using; illustrations may sometimes simply decorate the text that they accompany, but at other times they appear to reinforce, or even to subvert, the written word. Another factor to be considered is the evidence may have been filtered through different levels of recording (the dates of the performances of the Lydd play are noted in the parish churchwardens' accounts, a source that would been more concerned with financial aspects, for example, than with the niceties of the theatrical form used).

Cross-category evidence needs to be treated very carefully, but, as with the use of the evidence of veneration drawn from accidental survivals discussed above, it does seem essential to make this study of the cult of St George inclusive rather than exclusive. Hence, as readers and researchers, we should always consider that the readings offered by students of saint cults cannot and do not pretend to the status of 'truth'. This book is written in a spirit of such investigative detection, with due allowance to the fact that alternative readings can and should also be sought through further research into this saint and devotion to him.

CHAPTER ONE

THE DEVELOPMENT OF THE CULT OF ST GEORGE

St George is enigma personified. He is one of the most widely recognised hagiographical figures in the canon of the Church – the legend of his encounter with the dragon is common currency – yet he is far more than a mere romantic hero 'skilled in Dragon Management and Virgin Reclamation'.[1] Close investigation of the literature and iconography of his cult soon reveals that this saint is a highly complex figure. In the sub-title of his 1983 study, Sir David Scott Fox calls St George 'the saint with three faces'; I fear that he does our hero an injustice with a partial truth. For St George appears in many more guises than three. He is, of course, the chivalrous knight who rescues the fair lady from certain death, but he is also an ancient symbol of light and power engaged in perpetual struggle with the forces of darkness and chaos. He is the Christian hero who demands the conversion of an entire town before he will despatch the dragon who has claimed so many lives, yet he is also Al Khidr, the mythic hero of Islam. His legend is deeply concerned with the power of chastity to overcome evil, but he is also a strong symbol of fertility. Equally, he is the patron saint of England, and is often thought to be an honorary, if not actual, son of this country. However, he is also patron of places ranging from Catalonia to the Danish town of Holstebro, while the Black Sea state of Georgia is actually named in his honour.

St George was a hugely popular saint throughout the Middle Ages: over 100 visual cycles of his legend, dating from the early twelfth century to the end of the sixteenth century, are still extant throughout Europe, besides countless individual images, almost all of which depict his combat with the dragon. In England alone almost 100 medieval wall paintings of St George are known, around half of which are still legible to some extent. In addition, a considerable number of literary versions of his life survive, including eight English and Scottish versions dating from between the eleventh and sixteenth centuries. Over the course of the 1,700 years that have elapsed since the probable date of his death there have been innumerable, sometimes quite startling, variants of St George's legend. These are found in both the literary and visual records of devotion to him, and several of the most interesting variations were apparently well known in late medieval England but have subsequently been largely forgotten. These aspects of the cult form a major part of this study, but a secondary theme is concerned with the comparisons that can be drawn between St George and his analogues throughout the cultures of the world: the fundamental concept of the mythic hero who overcomes a monster is both widespread and long-lived. It seems very likely that the story of St George has been informed by the legends of these non-Christian figures, and when viewed in this light it is evident that the roots of his cult penetrate the deepest realms of religious belief.

As St George embodies such a diverse group of themes and patronages, we need to be certain which aspects are being presented when we examine the role he plays within any one image or narrative. We need to be careful to consider not only the date and provenance of the work, but also the audience for which it was intended. Given that there is this multiplicity of factors at work in the presentation of the saint, it is essential to have a grasp of the history of the cult in order to be able to make some sense of it. This chapter considers the genesis of reverence of St George and the spread of this devotion to Western Europe during the early Middle Ages. The evidence for the 'real' life and death of the man identified as St George is assessed, alongside the probable reasons for the development of his 'fictional' story and the impact of imagery and ideas associated with other figures, both Christian and non-Christian. But before we begin this detailed examination it will be wise to refresh our memories of the conventional history of the saint, beginning with the largest source of information, the hagiographical material.

St George's legend was very popular throughout the medieval period, but it was subject to a great deal of reinterpretation. Tables 1, 2 and 3 (see pp. 218–21) summarise the various extant accounts in Old English, Middle English and a Scottish dialect, along with two Latin versions. It is readily apparent that there is a marked disparity between the different retellings. For example, the dragon episode, which is now generally assumed to be *the* legend, does not appear at all in Ælfric's version of the *Life*, and the tortures inflicted on St George vary a great deal. Yet some aspects are relatively consistent, and the basic medieval written legend can be summarised as follows:

> St George, whose name is derived from the Greek term for 'a tiller of the soil', a Christian and an officer in the Roman army, is called upon to sacrifice to the Roman gods. He refuses to do this, and is then detained and tried before a heathen ruler (usually

> called Dacian). St George is tortured on the rack and the wheel, and is subjected to other improbable torments such as being dismembered and boiled (see, for example, illustrations 3.5 to 3.9 and 3.20). He steadfastly refuses to sacrifice, and many onlookers are converted to Christianity. He is also given a poisoned drink by a powerful magician named Athanasius (illustration 3.9); when this fails the magician himself is converted. St George is ultimately beheaded (illustration 3.10), and the heathen ruler is often said to die immediately afterwards.

The story is enhanced by variations such as the conversion of the heathen ruler's wife and an episode where St George pretends to recant, visits the heathen temple and then throws down the idol, which is usually said to be Apollo or Bacchus (illustration 3.11, the late fifteenth-century Borbjerg retable, depicts St George before the heathen temple in the central panel). This story of the witnessing, torture and death of St George can be characterised as the 'martyrdom legend'; it demonstrates a direct conflict between Christianity and the classical Graeco-Roman religions, which is typical of the lives of early Christian martyrs.

In most versions of St George's legend an episode is included where he rescues a princess, and this is a clear deviation from the standard model of a Christian martyr. This story was apparently not recorded before the tenth century, but its inclusion in the mid-thirteenth-century *Golden Legend* version of the Life of St George ensured that it became a standard motif in subsequent treatments of the legend of the saint even though the order in which these events were thought to have occurred relative to the martyrdom is often uncertain. The basis of this story is that a water-dwelling dragon has been threatening a town in Libya, usually called Silene, with its pestilential breath and, in order to keep it away, the people have been giving it sheep. When the supply of sheep begins to fail the people agree to sacrifice one child and one sheep each day. Lots are drawn, and eventually the king's only daughter is chosen. The king asks for her to be spared, but the people threaten to burn him and his palace if he refuses to give her up to the dragon. In most accounts a grace period is agreed, and then the princess is sent out with her sheep. She is wearing her best clothes, but sometimes is explicitly said to be dressed as a bride. St George, the knight-errant, then arrives and offers to kill the dragon. The princess protests but the saint insists on fighting the monster, and succeeds in wounding it with his lance or spear. He then instructs the princess to fasten her girdle around the dragon's neck, and she leads it back to the city as if it were a dog. Everyone is very frightened, but St George says that he will kill the dragon if all the people will convert to Christianity; in some cases the dragon is already dead when the baptism takes place. He then baptises the king and many thousands of his subjects, and asks for a church to be built. The king offers the saint a reward, usually money but sometimes land or the princess's hand in marriage. St George refuses, but teaches the king about Christian belief and then goes on his way.

Illustration 1.1 from the Salisbury Breviary, a French manuscript created for John, Duke of Bedford *c.* 1424–35 (Paris, Bibliothèque Nationale, MS Lat. 17294), illustrates several episodes of the dragon story within one image: St George meeting the princess, fighting the dragon, then accompanying the princess as she leads the subdued beast towards the city as the inhabitants flee in fear. St George wears armour throughout the narrative and is identified by a little crest of a red cross on a white background on his helmet. He carries a shield bearing the same device in the scene of the combat with the dragon. The story begins on the left side in the background, where the king, queen and princess look out of the window of a castle labelled 'Sylene'. In the centre St George, mounted, speaks with the princess who stands in the gateway of the castle. They each have a speech scroll; George's reads '*Filia quid p[rae]stolari*' (Daughter, what are you waiting for?), the princess's reads '*bone iuvenis fuge*' (Run away, nice young man!). Then, in the background, St George spears the dragon in the mouth while the princess kneels in prayer behind him. Finally, in the foreground, the princess leads the dragon with a girdle, while St George, having dismounted, spears the dragon through the neck from behind. A group of five citizens flee from them as they approach.

This presentation of several aspects of the narrative within one image, a relatively common device in late medieval art, also occurs in a late fourteenth-century carved chest-front (illustration 1.2). Here we find St George encountering the princess at the top of the composition, in the upper left corner. The combat is depicted immediately beneath, with the princess praying on the far left. In the centre we see St George riding back towards the city, following the princess who leads the dragon on a leash. Her watching parents are visible as two crowned heads, looking out from a tower in the midst of the town buildings. A large lion sits outside the town gates, looking back towards the town itself: his exact meaning is unclear, but he is one of a number of wild animals present in the image, and it seems likely that together they are intended to evoke a sense of the natural, uncultivated wilderness that lies beyond the safety of the city wall.

In common with those of most other early saints, St George's legend, or legends, have little grounding in historical accuracy. But not everyone has been dissuaded from belief in him, however slight the evidence. 'That St George is a veritable character is beyond all reasonable doubt, and there seems no reason to deny that he was born in Armorica, and was beheaded in Diocletian's persecution by order of Datianus, April 23rd, 303.' Brewer's *Dictionary of Phrase and Fable* (1894) could hardly be more wrong. Far from being a

Opposite: *1.1 The Salisbury Breviary, 1424–5: the narrative of St George and the dragon with images of the trial of St George. (Bibliothèque Nationale, Paris. MS Lat.17294, fol. 448)*

Sylene
puincia huc aduenisti: uel quo
nomine vocitaris. Sanctus ge
orgius dixit. xpianus ✝ dei
seruus sum: georgius nuncu
por genere capadocus prie mee
comitatum gerens. Elegi vero
temporali carere dignitate: et
inmortalis dei unpio deseruire.
Dacianus dixit. Erras
georgi: accede ✝ im
mola deo appollini.
Beatus georgius respondit. Do
mino ihesu xpisto exhibeo cultu
ram omnium seculor: non appol

1.2 Late fourteenth-century carved chest-front of the narrative of St George and the dragon. (Victoria & Albert Museum, London)

definitive statement on the saint, this commentary merely provides an opportunity for dissent among the cognoscenti, for there is no aspect of St George's life that is incontrovertible, whether his birthplace, profession, the year of his death or details of his tortures. Despite Brewer's bold assertion, St George is rarely hailed as a native of Armorica (an ancient name for Brittany), but is strongly associated with the Palestinian towns Joppa (the modern-day Jaffa) and Diospolis (or Lydda). Both claim to be the site of his martyrdom, and the latter claims to be his birthplace too. Furthermore, the fact that the saint is often given the appellation 'St George of Cappadocia' is recognition of a tradition that he originates from this area of central Turkey.

Confusingly, there is also an historical figure called 'George of Cappadocia', a character of somewhat different pedigree who is never likely to be canonised. He is quite well documented and is known to have pursued a career selling questionable pork to the Roman army, later rising to the position of Archbishop of Alexandria. A known adherent of the Arian heresy, a belief system that questioned the divinity of Jesus, he was murdered in AD 362 by an angry mob. A small group of commentators, notably Edward Gibbon in *The History of the Decline and Fall of the Roman Empire*, have attempted to identify St George with this George of Cappadocia, and succeeded in sullying the saint's reputation to a considerable extent. However, it seems unlikely that such a heretic could become a saint of orthodox Christianity, and the discovery during the nineteenth century of two churches dedicated to St George, at Shaqqâ and Ezra in Syria, effectively closed the question for they were built around AD 346 and hence predate the death of George of Cappadocia by some sixteen years. An inscription at the Ezra church stated that it contained 'the cherished relic of the glorious Victor, the holy Martyr George'. This statement clearly identifies *this* St George as a martyred Christian, which is entirely congruent with the 'original' martyrdom legend. However, although some commentators have claimed that the Ezra inscription is consistent with a date of AD 346, others have placed it as late as AD 515: this disagreement clearly throws the whole issue into yet more confusion. Despite this rather difficult, and perhaps self-contradicting, evidence, it is still quite possible that the life and exploits of George of Cappadocia had some influence on the emerging cult of St George. The Arian George seems to be the first person recorded bearing the Greek name 'Georgios', and given that there is no historically authentic reason to connect St George with Cappadocia it seems quite possible that a conflation of the two figures may have given rise to the tradition that locates the saint in this area. The dubious Archbishop George of Cappadocia did at least have the advantage of definitely having existed, something that cannot be claimed with any veracity of the 'actual' St George.

The story of the 'real' St George which seems to have the widest currency is set in Nicomedia, the town on the Asiatic shore of the Bosphorus which was one of the official residences of Emperor Diocletian (ruled AD 284–305). Towards the end of the third century, Christianity was generally tolerated in the Roman Empire, with the faith openly professed by many people of rank, up to and including Diocletian's wife and daughter. However, there was ill-feeling among non-believers, which seems to have been directed particularly at Christian soldiers who were thought to be breaching disciplinary codes as a consequence of their religion. Several were executed at the turn of the century, but then a subversive plot was discovered in which believers were said to be involved. All soldiers were ordered to sacrifice to the Roman gods, and on 23 February AD 303 the Praetorian Guard razed the Cathedral of Nicomedia. The next day saw the issue of an edict effectively outlawing Christianity: churches and writings were to be destroyed, meetings for worship were forbidden, and Christians who held office were stripped of their posts. Some commentators claim that those Christians who did not hold office were expected to submit to slavery, and all were to lose their civil rights, a change in legal status which meant that previously protected people could now be subjected to torture. The edict was ruthlessly enforced throughout the Empire, and many believers were martyred; in Britain St Alban was among those who suffered.

Eusebius, an ecclesiastical historian and Bishop of Caesarea who lived in the mid-fourth century, writes that when the decree was published in Nicomedia an unnamed man of high rank tore it down and publicly destroyed it. Eusebius records that he was the first Christian in that district to be martyred under the terms of the edict, and that he was tortured, imprisoned and executed but bore every torment with great courage. Some later versions of the story name the anonymous man as St Nestor, a close cognate of several aspects of St George in the Greek tradition, but most commentators claim that the man in question was St George himself. Established facts about the hapless martyr are undoubtedly in short supply in this story, but little time elapsed before extra material was grafted on to these bare bones, much of it probably drawn from the traditions of other martyr–saints. St George is said to have been a soldier native to Cappadocia, or perhaps Lydda, and early writers tend to picture him as a Roman officer of some rank. It is claimed that after his destruction of the edict he went to the Temple of Bacchus and threw down the statue of the deity; he is said to have later refused to sacrifice, and was then tortured and martyred on a date usually identified as 23 April AD 303. Sir Ernest Wallis Budge, keeper of near Eastern manuscripts at the British Museum in the late nineteenth century, and a noted authority on early Christianity, argued that the martyrdom is likely to have taken place some fifty years earlier, on the basis of inferences he drew from the *Chronicon Paschale*, a Byzantine work of the early seventh century. However, Budge remains isolated in this view. The cults of soldier–saints such as St Nestor seem to have been very influential on the development of St George's legend. St Menas, another very popular Eastern saint whose cult seems to predate that of St George, has a legend which is remarkably similar. In early versions of their lives the details of their military careers are virtually identical, and both were persecuted by a tyrannical heathen ruler. It is also notable that St Menas is associated with the cure of skin diseases, particularly 'the scab', which is remarkably close to St George's identification as a healer of scaly skin conditions; both are also strongly linked to the ideal of chastity. A third soldier–saint whose cult may have influenced St George's own is St George of Bydda. This obscure figure is noted by only one commentator, with little clear evidence, but claims of links to both Cappadocia and and Georgia may be significant.

Meanwhile, a group of fourth- and fifth-century Coptic texts provides very detailed information about the saint: he is said to have been born in AD 270 at Militene, a city in Cappadocia where his father, a Christian named Anastasius, was governor. Anastasius's own father, John – also a Christian – is said to have been the governor of the entire province. St George's mother is named as Kîra Theognôsta, the daughter of Dionysus, Count of Lydda: a neat device that allows the two main sites claiming St George to be given similar weighting. Even more interestingly, Kîra Theognôsta is said to be related to 'the saints that dwelt at Lydda' mentioned in the Acts of the Apostles (chapter IX, verses 32–5) as well as to Joseph of Arimathea: linking pseudo-historical saints with 'real' Biblical characters was a common medieval device aimed at substantiating the claims to sanctity of otherwise dubious figures. On the death of her husband Anastasius, Kîra Theognôsta returned to Lydda with her ten-year-old son George and his two younger sisters Kasia and Mathrôna (whose names are the Coptic forms of 'Katherine' and 'Martha', two saints whose legends bear striking similarities to some aspects of St George's legend, as we shall see). In one version no mention is made of the return to Lydda: instead, George was adopted on the death of his father by the new governor, Justus, who trained him as a soldier and betrothed him to his own daughter. But before the marriage could be formalised, Justus died and George entered military service under Emperor Diocletian, serving alongside the young Constantine in both the Egyptian campaign of AD 295 and the subsequent Persian War. The narrative then recounts the story of the purge of Christianity from the Roman army, George's tearing down of the decree at Nicomedia, and his subsequent martyrdom.

Despite the well-constructed legend set out in these Coptic manuscripts, a rather different story is found in a fragmentary manuscript dated to *c.* AD 350–500, which was discovered under a fallen pillar in the cathedral of Q'as Ibrim during the construction of the Aswan Dam in 1964. This version is written in Greek but was probably composed by a Nubian: it has been suggested that the historical saint may have originated from the kingdom of Nobatia in the Nubian region, an area of the Nile Valley between Aswan and Khartoum. Despite its probable provenance, in this version St George is again identified as a Cappadocian, but this time his Christian mother, Polychronia, secretly baptised her son against the wishes of her husband Gerontius. Some years later George entered the Imperial Service and rose quickly through the ranks of the local service. He travelled to Diospolis to seek further preferment, and was horrified to hear of the ruler's pagan beliefs. He openly criticised this unnamed ruler during a visit to the court and was then imprisoned and tortured with iron-spiked shoes, the crushing of his skull, scourging and other torments. St Michael intervened to free him from prison and cure his wounds, and many people, including the ruler's wife, were converted to Christianity when they heard St George preach. The saint also defiled the temples of Apollo and Heracles, and was then beheaded along with several thousands of the king's subjects.

The Coptic and Nubian narratives described above were undoubtedly linked to later versions of the life of St George, but it appears that the most influential version of the St George legend is a fragmentary fifth-century Greek palimpsest in Vienna which is presented as based on an earlier document written by, or at least with the assistance of, a servant of the saint called Pasicrates. This outlines the early life of St George in a story very similar to the Coptic tradition discussed above, but gives a much more detailed account of the martyrdom of the saint, which Pasicrates claims to have witnessed. He says the torture endured for seven years and led to the conversion of 30,900 people, including the Empress Alexandra. The villainous emperor is a Persian named 'Datianus', or 'Dadianus', a name that transmogrifies into the 'Dacianus' used by Ælfric and the 'Dacian' of later medieval tradition. This detailed version had an enormous impact on the subsequent hagiography of St George: it is the source of the traditions that St George was killed four times, only to be resurrected on the first three occasions, that he was given poison by a magician named Athanasius (who subsequently converted to Christianity and was himself martyred), that the saint was suspended over a fire, sawn in two, was dismembered and boiled (among many other torments), that he performed healing miracles and a miracle of making seventy wooden thrones take root and bear both blossom and fruit, and that he resurrected the dead.

The problem with this apparent eyewitness account, aside from the somewhat fantastical nature of the saint's experience, is that 'Pasicrates' was almost certainly an invention of hagiographers. It seems that the persona of the servant of a martyred saint was commonly adopted by early writers of martyrdom legends and this finding tends to suggest that it was *the story itself*, and the general Christian truths it espoused, which was significant rather than any claim to be presenting the literal truth about St George. Hence the serious inconsistencies in this version of the legend, such as the contentions that a Cappadocian should not have been answerable to the King of Persia and that the profession of magician was outlawed in Classical Rome, need not have been an issue for the first readers of this text. Such 'problems' could have arisen from a simple lack of knowledge about geography, or a tendency to treat all foreign races as interchangeable: again, the impression given is that these 'minor details' are simply irrelevant to the main purpose of the work, which was to encourage devotion to the saint.

A Vatican manuscript, almost certainly of a somewhat later date, and possibly as late as the eighth century, names Diocletian as the heathen emperor, and incorporates three miraculous cures rather than actual resurrections. Otherwise it is very similar to the earlier work, but the problem of its date throws into question the proposition that the anonymous martyr of Nicomedia was in fact St George: if this identification is accurate, why was Diocletian not named as the ruler in the earliest sources? In an attempt to resolve the problem, Datianus/Dacian is sometimes identified with the historically authentic Maximinus, Diocletian's co-emperor, possibly on the grounds that he also bore the name 'Daza'. One other possibility is that the emperor in question was actually Decius (ruled AD 249–51), another renowned persecutor of Christians, but the fact that he reigned over half a century before the generally accepted date of St George's martyrdom does tend to undermine this contention. The net result is that none of the competing camps are able to offer a truly convincing explanation of who St George was, or, indeed, if he actually existed at all. Gelasius, a late fifth-century pope, recognised the extent of the problems associated with the saint, and decreed that the hagiographical legends should be treated with extreme circumspection. His Church Council of AD 494, which formulated the first *Index* of forbidden books, trimmed the number of St George's tortures and removed all references to resurrection. The evidence of later images and literature concerned with the lengthy martyrdom clearly demonstrates that their efforts were not well rewarded. The discussion below (see Chapter Two) of the construction of St George as a martyr outlines the significance of the large number and variety of tortures associated with the saint. Although resurrection does not appear as such in the literary lives outlined in Tables 1, 2 and 3 (see pp. 218–21), miraculous cures are performed on the tortured saint in several versions, while the visual motif of the resurrection of St George by the Virgin, discussed below (see Chapter Three), is a clear example of resistance to this official proscription.

Despite the apparent uncertainty over the precise nature of the physical saint, there is clear evidence that a cult of St George existed from the earliest times, regardless of the veracity of his legend. We have already referred to the mid-fourth-century churches at Shaqqâ and Ezra, but Lydda was undoubtedly the most famous seat of his devotion. Unfortunately, the evidence here is relatively late: around AD 530 Theodosius, a deacon and pilgrim, wrote about the saint's tomb at Lydda, and mentioned the miracles that were said to have been witnessed there, but it is at least possible that pilgrimage had already been taking place for many years. Certainly the shrine here is generally recognised as the epicentre of the medieval cult; Constantine, the first Christian Emperor of Rome, was said to have built a basilica over the saint's tomb.

Lydda was to prove important in fostering St George's devotion much later, as some Crusaders are known to have visited the shrine there. It is claimed that the church built by Constantine was destroyed by Khalif Hakem in 1010 but was restored by King Etienne of Hungary. This building reverted to the use of Muslims, but during the First Crusade a cathedral was raised on the site between 1150 and 1170. Saladin subsequently destroyed this building in 1191; some traditions suggest that Richard Coeur-de-Lion (d.1199) rebuilt the cathedral, but there is little evidence for this. As we shall see it is incorrect to claim (as some studies of the cult have done) that the returning Crusaders introduced the cult of St George to Europe, for there is ample evidence of an established devotion well in advance of this date, but it is clear that the Crusades added impetus to the growth of the Western cult. Stories abounded of soldier–saints appearing to aid the Christians at critical moments in the various campaigns. These heavenly warriors included Theodore, Demetrius and Mercurius, warrior saints who, along with St George, were identified as the assistants of the Archangel Michael and were all believed to have died in the persecutions of Decian and Diocletian. They are all thought to have originated from the kingdom of Nobatia, a location which, as already mentioned, was also specified in one tradition of St George. Of this group of soldier–saints, which also included St Maurice on occasion, St George was perhaps the most famed; his first ghostly appearance was probably to aid the Normans against the Saracens at Cerami in 1063, but the subsequent manifestations at Jerusalem and Antioch in 1098 were the most often recounted.

The Jerusalem episode is told in the *Golden Legend*: a very beautiful young man appeared to a priest and identified himself as St George, the captain of the Christian host. He said that he would accompany the Crusaders to Jerusalem if they would carry his relics. Later, when they had the city under siege, the Christians did not dare to mount their scaling ladders for fear of the Saracens' resistance until a figure in white armour marked with a red cross appeared and led the invaders safely over the walls to slaughter their enemies. The Antioch story was recorded in the anonymous *Gesta Francorum*. This account claims that a numberless host of men on white horses, all bearing white banners, appeared from the mountains to help the Crusaders, and that 'many of our men saw them'.[2] This story was subsequently recounted by William of Malmesbury and several other chroniclers.

The oldest extant image of St George is a sixth-century Byzantine icon of the Virgin with saints and angels (illustration 1.3). Here we see St George paired with St Theodore, another of the group of soldier–saints, although by the later Middle Ages it is far more common for St George to be paired with St Michael – see, for example, the Borbjerg retable (illustration 3.11). In this Byzantine image St George, on the right, appears as a beardless young man with fair hair, a stylisation that was to reappear many times in subsequent images of the saint in an apparent evocation of the 'very beautiful young man' described in the *Golden Legend*. Like St Theodore, on the left, St George holds a cross and is not obviously presented as a military figure, although it has been argued that armour is discernible beneath their robes.

1.3 Sixth-century Byzantine icon of the Virgin Mary and saints. (St Catherine's Abbey, Sinai)

By contrast, other images of St George from the early and high

Middle Ages are generally unequivocal about his status as a soldier–saint: an anonymous Georgian silver icon, dated to the eleventh or twelfth century, presents him as a classical Roman soldier (illustration 1.4), while a second Georgian icon of a similar date shows him in combat with a human enemy (illustration 1.5). That said, some images of this time do not present St George as an overtly military saint: a Georgian liturgical cross, also of the eleventh century, focuses on the martyrdom of the saint (illustration 1.6), and, although his trial before the heathen ruler is depicted, the saint does not appear to be wearing armour in any of the scenes.

1.4 Eleventh- or twelfth-century Georgian silver icon of 'St George'. (Sujuna, Georgia)

1.5 Eleventh-century Georgian silver icon, St George overcomes the tyrant. *(Nakipari, Georgia)*

1.6 Eleventh-century Georgian liturgical cross of the martyrdom of St George. (Georgian Museum, Mestia)

The *raison d'être* of this cycle of the saint's life is perhaps the depiction of torture rather than St George's role as a soldier: it is discussed further in Chapter Two.

By the later medieval period St George's status as a military saint is always an integral part of his legend. Some visual cycles contain a considerable amount of martyrdom imagery, such as the mid-fifteenth-century Stamford cycle (illustrations 3.5 to 3.10) and the early sixteenth-century St Neot cycle (illustration 3.15), but this presentation is always allied to a depiction of St George as a soldier, invariably in his combat with the dragon but sometimes also in his role as the champion of the Virgin (see Chapter Three). In these later images St George is generally not represented as part of the coterie of Eastern soldier–saints, despite the chroniclers' accounts of the Crusades. He either fights the enemy host single-handed, as, for example, at Stamford (illustration 3.1), or he leads the Christian army against their heathen foes: St George's miraculous appearances to aid Crusaders at Jerusalem and Antioch were only two of many such manifestations. The panel of the battle scene in the Valencia altarpiece (illustration 2.4) depicts St George at the battle of Puig (1237), where he is said to have aided James the Conqueror, King of Aragon, to defeat the Moors, but the saint is apparently recorded in accounts of every victory of the Christians over the Spanish Moors from the battle of Alcoraz (1096) onwards.

Despite this strong evidence of the identification of St George as the premier soldier–saint, he does appear in company with other martial saints on occasion. The panel of 'The Warriors of Christ', which forms part of Jan and Hubert van Eyck's Ghent Altarpiece (1432), depicts St George on horseback, bearing a shield and banner of his red cross on a white field (illustration 1.7). He is flanked by two other soldiers, St Sebastian (on the right) and a figure who may be either St Martin or St Victor (on the left). The two flanking soldiers form a kind of escort for St George: they each hold shields that are not marked with a device, in sharp contrast to the prominence given to the red cross on St George's shield. This red cross is echoed in the red poles of the banners held by all three saints, and also in the devices of the other flags: the unidentified saint carries a white cross on a red field (the inverse of St George's emblem) while St Sebastian holds a gold cross on a red field, quartered with smaller gold crosses. This unified presentation implies that the three saints are brothers-in-arms, fighting together to uphold the law of God, with St George as their captain, but it seems that this idea was not used by other artists. St Sebastian is identified as an officer of the Imperial Guard who served under Diocletian: like St George, he is said to have been martyred when he refused to abjure his Christianity, but he does not seem to have been a popular saint in the early Church. Indeed, it is likely that his cult only really developed

Interestingly, St George seems to have been invoked by *both* sides during the battle between the Swedes and the Danes at Brunkenberg (1473): the Swedish victory led directly to the commissioning of the sculptor Bernt Notke to produce a large statue of St George and the dragon, plus a narrative of allied imagery, for display in St Nicholas' Church, Stockholm. It is unclear whether their defeat led the Danes to reconsider their devotion to St George.

Alongside these localised traditions there is also considerable evidence (much of which has never been collated) of areas or towns where devotion to St George was particularly strong. For example, in late medieval Normandy there were nearly seventy parish churches dedicated to St George, with four sites holding relics of the saint, two healing wells or springs where he was invoked, seven settlements where an annual fair of St George was held, three towns with confraternities (or 'associations' of St George) and a further community where an annual feast of St George was held. One town, Fontaine-le-Bourg (Seine-Maritime *département*), had a localised legend of St George in addition to a healing well dedicated to him, while Colomby (Manche *département*) even had a special song of St George which was sung on his feast day. Several local sayings invoking St George also survive: they primarily relate to agriculture, and hence utilise a memorable feast day that falls in the spring in order to record advice about planting days through an oral tradition. The importance of St George in Normandy is quite remarkable, and it is sometimes thought that it might be a legacy of the English occupation of this area in the early fifteenth century. However, there is clear evidence that the cult was well established far in advance of the English arrival: indeed, Normandy is the area where St George's cult seems to have really taken root in France.St George was known and venerated in Gaul from at least the sixth century, and in the middle of the eighth century an apparently miraculous event took place that seems to have led to a marked upsurge in the cult. A contemporary chronicler relates that during the time of Abbot Austrulph (AD 743–53) a coffer was washed up on a beach near to Portbail in the Cotentin region of Normandy, and was retrieved by the local people. When opened by the religious and civic authorities, the coffer proved to hold a beautiful parchment book of the Gospels in Latin and a reliquary, which contained part of the jaw bone of St George, relics of various other saints and a piece of the True Cross, as well as letters to authenticate all the treasures. Suitably impressed, Count Richwin, the governor of Cotentin, and the religious leaders decided to allow God to choose where these gifts be should be taken. They placed the coffer and its contents in an ox cart, let the animals wander at will, and followed as the cart was pulled inland to the hilltop settlement of Brix. It was decided to build a church to the honour of St George there, and at Richwin's insistence two further sanctuaries were built, one in honour of the Virgin, and one toSt Cross; many miracles were witnessed at the new church complex.

One (French) commentator has claimed that the coffer was being sent by Pope Zacharias, the discoverer of the skull of St George, as a gift to the English Church when 'the hand of God' redirected it to the Normans, who were presumably thought to be more deserving! There appears to be no evidence to uphold either this assertion or the tradition that St George's cult reached Britain in the sixth century when Antonius, a probably mythical Count of Britain, chose the saint as the patron of the brigade of heavy cavalry that later inspired the Knights of the Round Table, but it is still clear that the saint was recognised in England well before the Norman conquest. In AD 679 Adamnan, abbot of Iona, related a miracle of St George which he had heard from a traveller named Arculf, concerning a man who had made a vow to give his horse to St George in return for protection on a journey from Diospolis: the man broke his vow and St George took revenge by making the horse unbiddable until he repented. Bede mentions this story in his *Ecclesiastical History* and included St George in his martyrology. He uses the name Dacian, or Datian, for the Persian king, which indicates that this is the source of the 'English' name of the tyrant. St George also appears in a ninth-century Anglo-Saxon ritual at Durham, and a Saxon martyrology from around the mid-tenth century. Ælfric's *Passion of St George* was written at York around 1000. There is also some evidence of pre-Conquest foundations dedicated in honour of St George. He was the titular saint of the church at Fordington (Dorset), mentioned in King Alfred's will, and Knut (also known as King Canute), or perhaps his father Sweyn, founded a house of regular canons at Thetford under his patronage; the late eighteenth-century commentator Samuel Pegge credited Ulvius, the first abbot of Bury, with this foundation. A church in Southwark was dedicated to him in Anglo-Saxon times, and a church in Doncaster was dedicated to St George in 1061.

Robert d'Oiley, a Norman nobleman, continued this trend after the Conquest. He built a castle in Oxford in 1074, complete with chapel dedicated to St George (some commentators claim that the St George dedication was held by a parish church built by d'Oiley close to his castle, rather than a chapel within the castle). The 'Lewes Group' of wall paintings in Sussex, dated to *c.* 1080–1120, include the earliest cycles of St George in England, probably based on Byzantine wall paintings. One of the better known images from the 'Lewes Group', at Hardham on the north wall of the nave, shows St George in battle. It has now been convincingly demonstrated that it is likely to represent the saint's appearance at Antioch, although earlier commentators, working before serious conservation was carried out on the image, interpreted this scene as the combat with the dragon. This would be an exceptionally early date for a Western European subject of St George and the dragon, and the work makes much better sense as a crusading image, but the erroneous identification of the Hardham wall painting as a scene of the dragon fight is still given by some modern writers.

As the English cult became more firmly established through the later medieval period, strange variations on St George's legends began to spring up that seemed to confirm his links with the country. He was said to have visited England as a tribune of Beirut, on the orders of Diocletian, and to have formed a friendship with Queen Helen, Empress of Britain, who has been identified with St Helen, the mother of Constantine the Great and the purported discoverer of the 'True Cross' (*c.* AD 255–*c.* 330). This story has been supported, by at least one commentator, with the interesting, if somewhat bizarre, idea that the friendship with Helen forged on this trip led her, some twenty years later, to found a church adjoining the Rotunda of the Holy Sepulchre with a dedication to St George. It has been maintained that Constantine himself was a great friend of St George when they were in service together under Diocletian, an interesting reversal to the Coptic tradition discussed above, and further alleged that the two soldiers spent some time together in York during St George's posting to this country.

It is also claimed that the saint visited the tomb of Joseph of Arimathea (his putative kinsman in Coptic tradition) at Glastonbury, as well as Caerleon-on-Usk, which is said by Gildas to have been a centre of Christianity in England in the early fourth century. Doubtless it was on this same trip to England that he killed the dragon at one of the places to claim the combat. Several English towns and villages vie for the honour of being identified as the site of the encounter with the dragon. Dragon Hill in Berkshire, which stands alongside the White Horse of Uffington, has a bare patch at the summit; it is said to have been made barren by the dragon's blood spilt there by St George. Other places, such as Dunsmore Heath (Warwickshire), Brinsop (Herefordshire) and a Welsh hamlet of St George (Denbighshire), also claim the encounter, but they all seem to a follow a highly developed tradition related in Richard Johnson's *The Most Famous History of the Seven Champions of Christendome* (1576–80). This version, discussed in Chapter Six, claims that St George was a native of Coventry who rescued the daughter of an Egyptian sultan from a dragon and then married her; they went on to have three sons, one of who is named as Guy of Warwick. After a long and happy marriage the princess died in a riding accident. St George then journeyed to Jerusalem before returning to fight a second dragon that was terrorising an English town, and in the battle both dragon and knight were killed in a close parallel to the death of Beowulf. This treatment underlines the romantic aspects of the dragon legend and also demonstrates the extent to which St George's story changed over time: there is no mention of a martyrdom at the hands of a heathen emperor in this version.

The reference to Guy of Warwick, another English slayer-of-monsters, is a development that underlines the all-inclusive nature of these romantic treatments: the telling of a good story was Johnson's paramount aim, and by bringing in material from other legends he was able to place his legend of St George in a familiar context. Johnson's work is largely based on the Middle English poem *Sir Bevys of Hampton*, and this was the source of most of these later variants. It has been observed that a carving, *c.* 1533–6, on the provost's stall in King's College, Cambridge, which features an image of St George in conjunction with a lion carrying off a newborn child, indicates that some of the imagery employed by Johnson (and not deriving from *Sir Bevys*) was already associated with the saint some fifty years earlier. Taken in conjunction with the English version of the legend of the resurrection of St George by the Virgin, visible in the fifteenth century (see Chapter Three), this indicates that there was a strong, and long-standing, tradition of embellishment of the basic narrative in England. The story of St George given in an eighteenth-century chapbook goes so far as to claim that he was descended from Æneas, though of English birth, and that he was buried at Windsor, an assertion that was presumably based on the dedication of St George's Chapel at Windsor Castle.

St George is primarily recognised now by English people as their patron saint, but it is by no means clear when he was assigned this particular role. The first explicit reference to naming him as the patron saint of England occurred in 1351, when it was written that 'the English nation . . . call upon [St George], as being their special patron, particularly in war'.[5] This invocation of St George as a martial saint fits in with the pattern of devotion to the saint during the early and middle years of the fourteenth century in England, for military imagery was a dominant feature. The peculiarly English visual narrative of St George raised from the dead and armed as a knight by the Virgin appears from the early fourteenth century (this tradition is discussed in detail in Chapter Three), and it is likely that this story was especially resonant for patrons who were themselves knights. Other aspects of the saint's legend and iconography would also have been attractive to this kind of devotee. A fragmentary brass at Elsing (Norfolk; illustration 5.5) commemorates Sir Hugh Hastings (d.1347), who was a distinguished leader in the early years of the Hundred Years' War, notably the Gascony campaign of 1345–6; it features an image of St George mounted on horseback in a strongly military context, and suggests that the soldier–saint was invoked as an example of bravery and nobility. St George's presentation as an armed equestrian figure made him particularly attractive as a patron to knights who fought on horseback, but he did not always appear in this guise. For example, a standing image of St George without his dragon in stained glass at Barton-on-Humber (Lincolnshire), dated to *c.* 1334–40, still presents St George as a strongly military figure. It is likely that this image is linked to the idea of the *miles Christianus*, the 'soldier of Christ', which probably derives from St Paul's use of terminology such as the shield of faith and the helmet of salvation. Another standing figure of St George, in armour but again without his dragon, appears in a South English Legendary, *c.* 1400–20, which probably originates from Cambridgeshire (Oxford, Bodleian Library, MS Turner 17, fol. 91v). The relatively late date of this work indicates the longevity of interest in the iconography of the saint as an isolated armed soldier, rather than specifically as a knight on horseback. An image of St George in glass at Heydour (Lincolnshire), dated to *c.* 1360, also shows the saint without his dragon, but accompanied by the traditional English patrons SS Edward the Confessor and Edmund. All three are wearing armour, and this unique presentation tends to emphasise their joint role as the protectors of England from its earthly enemies.

St George's appeal to English kings, and to the knights who served them, seems to be based on his status as a model of chivalry. Quite why he was perceived in this way is unclear, as St George has no well-founded claim to be a military saint. As stated earlier, he is reputed to have been a tribune in the Roman army, but Ælfric's Old English life of the saint merely refers to him as a 'rich nobleman', a description that probably comes closest to the original anonymous 'man of high rank' who tore down the anti-Christian decree at Nicomedia. Certainly, there is little to link this pseudo-historical figure with the dashing knight on a white charger so beloved of the popular imagination, despite the enormous number of images of St George that portray him in this way. As with so many other aspects of his cult, it is difficult to be sure when the chivalric ideal became important as an adjunct to his legend, but even the earliest English images certainly present him as a soldier. Besides the 'Lewes Group' wall paintings, the oldest image of St George in England is found on the tympanum of St George's Church at Fordington (Dorset; illustration 1.8). It is dated to *c.* 1100, and is thus almost exactly contemporaneous with the reported sightings of St George aiding the Crusaders at Jerusalem and Antioch. Like the Hardham image, the saint is shown engaged in battle with an enemy army. Interestingly, at Fordington, St George is not himself wearing armour, but he holds a lance that is thrust into the mouth of a fallen knight. This may have been a copy of a similar carving on the tympanum of Constantine's Church at Lydda, which is said to have been in existence in the Crusaders' time; we should note the similarity of presentation found in the eleventh-century Georgian

1.8 St George overcoming the pagans, *sculpted over the doorway of Fordington church (Dorset),* c. *1100.*

icon (illustration 1.5) where St George spears his human enemy in the mouth or throat. A cognate image occurs on a Norman tympanum at Damerham (Hampshire; illustration 1.9); this time St George appears to be wielding a sword rather than a lance. A further example of this subject may well occur on the capitals of the chancel arch in the parish church at Wakerley (Northamptonshire). We should note that the Damerham image shows the human enemy being trampled by the hooves of the horse: this is very similar to the conventional position of the dragon in later images (see illustrations 3.4 and 5.24, for example). One problem with this group of images is that, in the absence of inscriptions or clear identifying attributes (a very common problem in images of this date), it is impossible to be sure that this actually is St George: it has been suggested that the trampling of the fallen human figure is the strongest means of providing a positive identification of St George in Norman imagery.

The subject of St George attacking a *fallen* human enemy seems to be generally superseded by the saint fighting a dragon in later imagery, although there is clear evidence of the persistence of traditions of St George leading armies, or at least engaging an enemy host on his own (see, for example, illustrations 2.4 and 3.1). However, the extension of the saint's legend to include the dragon

1.9 Sculpted tympanum of St George in battle, Damerham (Hampshire), c. *1100.*

episode in the twelfth century seems to have been essential in the development of St George as a chivalric model, as it presents him in the guise of a gallant Christian knight who defeats the ultimate enemy, the Devil, rather than a mere heathen host. The motif of St George fighting the dragon is by far the most frequently depicted subject drawn from his iconography; indeed, it is one of the most popular images in Christian art, with several hundred medieval examples extant.

Although traditions such as those that locate the scene of the dragon fight to various places in England, Denmark, Egypt and other countries imply that during the medieval period St George's dragon was generally perceived as being a 'real' animal of flesh and blood, we should be aware that the dragon story almost certainly derives from ideas about the embodiment of good and evil. St Michael is another well-known saintly dragon-slayer, but his monster is explicitly described (in the *Golden Legend* at least), as the Devil in the guise of a dragon. The Devil also appears in the form of a dragon in the legend of St Margaret, another victim of a heathen emperor who wished her to renounce her Christianity. While imprisoned, she asked God to show her the enemy who was opposing her, whereupon a hideous dragon appeared in her cell. According to some sources, it swallowed her, but all are agreed that it vanished when she made the sign of the cross. St Margaret's dragon has a metaphysical, even hallucinatory quality, but some medieval dragons were distinctly corporeal. St Martha killed 'a whelp of Leviathan' in the Rhone valley near Arles, which had been terrorising people who wished to use the river. The saint subdued the beast with holy water and the sign of the cross, tied it up with her girdle, then stood aside while the locals killed it with lances and stones.

It is significant that in the earliest written version of his dragon legend, dating from the twelfth century, St George is also said to have subdued the dragon with the sign of the cross, but this tradition quickly gave way to a full-scale battle between the two foes, where the emphasis is on brute force and knightly skill rather than supernatural intervention. This model is certainly closer to that provided by St Michael, who is invariably shown engaged in physical combat rather than simply using the sign of the cross, but St Martha's legend may well have influenced St George's story. One good example is the motif of the girdle: in the earliest written version of the legend of St George and the dragon, the princess gives the saint a strand of her hair to tie around the defeated monster's neck: it is quite possible that the girdle which features in subsequent retellings may have been 'borrowed' from St Martha's legend, or that both instances of the motif derive from the same source. It is certainly probable that St George's legend was influenced by the stories of other saints: there was a strong tradition of dragon-slaying saints within the medieval Church, and it may well be significant that St Theodore, one of the soldier–saints associated with St George in the Eastern Church, is frequently credited with killing a dragon in some Orthodox Christian traditions. It has been suggested that St Menas, a soldier–saint whose cult is based in Egypt and who probably influenced the traditions around the martyrdom of St George, absorbed an ancient cult relating to the triumph of Horus over the monster Set: as we shall see, Horus himself is also identified as a source of the legend of St George and the dragon.

A tombstone in Conisbrough parish church (Yorkshire, illustration 1.10), roughly contemporary with the first written account of the dragon episode, is conventionally identified as the earliest English representation of St George and the dragon. However, some peculiarities in the iconography may imply that this is an image of another story entirely. To the left of the solider stands something which may be a font, alongside a second figure. This man seems to be an abbot or bishop, as he holds a crozier: these motifs are not associated with the iconography of St George, and they may perhaps identify this as an image of the narrative of St Carantoc, an early Celtic holy man who intervened with a dragon which King Arthur had failed to kill in Somerset. Despite the uncertainty with these English images, it is clear that visual references to the story of St George and the dragon elsewhere in Europe, and in Asia too, can be much older that the earliest textual references. Although it is sometimes claimed that the first image of St George and the dragon with a certain date is a coin of Roger of Antioch (1112–19), it has been persuasively argued that there is considerable evidence predating

1.10 St George and the Dragon *sculpted on a monument at Conisbrough (Yorkshire), twelfth century.*

this find. A seal of St George and the dragon was adopted as the arms of Moscow in the ninth century, and in the first years of the tenth century the same subject was carved in St George's Church, Prague. This iconography seems to be derived from a Byzantine symbol of a double-headed black eagle holding a shield charged with a scene of St George and the dragon, a motif that is said to have entered Russia with Slavic pilgrims to Constantinople. The same badge may also have been the source of the motif in France: the arms of the Russian princess Anne, who was a daughter of the King of Russia and Muscovia, and who married the French king, Henri I, in 1051, were St George killing the dragon. Meanwhile, Constantinople had several early monuments to the saint, including a ninth-century bronze door representing St George in combat with the dragon. All these examples are likely to have been influenced by Greek iconography. From very early times the Greek Church represented St George trampling the dragon of the Apocalypse, representing the Devil, accompanied by a crowned virgin, representing the Church. Here perhaps we have the kernel of the tradition of St George's combat: it began as a stylised way of representing the saint overcoming evil, in almost exactly the same way as St Michael with the Devil/dragon, but gradually came to be treated as a legend in its own right. The evidence is even clearer when we return to the disputed testimony of 'Pasicrates'. In this early written source there is certainly no literal dragon, but the heathen emperor is explicitly called a dragon in some revised versions of the 'eye-witness account'. It is easy to imagine that this slight allegory, taken with the Biblical references to the Devil as dragon, gave rise to the early Greek images. Add in the Church represented as a crowned virgin, and the legend of St George and the dragon is born as an adjunct to, and an explanation of, the visual images.

It is also significant that this iconography bears a strong similarity to pre-Christian legends of combat between heroes and monsters and it is likely that the legend of St George and the dragon is a manifestation of these ancient ideas. Analogy cannot be taken as proof of evolution, but even if there was no direct developmental link it does seem reasonable to suggest that his story may have common roots with at least some of these myths: virtually every recorded human culture seems to have had at least one version of the story of the hero and the monster. For example, in Classical mythology Zeus subdues the monster Typhon, Bellerophon kills the fire-breathing Chimera, Apollo overcomes the dragon Python, Jason kills the dragon guarding the Golden Fleece, Theseus kills the Minotaur, Heracles defeats the Hydra and Cadmus slays a dragon during the founding of Thebes. In ancient Teutonic and Scandinavian belief Sigurd overcomes Fafnir, while in Persian tales Mithra overcomes Ahriman and Thraetana is victorious over Dahak. In ancient Egyptian belief the god Seth subdues the dragon Apep each day as he tries to halt the progress of the sun god Ra across the dawning sky, while in Hittite tradition, which originates from the region of Anatolia in eastern Turkey, the mortal Hupasiyas is called upon by the goddess Inaras to despatch the dragon Illuyankas. This later tale forms part of a belief system related to weather, for it seems that Illuyankas was killed in retribution for his defeat of a weather deity; similar associations occur elsewhere. In Canaanite mythology the god Baal, who is also known as Haddad, or 'the Thunderer', is a fertility god responsible for rainfall; in one of his adventures he overcomes the giant serpent Lotan. A similar belief system underlies the Indian myth of the battle between the god Indra and the dragon Vittra, a monster that is depicted as a cloud serpent, holding vast quantities of water in its belly. Again, Indra is a weather god. He defeats Vittra by launching a thunderbolt at it, whereupon the dragon bursts open and rain streams down on to the parched earth. Thor, the Nordic god of thunder and lightning, is another dragon-slayer: he is named as the hero who will overcome the

Midgard Serpent at the time of Ragnarock, or apocalypse.

The links between these pre-Christian myths and the St George legend are difficult to prove, but it does seem reasonable to suggest that the story of the saint's combat with the dragon may have been influenced by a shared formulation of the archetypal hero and monster. One possible example of such connection is found in a twelfth-century scultped tympanum – an image designed to be placed over the main door – reset into the wall of the north nave aisle of the church at Brinsop (Herefordshire). It seems to depict a mounted St George overcoming the dragon, and has been conventionally associated with the style of imagery in western France at this date, in consequence of travels made by English pilgrims. However, it has recently been suggested that this sculpture is actually more strongly influenced by surviving artefacts relating to the Roman Mithraic cult in the local area such as a sculpted tombstone at Gloucester. The Persian deity Mithra is often cited as an analogue of St George as both a slayer of monsters and a figure associated with agriculture; it is unclear whether the Roman god Mithras was a form of this Persian figure, but even if they are completely unconnected the fact that a Mithraic image has been rethought as a Christian figure, St George, is very telling in the context of an attempt to uncover the roots of the dragon narrative related to this saint. Some of these ancient stories of heroes and monsters are simple paradigms of Good overcoming Evil, but others are more developed, with the inclusion of motifs such as a young woman in distress, and here the parallels becoming increasingly clear. For example, Perseus rescues Andromeda from a sea monster (illustration 1.11) while Heracles saves Hesione from another sea-creature at Troy in one of several dragon-killing exploits; this paradigm has almost certainly informed the St George legend. Indeed, if Perseus' flying horse, Pegasus, was not identified by his wings in the fifteenth-century image of Perseus and Andromeda used to illustrate Christine de Pisan's version of the story (illustration 1.11), it would be easy to mistake this subject for that of St George rescuing the princess. It may be significant that Perseus is said to have slain the sea monster at either Arsuf or Joppa, towns that are both close to Lydda: as we have seen, this site is often identified as the location of St George's tomb. Some commentators have claimed that the parallels between the two narratives indicate that a local legend has been Christianised, but it is important to remember that the dragon story was not associated with St George until at least six centuries after the proclamation of the tomb site at Lydda. Another common motif is the identification of the dragon with water: the myths of Perseus and Thor include sea monsters, while Cadmus kills a dragon guarding a spring and the Hydra, killed by Herakles, infests a swamp: in virtually all versions of the legend of St George and the dragon the monster lives in either a lake or marsh. Grendel, the

1.11 Perseus and Andromeda from The Epistle of Othea *by Christine de Pisan* (c. *1364–1430). (British Library, London, Harl. 4431, fol. 98v)*

monster overcome by Beowulf, was also the inhabitant of a swamp. This early medieval English story has further parallels with later traditions of St George. At the end of the story, Beowulf fights a dragon. During the struggle both Beowulf and the dragon die, a motif that also appears in an English version of the life of St George found in an eighteenth-century chapbook. In this account the first battle with a dragon occurs in Egypt, leading to the death of the dragon and the saint's marriage to the rescued princess, but the second encounter, fatal for both parties, occurs on English soil.

Another factor common to the Beowulf legend and some versions of the story of St George is the killing of a specifically female monster: Beowulf despatches not only Grendel but his mother too, and the identification of St George's dragon as female is an important development some late medieval versions of the saint's legend (this is discussed in Chapter Five). Another interesting parallel of this construction of the monster occurs in an ancient Babylonian creation myth. In this story the deity Marduk overcomes and kills the monstrous Tiamat. This water-dwelling creature is identified as a female spirit of primeval chaos, and seems very reminiscent of some of the associations made with St George's dragon in the later medieval period. Another water-dwelling monster overcome by a hero is the crocodile subdued by the Egyptian deity Horus. This combat was commonly depicted in visual imagery, and it has been suggested that this manifestation was a direct influence on the Greek image of St George and the dragon.

Another possible set of parallels with the story of St George seems to occur within the field of English folk tradition. This area, which encompasses apparent survivals of native pre-Christian belief systems, is notoriously difficult to research as it is associated with an oral tradition that is recorded only through folksongs and localised festivals, many of which will have changed considerably over time so that their original purposes and meanings are now obscure. Furthermore, it is likely that a considerable number of traditional folksongs were bowdlerised both by prudish Victorian collectors and some singers who refused to allow their 'betters' to hear the full, unexpurgated versions. However, the incomplete evidence that is available to us indicates that St George appeared in English folk ritual as an important character, with his stories and attributes derived from both the 'conventional' Christian legend and earlier, pre-Christian belief.

In a parallel with the ancient dragon-slaying weather gods, this version of St George is deeply concerned with the fertility of both the soil and animals. As noted above, his very name is derived from a term meaning 'a tiller of the soil', the same name that is used for the Persian deity (and dragon-slayer) Mithra. In spite of his role as a military saint, the identification of St George with agriculture is very strong, to the extent that he is sometimes claimed as the patron saint of farming. Although there appears to be no tradition that he actually worked the land himself, he is described as a signifier of the spring by Peter Damian (1007–72), who makes no mention of any military connections. St George is also sometimes linked with the ceremonies of early May that celebrated the imminent return of summer, perhaps because his feast day was moved by the reform of the calender effected in 1752 and 'old' St George's day then fell on 4 May, the traditional end of the May ceremonies. As noted above, one of the aspects of St George's cult in Normandy relates to agriculture: his feast day is used as a marker for planting several crops, and also for forecasting the weather for the year. Besides the derivation of his name, the reasons for this association with agriculture are obscure. However, St George did perform two interesting miracles of fruitfulness, according to Pasicrates' version of his life, when he induced both wooden thrones and architectural timber in the house of a widow to blossom and bear fruit. This story seems to disappear from later accounts, but a more significant feature of Pasicrates' account, the motif of the death and resurrection of St George himself, does indeed appear in some later medieval lives. This trope is strikingly reminiscent of the 'ancient customs' that some – but by no means all – historians claim were enacted in the pre-Christian period to ensure the fertility of soil, animals and people. These putative belief systems demanded that the spirits of nature should be honoured and their favour entreated through rites involving such practices as sacrifice of blood or crops, the lighting of fires, the decorating of trees and sexual activity. The archaic Spring Festival, forms of which are though by some to have taken place in many parts of Europe, are alleged to have featured dramatic rituals such as the King of the Year, a male figure who was said to symbolise the annual cycle of seasons. At his ascendancy he killed his predecessor, and was killed in turn one year later. If this 'tradition' ever existed, it is possible that it was initally practiced literally but later treated in a metaphorical sense, with a symbolic battle between the outgoing and incoming kings, and a recognition that this was the eternal essence of spring, rising phoenix-like from the ashes of the winter death. Proponents of these theories have tended to claim that such pre-Christian beliefs were largely stamped out by the medieval Church, and suggest that traces of them are still discernible in some aspects of folk culture. English mumming plays largely date from the nineteenth century, but some scholars claim that they draw on much earlier dramatic traditions: they feature St George or his analogues 'Sir George', 'King George' or 'Prince George' in a leading role, and place much emphasis on the resurrection motif. For example, in the Lutterworth St George play (published in 1865, from a version performed at Christmas 1863)

Prince George is killed by the Turkish Champion but subsequently resurrected by 'the Doctor', a figure who can be read as a version of the resurrecting St Michael in the life of St George by Pasicrates.

The motif of the combat between St George and his various human foes in these folk dramas can in itself be understood as a form of a pre-Christian tradition. This dramatic trope has been likened to the ancient theme of 'the two brothers', symbolising light and dark, summer and winter, mutually dependant forces locked in a struggle where each temporary victory is merely the forerunner of temporary defeat. One aspect of this story includes the idea that the defeated party journeys to the underworld, or 'Other-world'. It has been claimed that the reference to St George in the Cornish tradition recounted in the Padstow May Song is a version of this:

> Oh where is St George, where is he oh?
> He's out in his longboat,
> All on the salt sea oh!

This explanation of the song identifies the sea as a form of the 'Other-world', with St George preparing to return to land and usher in the Maying. There is little concrete evidence to substantiate this reading, but it may be significant that there seem to be no references to St George as a sailor or seafarer in any of the more orthodox legends. However, he is sometimes claimed as a patron saint of seafarers – St Nicholas of Myra is the more usual choice – and it is notable that the stretch of water in the Irish Sea that separates Wales from Ireland is known as 'St George's Channel', although this name seems to be relatively late and probably derives from a form of his legend entering Britain from the West.

Equally, the motif of the battle between St George and a human enemy does not appear in extant medieval written lives of the saint, but it is a feature of visual cycles of St George, such as the Borbjerg retable (illustration 3.11), the St Neot glass (illustration 3.15), and the Valencia altarpiece (illustration 2.4), as well as the early imagery noted at Hardham, Fordington (illustration 1.8) and Damerham (illustration 1.9). In Northern English folk drama the Turkish Champion is generally substituted by a similar character known as the Black Prince of Paradise, Paradine or Paladine, who is also known as the 'Morocco Dog' or 'Morocco King'. This may be an allusion to the visual imagery, or, more credibly, to common literary sources, for St George's human foes vary according to where the tale is told. Hence, in Denmark he fights the Swedes while in the Valencia altarpiece he fights the Moors, a very suitable opponent for work with a Spanish audience, and it is not impossible that a version of this latter tradition influenced the identification of the 'Morocco Dog' or 'Morocco King' in the Northern English folk drama. One intriguing aspect of the combat motif in folk drama is that St George is rarely portrayed actually fighting the dragon, despite the fact that this is undoubtedly his best-known opponent. The dragon-fight is certainly alluded to, for example, in the Lutterworth text where the St George character recounts the tale:

> I am Prince George, the Champion bold,
> And with my sword I won three crowns of gold;
> I slew the fiery dragon and brought him to the slaughter,
> And won the King of Egypt's only daughter.

It has been suggested that another character, known as the 'Bold Slasher' or 'Captain Slasher', may be read as a form of the dragon, but the existence of dragon costumes such as the Civic Snap at Norwich (illustration 4.16) imply that staging a dragon fight need not have presented particular difficulties to a determined group of actors. The most likely explanation is that the dragon was simply unimportant in the specific traditions of St George which informed these folk dramas: either it was subsumed into the motif of the combat with the human enemy, or, perhaps more plausibly, priority was given to a restaging of the fertility myth of the battle between two equal opponents, with its concomitant aspects of defeat followed by resurrection.

The haunting image of the 'Green Man' – the foliate face, redolent of the natural world, which sits so uneasily in Christian churches – has been identified as a pre-Christian form of St George. It acts as a reminder of his role as an icon of fertility; in fact, 'Green George' is a name sometimes given to this image, which may act as a symbol of the return of spring after the temporary triumph of winter. An interesting echo of this aspect of St George is found in an Islamic analogue known as 'Al Khidr', 'Al Khadir', 'El Khudr', 'Khizr' or 'Jiryis Baqiya'. This figure is particularly associated with the area around Palestine, Lebanon and Syria. He is also recognised by Jews in this region under the name 'Eliyahu ha Navi', who is considered to be a special guardian of Israel, and by local Christians as 'Mar Jiryis'; much of the rebuilt church over the shrine at Lydda was converted to a mosque, and it seems that the tomb was positioned squarely between the two sections of the building and was thus available to both Christian and Moslem devotees. The various names applied to this holy character equate to terms such as 'the Living', 'the Green One' and 'the Evergreen One'; he is thought to derive from the Greek sea god Glaucos, whose name means 'the Blue One' or 'the Green One', a fisherman who achieved immortality, and hence the status of a god, after eating a seashore herb that he had noticed restored his fish to life. Utnapishtim, a character in the Gilgamesh epic, attained immortality in a remarkably similar way, and this parallel may indicate another influence.

Al Khidr (and his alternative appellations) is reputed to have found the Fountain of Youth, or the Well of Life, which is said to be located near the confluence of the Mediterranean and the Red Sea. Drinking from this fountain confers immortality, and it is claimed that Al Khidr has been repeatedly killed and resurrected; one story involves a martyrdom at the behest of a pagan king. Some traditions state that Al Khidr bathed three times in the Well of Life: in consequence, his skin and all his apparel turned entirely green, and he leaves green footprints wherever he goes. Like St George, this figure is invoked as a healer: one of his shrines, visited by adherents of all three religions, is known to have been located at a kind of psychiatric asylum near Bethlehem, where several miraculous healings were claimed. Another healing shrine was located on the slopes of Mount Carmel, whilst in the early twentieth century it was noted that those suffering from 'fever, quaking and fear' resorted to a shrine of Mar Jiryis at Urmi in Persia.[6]

One Middle Eastern story about the power of Al Khidr is more equivocal about his thaumaturgic powers, a story which is set in a Christian church dedicated to him under the name Mar Jiryis. A priest was administering communion in the 'Greek fashion', where the bread is crumbled into the wine and the mixture is spooned into the mouth of communicants. The priest contrived to spill some of this holy substance on to his foot, where it burned a hole right through to the floor and left a mark on the flagstone below. The unfortunate priest died of his wound, but a diseased man later knelt on the stained flagstone, quite unaware of its significance, and was miraculously healed. Many other healings subsequently took place on this stone, until the Sultan of the Muscovites decided that he must have the stone for himself. The local Patriarch, a friend of the Sultan, agreed, and the stone was extracted from the floor and taken overland to Joppa without incident. However, once it had been loaded on to a boat Mar Jiryis himself appeared in the sea and pushed the boat back to the shore with his lance. The Sultan then realised his mistake, and arranged for the stone to be returned to its original place with all due ceremony.

Mar Jiryis, under his various appellations, also has strong associations with fertility, particularly in terms of stories linking him with the weather. One example dates from as recently as 1906, when the failure of winter rains led to famine and poverty. It is claimed that a woman was slowly filling a pitcher from a scanty spring at Ain Kârim when she was accosted by a horseman holding a long lance who ordered her to water his horse. She objected to his command, but obeyed him, and was horrified to discover that blood, and not water, streamed from the pitcher. The horseman then revealed his identity as Al Khidr, and ordered the woman to tell everyone that if Allah had not sent the drought there would have been a great pestilence and other grave misfortunes. He then appeared to another woman at Hebron with a similar message, promising that the rains would come after the Greek New Year. It seems that his prophecy came true. This story clearly demonstrates the longevity of this particular cult of St George. It also serves as an example of the way in which Al Khidr is recognised as an eternal wanderer who helps people in trouble. The Old Testament prophet Elijah is a related figure who also fills this role and he too is claimed as an influence on the cult of St George. A good example of this aspect of the saint is his miraculous appearances during the Crusades and other military campaigns. Interestingly, Al Khidr is sometimes claimed as a figure of sexual chastity: as argued below, this too is a defining feature of St George during the late medieval period.

Another potentially important influence on the development of St George was the derivation of motifs from other cults. Constantine is a particularly interesting example of a figure who is sometimes presented in a way which is strongly reminiscent of some aspects of the story of St George. As we know, he is closely linked to the early cult, being credited with erecting a church over the tomb of the saint at Lydda, as well as the rather more spurious traditions which claim that the emperor and the soldier–saint were brothers-in-arms, and even close friends, in the Imperial service. The mid-fourth-century historian Eusebius, in his life of Constantine, notes that the emperor had caused to be created an image of himself overcoming a dragon, as a symbol of the Devil. This image may well be, or be similar to, a bas-relief that is thought to have existed in Constantine's church over the tomb at Lydda, which is described as showing the emperor holding a banner of the cross in his right hand, standing on a dragon or serpent. A coin minted during Constantine's reign also depicted the emperor with a fallen dragon, apparently as an allegory of his suppression of some elements within Imperial Rome, and it has been claimed this iconography of Constantine may have led directly to the genesis of the story of St George and the dragon. However, we should note that this initially rather persuasive idea is undermined by the fact that so many centuries elapsed between the time when Constantine's church was built and the addition of the dragon story to the legend of St George; the suggestion that the myth of Perseus was a strong influence is open to the same criticism. As we have seen, St George's iconography and legend bear strong resemblances to the images and stories of other saints, particularly dragon-slayers such as St Michael. In Chapter Two we will examine the ways in which the legends of other martyrs have also affected the figure of St George: overall it seems clear that a veritable array of Christian and non-Christian influences have meshed together to produce this many-faceted figure, who is a far cry from the putative 'original', anonymous hero of Nicomedia.

CHAPTER TWO

ST GEORGE THE MARTYR: TORTURE AND RESURRECTION

As Chapter One has demonstrated, the early versions of the legend of St George clearly present him as a martyr: the cycle of images on the eleventh-century liturgical cross from Georgia (illustration 1.6), which illustrates nine episodes in his martyrdom, is a good example of the narrative form, both visual and literary, used in connection with this saint in the early medieval period. The iconography of the work indicates that the sequence reads first on the horizontal plane, across the left arm, then down the vertical plane, and finally across the right arm:

(1) The first image is rather unclear. St George, on the left, is probably performing a miracle of healing on three people, two of whom have walking sticks. Alternatively, he may be giving alms to them, although there seems to be no tradition of identifying St George as an almsgiver.
(2) St George stands before the heathen ruler, who sits on an ornate throne. A third figure pushes, or holds, the saint.
(3) St George is beaten with sticks by two assailants.
(4) He has been bound to a wheel. The torturers are pulling on ropes that are bound to his hands and feet, apparently in an effort to stretch his body.
(5) St George is bound to a post. The torturers, standing on what is probably meant to represent steps, attack his body with implements, probably small rakes to tear his flesh.
(6) This is a rather indistinct subject. It may represent St George being burned on a pyre, with a torturer stirring up the fire with a long pole, but it is perhaps more likely that the saint is shown being put into a lime kiln. The figure on the right, who is haloed and is probably to be identified as Christ, is shown comforting the saint.

(7) The final image of torture is again indistinct but probably shows St George being crushed by a millstone, which is rolled on to his chest by a torturer. A hand from Heaven blesses the saint in the top right corner.
(8) Alongside the scene of the raking, we see St George with three other figures, two of them haloed, who stand behind a small cow or ox. This is likely to show St George with bystanders who were converted by his ability to overcome the magical powers of Athanasius, the sorcerer who tried to poison him. Athanasius himself may well be represented: the cow or ox is probably a reference to a magical act that the sorcerer performed – splitting an ox into two parts, then uniting the two pieces – in order to prove his power before his attempt to poison the saint.
(9) The final scene shows St George twice; firstly, being blessed by the hand of God and, secondly, about to be beheaded.

The five tortures depicted in this cycle clearly dominate the composition. The subjects on the vertical plane all occupy panels that are obviously larger than those images on the arms of the cross – the lowest image, of the torture of the millstone, is a possible exception. The positioning of the torture images on this central axis also gives them greater prominence: four subjects associated with the trial of St George depicted on the horizontal plane act primarily as an adjunct to the images of torture, and it is likely that this construction of the saint – St George as a martyr, one who suffered great physical torment as he refused to submit to the will of heathen ruler and was ultimately vindicated by a recognition from Christ himself – was the most significant aspect of the cult during the early medieval period.

The subsequent introduction of the dragon legend obviously led to a broadening of the narrative, with the introduction of the idea of St George as a *miles Christianus* – a soldier of Christ – engaged in a battle with a tangible, monstrous form of the forces of evil. However, although the dragon legend was to prove very important in the iconography and hagiography of the saint, it would be untrue to claim that the concept of the saint as martyr was totally superseded in the late medieval cult. If we consider, for example, the panel paintings of eight scenes of the martyrdom of St George created by a master from Bruges at the beginning of the sixteenth century (illustration 2.1) we see that no fewer than five of the eight subjects are concerned with the torture of the saint, besides the actual execution:

(1) The saint is shown baptising the king, queen and rescued princess.
(2) He is suspended by his hands while one torturer attacks his skin with a small rake and another prepares to burn him with a flaming torch.

2.1 Scenes of the martyrdom of St George, early sixteenth century. (Groeningemuseum, Bruges)

(3) St George drinks from a goblet, which shows that he has nullified the attempt to poison him.
(4) A further attempt at torture fails when a wheel on which he was about to be tormented breaks apart under the influence of rays of light descending from heaven.
(5) The saint is 'baked' in a metal bull-shaped vessel over a fire.
(6) He is dragged through the streets by a horse;
(7) executed;
(8) and finally buried. The disabled supplicant in the foreground alludes to the miracles of healing which are routinely associated with the tombs of saints.

These panels, along with many other similar cycles, clearly demonstrate that motifs of torture continued to be an important aspect of St George's cult throughout the Middle Ages. This similarity

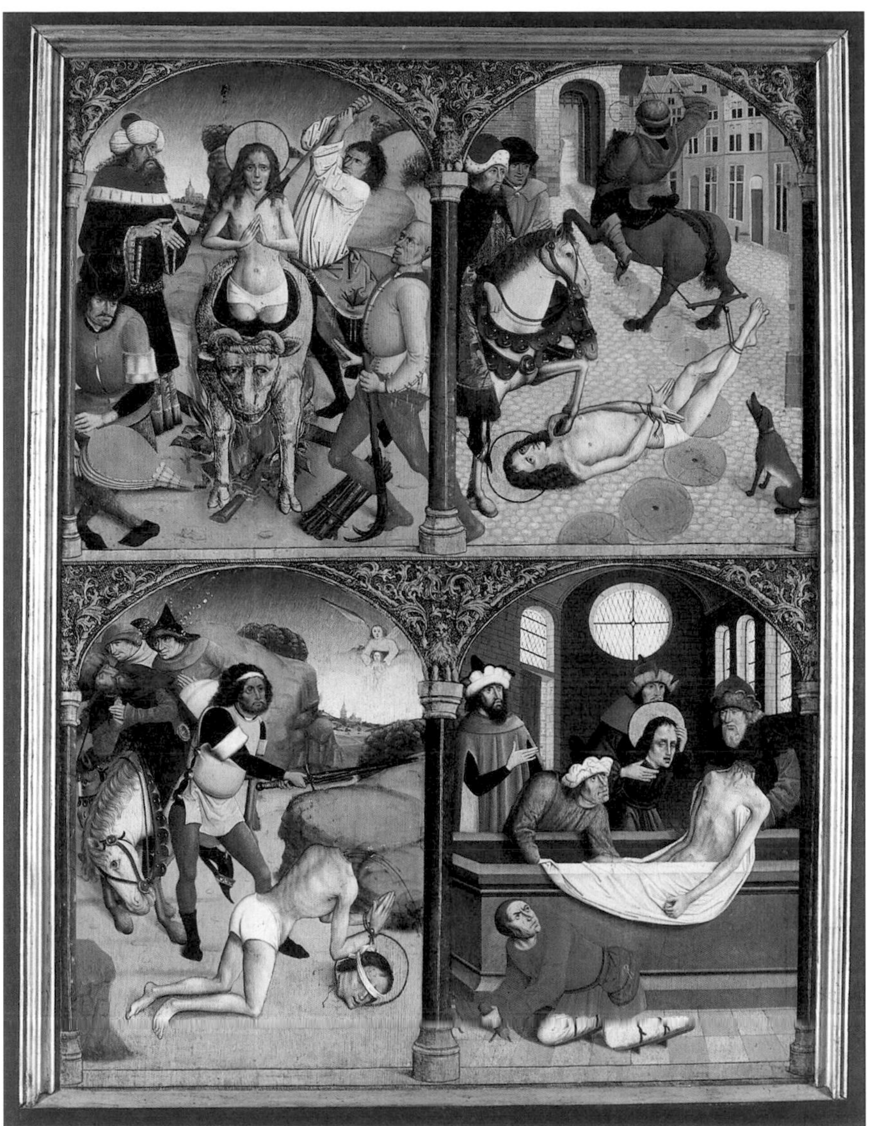

of motif may be due to some extent to the simple persistence of a well-established tradition, but close examination of the differences between the treatments of the saint's legend tends to suggest that more complex issues are involved. In Eastern Orthodox Christianity, particularly the Greek Church, St George is still hailed today as a *megalomartyr*, a term that signifies his position as a martyr among martyrs, a Christian who suffered so extraordinarily at the hands of his heathen adversaries that his legend stands out from the mêlée of other, more limited, martyrdoms. To some extent this Eastern tradition will have informed the Roman Church's view of the saint, but it seems necessary to ask why this particular formulation seemed so attractive to Western European Christians, particularly in the light of the proscriptions of Gelasius, which sought – apparently in vain – to remove many of the references to torture from the martyr's legend. As we shall see, the specific meanings apparently attached to the motif of torture in the various late medieval treatments may be attributed to more than one underlying theological or philosophical construction.

If we compare the use of torture in several treatments of the legend of St George the main issues become very clear. The Georgian cross and the Bruges panels show some interesting differences in the tortures: the only common motifs are the use of the rakes and the wheel. However, if we turn to the Valencia altarpiece (*c.* 1410–20; illustrations 2.2, 2.3 and 2.4) we find a set of tortures with only limited correspondences to either of the other two cycles.

The Valencia altarpiece was almost certainly created by the German artist Marzal de Sas for a confraternity of St George in Valencia; it devotes two large panels and sixteen smaller panels to the legend of St George (illustration 2.2 shows subjects 1, 2, 6 and 10; illustration 2.3 shows subjects 7, 9, 12 and 16). The central panel (illustration 2.4) of the retable shows St George amid a group of mounted knights, assisting James the Conqueror, King of Aragon, to defeat the Moors at the battle of Puig (1237). The lower central panel shows St George, again presented as a mounted knight, spearing the dragon. The princess looks on with her lamb from the background on the left side, and the hand of God blesses him from above. The placement of the small panels has evidently been disrupted at some point in the altarpiece's history, but the logical ordering, suggested by C.M. Kaufmann,[1] is used here:

(1) St George is armed by the Virgin and angels. Christ looks down from above and blesses the saint.
(2) This subject depicts the sacrifice of a child and a lamb to the dragon. A man leans through a door in a woodenfence and lowers the child feet first into the unwinged, lizard-like dragon's mouth.
(3) The lot falls on the princess, who stands in the foreground on the right, next to the king on his throne amid a throng of citizens.
(4) Following on the narrative from the central panel of the combat with the dragon, St George is shown harnessing the subdued beast. The princess stands alongside him with her lamb.
(5) The baptism of the king, queen and princess.
(6) The trial before Dacian. The emperor sits with crossed legs on the right side, amid a group of attendants which includes a golden demonic monster who whispers into his ear.
(7) The first scene of torture shows St George tied to a saltire cross. He now wears white shorts; two torturers rake his flesh while a third tightens his restraints and a fourth uses a hammer to work on the cross. Dacian, holding a sword, looks on from the right side with two companions.
(8) St George is depicted nailed and tied with chains to a table. Two torturers secure the bindings while Dacian and a group of attendants observe from the background.

Opposite: 2.2 *Marzal de Sas (attributed),* The Valencia Altarpiece, c. *1410–20: details of narrative panels. (Victoria & Albert Museum, London)*

2.4 The Valencia Altarpiece: *detail of panel of St George in battle. (Victoria & Albert Museum, London)*

(9) St George is shown imprisoned, visited by Christ and a bevy of angels. Three guards outside the prison on the left side pay little attention.
(10) The torture of the poison. St George, still in armour and a long robe, stands in the centre before Dacian and a group of attendants. He holds a small chalice containing a dragon – a conventional marker of poison. In the foreground a man kneels in prayer; he is being strangled by an executioner standing behind him. This seems to be the execution of the magician Athanasius when he converted to Christianity.
(11) St George is tortured on a mechanism of two large wheels with sharpened points. One torturer operates the mechanism while Dacian and his attendants observe from the right side.
(12) This particularly gory scene depicts St George sawn in half vertically. He has been tied to a wooden frame, and is being cut apart by two torturers wielding a double-handled saw; his

Opposite: 2.3 The Valencia Altarpiece: *details of narrative panels. (Victoria & Albert Museum, London)*

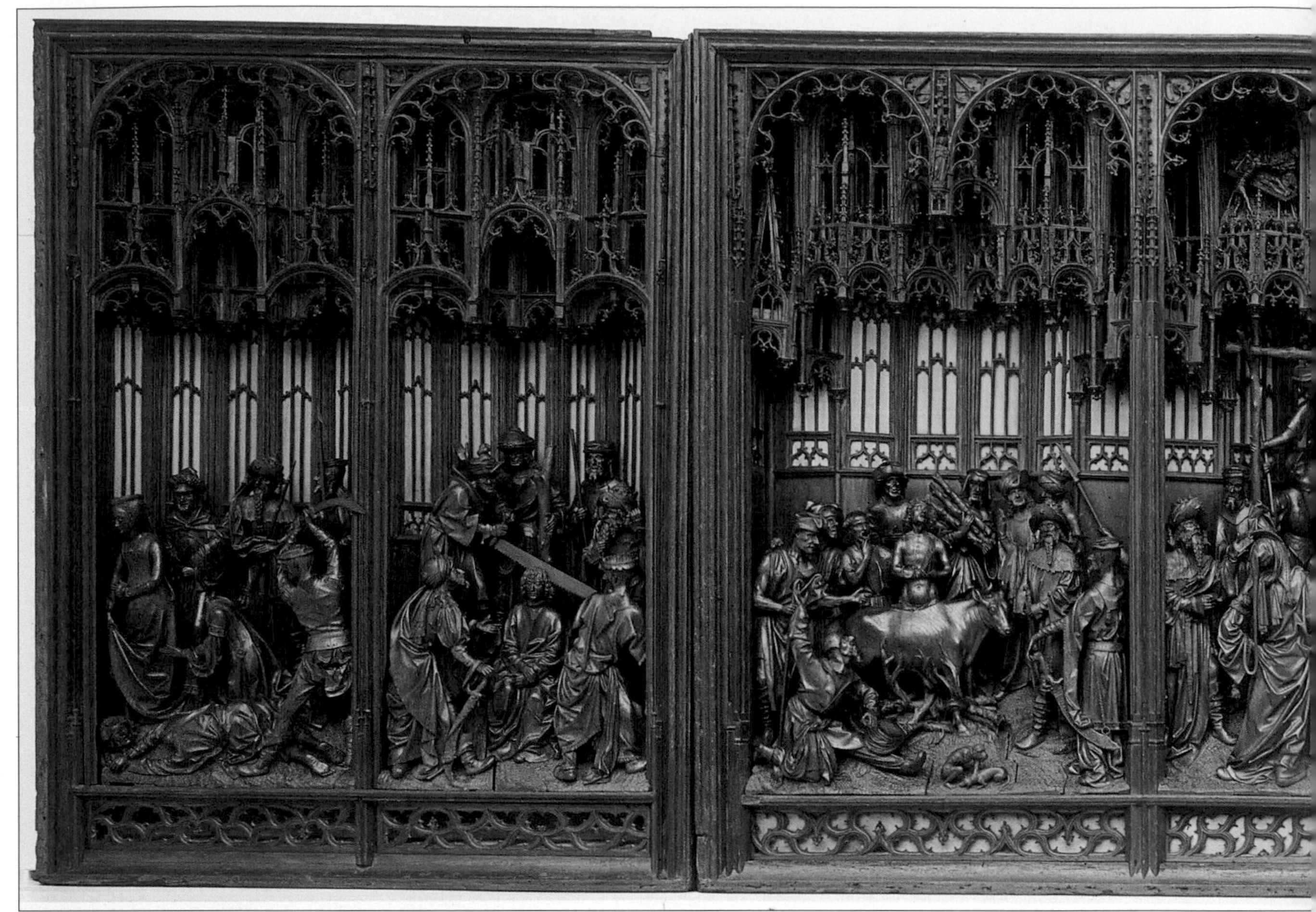

2.5 Jan Borman, altarpiece of the martyrdom of St George, 1493. (Musée royaux d'Art et d'Histoire, Brussels)

intestines are spilling from the lower part of his abdomen. Dacian and a group of attendants look on from behind a low wall, and the hand of God blesses the saint from above.

(13) St George is shown in prayer, in a cauldron of molten lead over a fire. One torturer tends the fire while a second stirs the cauldron. Dacian and a group of attendants look on from the background on the left side.

(14) This subject shows the episode in the heathen temple. St George, in a long robe, stands in the foreground looking up to heaven. The idol topples from its pedestal and fire from heaven burns the temple, the idol and its priests.

(15) St George is dragged naked through the city. His feet are tied to a horse, which is ridden by a torturer. Dacian observes from the right side.

(16) St George, kneeling in prayer, is beheaded by an executioner. This man's face is attacked by a small winged demon, whilst the saint's soul is carried up to heaven by two angels on the left side. On the right side Dacian looks up to see the fire from heaven which is descending to kill him and his companion.

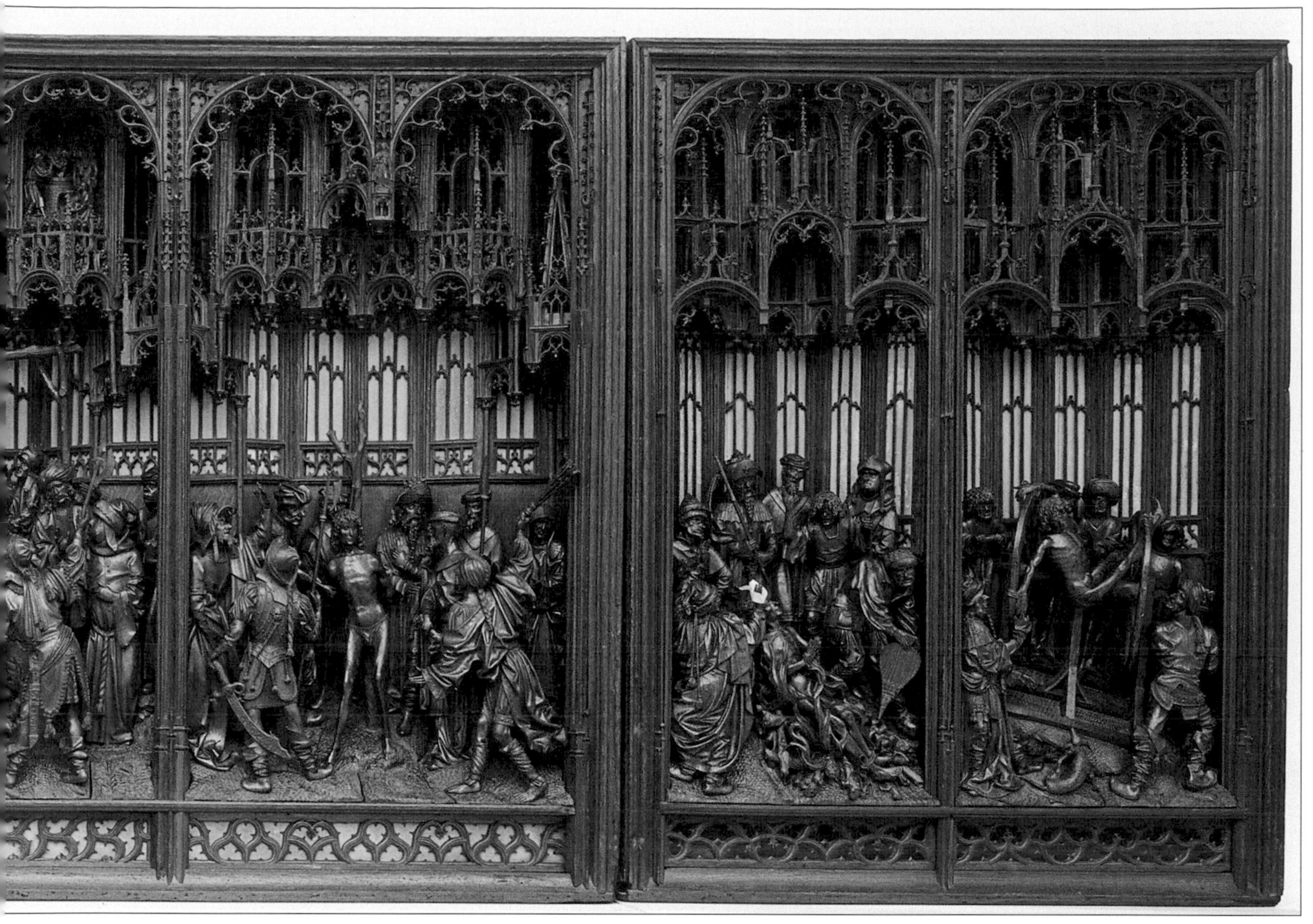

It is notable that in the Valencia altarpiece there is no sign of the beating, the pyre or lime kiln, the millstone found on the Georgian cross, or of the bull-shaped vessel or the burning torch found on the Bruges panels. Furthermore, the wheel torture is presented quite differently; for the Valencia version *two* wheels are employed, both equipped with sharpened points. Another difference is found in the motif of the raking: in the Valencia panel St George is shown tied to a saltire cross rather than to a post or suspended by his hands.

The apparent lack of consistency between the eleventh-century Georgian cross, the fifteenth-century German altarpiece made for a Spanish audience and the sixteenth-century Flemish panels could be explained by either the differences in date of creation or the fact that they originate from, and were made for patrons in, different geographical areas. However, the same trait of inconsistency is found when comparisons are made between cycles of the saint which are demonstrably close in date and provenance. For example, in the wooden retable, or altarpiece, sculpted by the Flemish artist Jan Borman in 1493 (illustration 2.5) we find St George being roasted in a metal bull-shaped cauldron in a close analogue of the subject from the early sixteenth-century Bruges panels, but he is also shown suspended upside-down over a fire and beaten with cudgels, a motif that does not appear in the Bruges imagery.

Some cycles of St George's life survive in only a fragmentary or heavily restored form; these versions obviously cannot provide such useful evidence as complete cycles, as we usually cannot know either the subject matter of lost scenes or the original forms of subjects that have been changed by a restorer, but they do constitute a very useful source of information when cataloguing new types of torture or different treatments of 'established' tortures. They can also help to address the significance of geography and chronology. A useful case study can be made by comparing two cycles that exist in Clermont-Ferrand Cathedral which seem to have been made within a fifty-year period. The earliest, a cycle in glass that survives in a restored form, dates from the mid-thirteenth century; with thirty-six panels it is one of the largest surviving medieval cycles of St George (illustration 2.6). Besides the restoration work there has probably been some disturbance of the sequence of subjects, and it is very likely that the five roundels relating to the dragon story are misplaced in relation to the basic story of the trial and torture of the saint. The subjects are described here following the interpretation given by Abbé Berger,[2] with restored subjects marked with an asterisk:

2.6 Detail of St George window, 1283–7. (Clermont-Ferrand Cathedral)

(1) St George before Dacian and his wife Alexandra.
(2) St George protests against the persecution of Christians.
(3) St George in prison.
(4) St George disputes with Dacian and Alexandra.
(5) Alexandra converts to Christianity.
(6) Alexandra is arrested;
(7) decapitated;
(8) and the executioner takes her head to Dacian.
*(9) The dragon story intervenes at this point, as the princess leaves the town of Silene.
(10) She meets St George.
*(11) He goes with her to face the dragon.
*(12) St George fights the dragon while the princess prays for his success.
*(13) She then leads the vanquished dragon back to Silene.
*(14) The story of Dacian now recommences, with the scene of Athanasius failing to poison St George.
*(15) Athanasius converts to Christianity and throws down the idols. (If this reading correctly reflects the original version it is unparalleled, for St George is conventionally depicted overcoming idols without reference to any converts.)
(16) Dacian offers a banquet to his high priest if he will remove St George.
(17) The priest goes to thank the idols for his success;
(18) and converses with them in a satanic manner.
(19) St George asks to be taken to the temple, where he makes the sign of the cross and the idol of Apollo falls.
(20) St George is taken back to prison.
(21) He is given to the torturers;
*(22) burnt with torches;
*(23) dragged through the streets;
(24) and thrown into quicklime.
(25) But he jumps out unharmed, and a demon jumps into the limepit in his place.
(26) St George is seen entering the prison again.
(27) He is stripped naked and shod with hot iron shoes.
(28) A woman prays whilst an angel and someone who seems to be a king – an unparalleled figure – remove the shoes.
(29) Starved by Dacian, he is brought food by a holy woman.
(30) Dacian decrees that St George must die.
(31) He is decapitated;
(32) and as a precaution his body is dismembered.
(33) After his death St George appears to a woman and heals her son.
(34) Angels reassemble St George's dismembered body on a wagon;
(35) and bury him;

2.7 Detail of wall painting showing the restoration of St George after dismemberment, c. *1300. (Clermont-Ferrand Cathedral)*

(36) whilst other angels bear his soul off to heaven.

The second cycle of the legend of St George in the cathedral is a fragmentary group of wall paintings dating from around 1300 (illustration 2.7). It includes a series of six subjects, all related to torture and resurrection:

(1) St George is bound to two trees, with the dove of the Holy Spirit over him.
(2) St George is cut into pieces on a wheel of blades, watched by the emperor and a group of some eight onlookers. Two men remove body parts from the wheel and pass them on to a group of three men standing by a well.

(3) The body parts are put into the well.
(4) St George appears restored, before the emperor and three companions seated behind a table, with an angel and a servant working to replace the saint's feet. A second angel is shown retrieving body parts from a cauldron.
(5) Christ, seated with an angel in a horse-drawn wagon, blesses the revived saint.
(6) St George is bound to a wooden beam and attacked with hooks by two torturers.

The absence of subjects of either the trial or the execution of the saint in the wall paintings strongly suggests that these images are drawn from the central section of the original cycle, and this implies that there may well have been further tortures in the original scheme. However, the extant subjects clearly demonstrate that the designer of this cycle of wall paintings did not slavishly copy the motifs of torture found in the St George window in the same building, even though we might expect that it would have been tempting to have used such an obvious source. With due allowance being made for the effect of restoration on the glass, it can be claimed with some certainty that none of the tortures found in the wall paintings occur in the window, for there is no sign in the earlier cycle of the binding of the saint to a tree, or of the wheel of blades or of the tearing of his flesh with hooks. The motif of the dismemberment of St George's body does appear in both cycles, but, significantly, in the glass it occurs *after* his execution by decapitation, while in the wall paintings it is strongly associated with a resurrection: according to the chronology of written lives of the saint these resurrections always occur before the beheading. Not only does this obvious difference in approach in the two Clermont-Ferrand cycles reinforce the impression that there was no strongly established canon of scenes which had to be included in a medieval version of the legend of St George, it also suggests that neither chronology nor geography were likely to be important determining factors in the scheme used in any particular cycle.

This brief survey of five medieval cycles of the legend of St George will hopefully have given some impression of the sheer number and diversity of physical torments that are associated with this saint. Indeed, it can be argued that this discontinuity is one of the most significant aspects of the presentation of torture in the medieval cult. The English and Latin texts of the life of St George that I have studied list no fewer than twelve separate tortures (see Table 2), such as beating, burning, scourging and being dragged by horses or bulls, while the visual imagery adds a further five torments, such as being sawn asunder, being raked, and being crucified on a saltire cross. One particularly striking factor is that no single torture motif appears in all, or even most, versions; and even allowing for losses of material when manuscripts or image cycles have been damaged it is still remarkable that there is so little consistency between versions. The tortures that are mentioned most commonly in literary lives are the rack, with or without the simultaneous burning of the saint's body with flaming torches, and the wheel, but these tortures appear in only a few of the visual cycles. Another example of a common written tradition which is reflected in only a small number of visual images is the dismemberment of the saint. For example, the late fifteenth-century cycle of carved wooden desk ends at St George's Chapel, Windsor Castle, includes a scene of St George lying on a board being dismembered while his body parts are cooked in a cauldron nearby (illustration 3.20). Dismember-ment is a common trope in the written lives, but occurs only rarely in the visual imagery (the Clermont-Ferrand cycle of wall paintings, discussed above, contains one example, although the body parts are put into a well rather than cooked); it is far more common for St George to be shown boiled entire, as in the Valencia altarpiece, the St Neot glass (illustration 3.14) and the records of the lost mid-fifteenth-century glass cycle at Stamford (Lincolnshire; illustration 3.7).

Meanwhile, there is some evidence of localised traditions affecting the presentation of torture in the legend: the Valencia altarpiece uniquely features a subject of the saint nailed and tied with chains to a table. The subject is unparalleled in extant visual imagery, but it does occur in a textual source, a Catalan version of the life of St George found in two late fourteenth-century manuscripts; this implies that the German artist would not ordinarily have considered using such a subject, but that it was included at the specific request of the patrons of this work. There may well be other incidences of localised traditions, suggested by the inclusion in a cycle or life of torture that seems to appear nowhere else. For example, in the early sixteenth-century cycle in glass at St Neot (Cornwall), St George is depicted being ridden like a horse by the emperor's son, a subject that seems to have no analogue. Another example occurs in the Bedford Hours (illustration 2.8), where St George is shown seated on a horse while being beaten. It seems unlikely that the designers or makers of these cycles deliberately invented new tortures – they may well have been influenced by lost works or even the simple misinterpretation of other traditions – but it is clear that there was a wide range of torture motifs available to be used in the construction of any one cycle. The same observation can be made of the treatment of other episodes in the legend: consider the frequency with which the subject of St George throwing down the heathen idol is used, or the baptism of converts. It seems that the trial scene and the beheading

Opposite: *2.8* The Bedford Hours, *1423: John, Duke of Bedford, before St George, with roundels of the torture of St George. (British Library, London, Add. MS 18850, fol. 256v)*

fourth century who insisted on the importance of *viginitas spiritu* ('virginity in spirit'). Indeed these authorities claimed that corporal integrity was of little merit if not accompanied by sanctity of life: in the words of St Jerome, 'it is of no value to have virginal flesh if one has wedded in the heart'.[3] This approach is clearly illustrated by *The Book of Margery Kempe*, the autobiography of a Norfolk woman (*c.* 1373–*c.* 1440) who became a pilgrim and visionary following several failed business ventures. Despite being married and having borne fourteen children, Margery sought to achieve the status of virginity, having already persuaded her husband to take a vow of chastity with her. Margery seems to have thought that it was possible for Christ to bestow virginity on favoured individuals, in recognition of their devotion and piety, and it is quite possible that some other late medieval people had a similar view.

It is perhaps unfortunate that St George is never specifically said to be a virgin in the English, Scottish or Latin texts of his life, but there are several aspects of his literary and visual presentation that combine to give this effect. St George's standard emblem, the red cross on a white field, asserts him as a *miles Christianus* – a knight of Christ – which would seem to imply a chaste state, but of potentially greater significance is his relationship to the Virgin Mary through his role as 'Our Lady's Knight', for the virginal Queen of Heaven would surely require a virginal champion. This important facet of the late medieval cult of St George is considered at length in Chapter Three. Another possibly significant presentation is the motif of St George fighting an apparently female dragon, a trope that appears to be charged with the symbolism of sexuality being overthrown by chastity. This aspect of the cult is considered in Chapter Five.

When considering the question of the similarity of St George to female virgin martyrs, and specifically the concept that he may 'borrow' the nature of other saints, we should remember that St George is established as a borrower *par excellence*, most particularly in terms of his tortures. With very few exceptions, such as the scene in the St Neot's glass of St George being ridden, and the subject of the nailing and chaining to a table that occurs in the Valencia altarpiece, it seems that all the tortures which appear in his legend, whether literary or visual, also appear in the legends of other martyrs. Hence he is boiled in oil and poisoned like St John the Divine, beaten and burned with flaming torches like St Margaret, tortured on a saltire cross like St Andrew and St Vincent, and broken on the wheel like St Katherine of Alexandria. (In fact, he is rather less fortunate than St Katherine, for in her narratives the wheel invariably falls apart before she can be tortured on it while St George almost always suffers its full effects. The treatment of the wheel torture in the Bruges panels (illustration 2.1) is perhaps closest to the archetype of St Katherine, for the wheel is shown breaking apart under the influence of heavenly rays.)

One cycle of the legend of St George that seems to exemplify the borrowing of torture motifs in general, and those of female virgin martyrs in particular, is a series of images used to illustrate a mid-fifteenth-century German life of St George (British Library, Add. MS 19462) that is based on the early thirteenth-century poem *Der Helige Georg* composed by Reinbot von Durne. There are twenty-one images in total:

(1) Fol. 4r: St George is shown with two 'brother knights'.
(2) Fol. 10v: The battle with the dragon (illustration 2.9), with St George on foot.
(3) Fol. 13v: St George and a nun, presumably one of his devotees.
(4) Fol. 25r: St George before Dacian.
(5) Fol. 26v: St George in the stocks (illustration 2.10), with Christ looking on.
(6) Fol. 29r: St George with a widow and her two children (illustration 2.11).
(7) Fol. 33r: St George with Dacian and his wife Alexandra.
(8) Fol. 41r: The widow appears with one of her children before Dacian.
(9) Fol. 42v: St George with an idol.
(10) Fol. 46v: St George is dragged.
(11) Fol. 48v: St George is tortured on a wheel fitted with blades (illustration 2.12).
(12) Fol. 50r: St George before Dacian.
(13) Fol. 54r: The Empress Alexandra is tortured (illustration 2.13).
(14) Fol. 57r: Alexandra is beheaded.
(15) Fol. 59r. St George, upside-down, is sawn asunder (illustration 2.14).
(16) Fol. 63r: St George resurrects a dead person from a tomb.
(17) Fol. 71r: Three towers, the middle one flying a banner with a device of a black cross.
(18) Fol. 74r: An ox on a mountain.
(19) Fol. 76r: St George before Dacian.
(20) Fol. 79r: St George is baked in an oven.
(21) Fol. 82r: St George is beheaded.

This cycle is unusual in several respects, particularly the inclusion of scenes relating to St George's miraculous healing of the widow's son (illustration 2.11), a narrative theme that was important in early versions of the saint's life but is generally absent from later visual and literary treatments. These relatively unusual subjects are

German Life of St George, mid-fifteenth century. (British Library, London, Add. MS 19462)

Top*: 2.9* St George fights the dragon. *Fol. 10v.*
Centre*: 2.10* St George on trial in the stocks. *Fol. 26v.*
Bottom*: 2.11* St George with a widow and her two children. *Fol. 29r.*

Top: *2.12* St George is brought for torture on a wheel fitted with blades. *Fol. 48v.*
Centre: *2.13* The Empress Alexandra is tortured. *Fol. 54r.*
Bottom: *2.14* St George, upside-down, is sawn asunder. *Fol. 59r.*

enhanced by the addition of extraneous imagery, such as the scene with the nun and the illustration of the towers. However, perhaps the most interesting aspect of this cycle is the sequence of images of torture. The subjects of St George in the stocks (illustration 2.10), sawn in half while upside-down (illustration 2.14), and burnt in an oven are all apparently unparalleled, but it is the image of the torture of the Empress Alexandra which is truly arresting (illustration 2.13). We see Alexandra, naked except for a loincloth and her crown, being tortured by two men who are cutting off her breasts. Copious quantities are blood are depicted: this may now provoke a reaction of revulsion in a viewer, but for the fifteenth-century patron of this book the effect was probably to produce a feeling of great respect for the forbearance of the unfortunate martyr. If this subject is viewed in isolation, separate from the cycle of St George images, it could easily be mistaken for an image of St Agatha, a virgin martyr who is said to have had her breasts cut off during her torture. Another cognate is the empress in the narrative of St Katherine, who similarly suffered the removal of the breasts. There seem to be no references to this type of torment in other medieval literary or visual versions of St George's legend – Alexandra is hung up by her hair and beaten in some accounts, although her breasts were crushed with a huge rock in one Coptic version – so it may well be that we are seeing a conscious borrowing from a female virgin martyr legend, albeit a borrowing that was applied to the empress, one of St George's converts, rather than to the saint himself. It would be very difficult to establish whether or not this subject was directly influenced by a specific image of the turture of St Agatha or St Katherine's empress: again, we are confronted by the loss of so much material. Likewise, the artist need not have made a straight copy of an image from another saint's life: indeed, it is perhaps more likely that it was the general concept of a Christian woman being tortured by the removal of her breasts which was invoked in this image. The overall conclusion that we can perhaps draw from this image is that artists concerned with the legend of St George had no compunction about borrowing imagery from other saints and applying them to the St George narrative, whether or not the imagery was sustained by the written tradition of the life of the saint.

Drawing together the different aspects of the visual presentation of St George's martyrdom, it is clear that this narrative strand retained its importance throughout the medieval period, even when the newly introduced dragon story threatened to oust it altogether. It is probable that images and accounts of the martyrdom had different resonances for different audiences: some patrons sought to hold up St George as a role-model of Christian forbearance while others may have been interested in the presentation of spiritual virginity. A third sort of 'reader', both of texts and images, may yet have existed: Chaucer's Wife of Bath spoke of her husband's delight in reading a 'book of wikked wyves', and it is surely possible that some devotees of St George were drawn to the written and visual imagery of the suffering saint and his converts – the torn flesh, the cascading blood, the gruesome tortures – and took salacious delight in contemplating this medieval version of the horror film. Yet another explanation defines St George as a willing victim. This reading draws not only on the model of Christ as one who suffered in order to ensure the salvation of his followers but also alludes to the pre-Christian traditions discussed in Chapter One, where fertility rites demanded that a man should fight the outgoing 'king of the year' in order to placate the spirits of the earth through a sacrifice. The new ruler fought in the knowledge that he too would be deposed in his turn, but offered himself as a kind of sacrificial victim for the good of the whole community. It is difficult to know which of these various readings may be intended in any depiction of the martyrdom of St George, but it is likely that the artists and patrons who created these images will often have been influenced, even if only on a subconscious level, by such considerations.

CHAPTER THREE

THE VIRGIN'S KNIGHT: ST GEORGE AND THE CHIVALRIC IDEAL

One of the most interesting facets of the late medieval cult of St George in England is the strong connection that existed between the saint and the Virgin Mary. This can perhaps be understood as an aspect of mariolatry, a term used by historians to describe the phenomenon of the increasing interest that the Virgin attracted from the twelfth century onwards. This new devotion is evident in many different forms, such as the introduction of litanies for feast days specifically associated with the Virgin from the thirteenth century and the development in the fifteenth century of concepts such as the *Madonna della Misericordia* (the Virgin of Mercy, who shelters supplicants beneath her cloak), a subtle shift in emphasis which speaks volumes about changing attitudes to the importance of the Virgin as a figure worthy of devotion in her own right, rather than simply as a functionary of God the Father and Christ.

The cult of the Virgin became increasingly visible through the High Middle Ages through large numbers of church dedications and the creation of many images featuring the Virgin, whether as a mother or with narrative scenes of her life, as a main subject. By the late medieval period mariolatry was a well-established devotion, and there is ample evidence to suggest that one of the reasons behind the rise of the concept of St George as 'Our Lady's Knight' was the opportunity it afforded to the pious to unite their interest in this very popular saint with the ultimate female figure of devotional fervour. St George was identified as the Virgin's champion, a knight who would represent his patroness in combat, publicly defending her honour when it was impugned by the unworthy. This particular construction of the saint as a hero clearly invokes the mores of 'courtly love', an important trope of late medieval literature where a man, usually a knight, expresses his love for an unattainable, noble woman through service but never seeks to consummate his desire for her. The reasons why the woman is unattainable can vary, but in the standard format she is married to someone else although she truly loves her champion; on the rare occasions where lust gets the better of them the story always seems to end unhappily. However, in the relationship between the Virgin and St George the conventions of noble behaviour are never broken, and this 'perfect', unconsummated love underlines the Virgin's status as a beautiful, chaste and noble woman, worthy to be the mother of Christ.

The precise origins of the motif of St George as 'Our Lady's Knight' are unclear, but the link is certainly evident in the late twelfth-century *Golden Legend* version of his story, for it is stated that the King of Silene built a magnificent church in honour of St George and the Virgin following the saint's victory over the dragon and conversion of the city. The eighth-century French chronicler Fontenelle relates that when a relic of St George was discovered washed up on a beach in Normandy three churches were built, one dedicated to St George, one to the Virgin and one to St Cross; it is certainly possibly that the choice of the first two dedications is a reference to the link between St George and the Virgin. The motif of the double dedication occurs in virtually all the medieval English lives that feature the dragon legend, and the relationship between the Virgin and St George is also stated explicitly in some versions: 'men callis hym oure lady knycht' (*Scottish Legendary*, l. 14); 'oure ladyes owen knyght' (Lydgate, l. 85).

Altars with a compound dedication to St George and the Virgin are known, for example in the early sixteenth century at the parish church in Towcester (Northamptonshire), and the link is also evident in pairings of St George and the Virgin in artefacts such the Great Seal used by Edward III towards the end of his reign and a fifteenth-century latten candelabra, around 1 metre (3 feet) high, recorded at the Temple Church in Bristol. This magnificent object, which had twelve branches arranged in two tiers, was destroyed during the Second World War. The ornamentation consisted of a figure of St George and the dragon, in the centre of the two tiers, and a statuette of the Virgin and Child at the top. The pairing of St George and the Virgin and Child also occurs on the decoration of a tomb niche at Ratcliffe-on-Soar (Nottinghamshire). The tomb is that of Ralph Sacheverell (d.1539) and his wife, but the niche decoration is clearly part of a different scheme, and hence likely to be earlier, as the tomb effigies currently obscure the figures of St George and the Virgin and Child. The connection between the Virgin and St George also appears in the dedication of the Priory of the Blessed Virgin Mary and St George, a small Augustinian foundation established in Gresley (Derbyshire) during the reign of Henry I, as well as in various medieval carols, notably the mid-fifteenth-century anonymous text quoted on p. v of this book. The full text is:

Enfors we us with all our might
To love Seint George, our Lady knight.

Worship of virtu is the mede,
And seweth him ay of right:
To worship George then have we nede,
Which is our soverein Lady's knight.

He keped the mad from dragon's dred,
And fraid all France and put to flight.
At Agincourt – the crownecle ye red –
The French him se formest in fight.

In his virtu he wol us lede
Againis the Fend, the ful wight,
And with his banner us oversprede,
If we love him with all our might.[1]

'mad': maid; 'crownecle': chronicle; 'red': read; 'Fende': Fiend, i.e. the Devil; 'ful': foul

This carol is strongly patriotic, if not nationalistic, in its tone, with a comparison being drawn between St George's defeat of the dragon and his 'appearance' at Agincourt in 1415, where the English won a famous victory over the French. He is twice explicitly referred to as 'Our Lady's Knight,' and it is worth remembering that this sobriquet would be particularly appealing to an English author and audience, for England was sometimes referred to as 'the Virgin's dowry', that is, a country that was owned by the Virgin and in which she had a special interest. This idea was invoked in a late fourteenth-century altarpiece, now lost but known to us through a seventeenth-century description. The altarpiece showed Richard II and his first wife, Anne of Bohemia, offering a 'globe or patterne of England' to the Virgin, while an inscription stated '*Dos tua Virgo pia haec est; quare rege Maria*' [This is your dowry O holy Virgin, therefore rule over it O Mary].[2] A number of other English carols also explicitly refer to St George as 'Our Lady's knight', while he is invoked under this appellation in several English charms to protect horses against the 'night-mare', or 'night goblin', which was conceived of as a hideous hag who would sit on and squeeze the stomach of a sleeper and thereby cause bad dreams, or bring a horse out from a stable and ride it all night so that it would be found exhausted in the morning. The following rhyme was to be written on a piece of paper (or perhaps parchment) and tied into the horse's mane:

In nomine Patris, etc. [i.e. 'In the name of the Father, the Son and the Holy Ghost, Amen', in Latin]

> Saint Jorge, our Lady Knight,
> He walked day, he walked night,
> Till that he founde that foule wight;
> And when that he her founde,
> He her bete and he her bounde,
> Till trewly ther her trowth she plight
> That she sholde not come by night
> Within seven rod of lande space
> Theras Saint Jeorge y-named was.
> St Jeorge, St Jeorge, St Jeorge.

In nomine Patris, etc.[3]

To ensure full power, an amulet of a piece of flint with a natural hole should also be hung over the stable door. The earliest references to versions of this charm date from the period *c.* 1425–50, but it also appeared in a book on witchcraft as late as 1584; this longevity gives some indication of the extent of belief in its veracity. Through his identification as a knight, St George was, of course, particularly associated with horses, but for our purposes it is the clear link with the Virgin Mary that is of particular interest.

Perhaps the most obvious connection between St George and the Virgin is found in various English images of the saint, dating from the mid-thirteenth to early sixteenth centuries. The earliest known examples of this tradition occur in early fourteenth-century sculptures in the Lady Chapel at Ely Cathedral; the same motif can be seen in the contemporaneous Queen Mary Psalter and Smithfield Decretals, and the rather later Carew-Poyntz Hours (*c.* 1360), and also on a carved ceiling boss (*c.* 1382) in the west walk of the cloister at Norwich Cathedral. The story is concerned with the resurrection of St George, a motif clearly related to the early versions of the life of the saint discussed in Chapter One, but rather than angels performing the resurrection, as occurs in Pasicrates' account, it is the Virgin Mary herself who restores the saint to life and then arms him as her knight-champion. This motif seems to be based on a legend of the Greek soldier–saint Mercurius, who was said to have been resurrected by the Virgin for the specific purpose of killing the apostate Emperor Julian (a historically authentic character who was actually killed in AD 363 by a Persian thrusting a spear into his liver during a military campaign on the Euphrates). The *Golden Legend* gives an account of the apocryphal assassination of Julian by St Mercurius, stating that Julian had threatened to raze the city of Caesarea in Cappadocia following an argument with St Basil over a gift of barley loaves. St Basil had a vision of the Virgin summoning St Mercurius to despatch Julian, and the following day he visited the soldier's tomb to find that his lance was covered in blood; shortly afterwards, he was informed that Julian had been murdered by a mystery assassin. Versions of the legend of St Mercurius circulated in Western Europe from the thirteenth century in collections of miracles of the Virgin, the *Speculum historiale* of Vincent of Beauvais and Gerald of Wales's *Gemma ecclesiastica*, among other texts; in England St George seems to have been substituted for this little-known saint, although this incident does not occur in any written life of St George and is not alluded to in the *Acta Sanctorum*, the encyclopedic reference work on saint legends and cults, even in the section specifically concerned with devotion to St George in England. The *Lambeth Apocalypse* (*c.* 1250–5) illustrates a legend of the Virgin resurrecting the soldier–saint (fol. 45); the device on his shield is very close to the cross of St George, and this may indicate the source of the English visual tradition that substitutes St George for St Mercurius.

However, in later English visual imagery, particularly narrative cycles of St George, the apostate Emperor Julian generally disappears from the story. Three extant late fifteenth-century cycles, all created by English artists and craft workers, include a story where St George seems to be resurrected in order that he should kill the dragon; this new narrative also occurred in the lost Stamford cycle (*c.* 1450), according to the records made of the cycle during the mid-seventeenth century. Furthermore, an interesting development also takes place at the beginning of the story, and the visual evidence suggests that the narrative of St Mercurius/St George and the Emperor Julian was adapted in fifteenth-century England to make the link between the saint and the Virgin Mary even stronger.

Despite the clear congruence between these four cycles, it is interesting to note that the late fifteenth-century wall paintings of the miracles of the Virgin on the north side of Winchester Cathedral Lady Chapel include three subjects from the story of St George resurrected to kill Julian the Apostate, and may well also have appeared in the wall paintings on the north side of Eton College Chapel, dated 1479–88. The re-emergence of this form of the narrative in English material at this late date tends to imply that the two forms co-existed, rather than that the legend of St George as a dragon-slayer necessarily ousted the legend of St George as the assassin of the heathen Emperor Julian.

Besides Stamford (illustrations 3.1–3.3), the cycles where the new story occurs are those at Borbjerg (illustration 3.11), La Selle (illustrations 3.12 and 3.13) and St Neot (illustrations 3.14 and 3.15). Before considering this aspect further it will be useful to review briefly the history and iconography of each cycle in turn.

As noted in Chapter Two, the mid-fifteenth-century Stamford cycle of the life of St George was formerly in the chancel windows of St George's Church, Stamford (Lincolnshire). It is known to us now through drawings made of twenty-one of the subjects in the seventeenth-century herald William Dugdale's *Book of Monuments*, but it is likely that there were a further eight subjects; the evidence concerning the placement of the lost images is inconclusive, but it seems likely that three or four are missing from the beginning of the cycle. The recorded subjects are:

(1) This is an apparently unparalleled subject of St George standing before a well brandishing a sword, with a woman and a water jug lying on the ground. It is unclear whether St George has cast them down or is about to raise them up. The saint is haloed, but is not identified by his red cross device: despite the presence of the sword, he does not wear armour. It seems likely that this is a subject drawn from the obscure early part of St George's career, and perhaps reflects a lost tradition.
(2) St George, still with a halo but now wearing armour with a red cross tabard and shield, is depicted on foot (illustration 3.1). He uses a sword to fight a group of six armed men, who are not identified by any device. Two of the figures are already falling, but the other four men threaten the saint with lances and swords.
(3) St George, wearing armour and a red cross tabard, kneels before an altar bearing a figure of the Virgin and Child (illustration 3.2). He is about to be beheaded by a bearded

3.1 to 3.10 William Sedgwick, sketches (c. *1641) in William Dugdale's* Book of Monuments *of the St George narrative cycle in the chancel glass of St George's church, Stamford (Lincolnshire),* c. *1450. (British Library, London, Add. MS 71474)*

Below left: *3.1 St George in battle. Fol. 152v.*

Below: *3.2 The execution of St George. Fol. 153.*

Above: *3.3 St George resurrected by the Virgin Mary. Fol. 153v.*

Above right: *3.4 St George fights the dragon. Fol. 154.*

man, in armour and a plain red tabard, who wields a large axe.

(4) St George is resurrected by the Virgin and three angels from a stone tomb-chest, which is depicted in an outdoor site beneath a substantial archway (illustration 3.3).

(5) St George, mounted and armed as a knight, fights the dragon. In the main, this is a very conventional treatment, with the dragon in the classic pose under the horse's hooves, the princess kneeling in the background and her parents watching from a fortified building (illustration 3.4). The only exceptional aspect is the lack of a lamb.

(6) This subject shows the baptism of the king, queen and princess by St George, who still wears his armour but now has a sleeved tabard. Five other converts are waiting their turn; they are all naked, and the foremost, a woman, covers herself rather ineffectually with a white sheet.

(7) A scene of the trial of St George, who is still in armour and tabard and is escorted by three armed guards. Dacian does not seem to be enthroned, but is seated before a cloth of honour. This is a rather unusual treatment, as Dacian has his hand on the head of a woman who appears to be denouncing the saint. Her identity is a mystery, as there is no known tradition that corresponds to this image.

(8) This subject is in two parts. On the left side, St George is shown being pushed into a prison by a guard while Dacian, holding a sceptre, looks on; on the right side, he is in prison,

Above left: *3.5 St George tortured on the rack.Fol. 156.*

Above: *3.6 St George is scourged. Fol. 156v.*

preaching to a wimpled woman who kneels in prayer outside. She is almost certainly to be identified as the Empress Alexandra, who was converted by St George.

(9) St George, now stripped and wearing only a loincloth, lies on a rack (illustration 3.5). Two torturers pull on the ropes tied to his body, and Dacian looks on amid a group of six other men.

(10) St George is tied to a cross and scourged by two torturers (illustration 3.6). Dacian and another figure look on.

(11) This subject appears to be St George raked or burnt by torches. He is seated and assaulted by three torturers, who hold indistinct implements against his body.

(12) St George is boiled in a cauldron, which seems to contain water rather than lead, placed on a fire (illustration 3.7). Two torturers stir the liquid while a third, seated on the ground, looks on.

(13) The torture of the millstones, in a rather unusual version (illustration 3.8). Rather than being suspended by his hands, St George has been seated on a mechanism with a large blade, a millstone tied to each foot. Two torturers are present, one of whom appears to be operating the mechanism in order to raise the blade and cut the saint in half. Dacian also looks on.

(14) St George is bound to a post and a torturer holds a chalice to his lips (illustration 3.9). This image is probably the poisoning of St George, although there is no sign of the conventional dragon in the chalice. Three other torturers, armed with large axes, look on.

3.7 St George is boiled. Fol. 157v.

3.8 St George is tortured with millstones. Fol. 158.

3.9 St George is poisoned. Fol. 158v.

(15) This is a curious image that shows St George baptising a figure of indeterminate gender while two people, one a bearded man, look on. It seems likely that the convert is Athanasius, the magician who became a Christian when his poison failed to kill the saint, but the fact that St George wears armour is rather troublesome. The purple of the robe held by the bearded man could be significant, although the only royal or imperial figure converted by St George, apart from the rescued princess and her family whom we have already seen, was Dacian's consort the Empress Alexandra. The short hair on the baptised figure, in stark contrast to the princess and queen's long hair in the previous baptism, makes it unlikely that this figure is female, although the short hairstyle on the near-naked woman in the first baptism scene (subject 6) could imply that this figure is a short-haired woman, or a woman with her hair tied up in some way.

(16) St George, again wearing only a loincloth, is suspended by his hands and sawn vertically in half by two torturers. It is interesting that the saw is not shown passing through the saint's chest; the torturers here are defying logic as they apparently float in mid-air to hold the saw at his head.

(17) This seems to be a second scene of resurrection. St George is shown lying in a similar chest-tomb to that in subject 4, but wearing a loincloth rather than graveclothes. St Peter stands on the left side, holding his key, and next to him stands a male figure, who is almost certainly Christ, raising the saint. Two angels also assist. This scene is problematic as it seems to have no analogues. St Michael, angels and the Virgin are variously credited with resurrecting St George, but there does not seem to be a tradition of Christ performing this function.

(18) A version of the torture on the wheel: St George is shown tortured on a machine that seems to work on a ratcheting system operated by two torturers. A third torturer, holding a large axe, looks on, as does the Emperor Dacian.

(19) St George, who kneels and has his hands tied to a post, is scourged by a torturer with a seven-headed whip. Two other torturers look on. Dacian is also present, and next to him is a man dressed in clerical robes, an iconographic convention which identifies a *clerk*, or secretary, rather than a *cleric*, in this context.

(20) St George kneels, awaiting his beheading by an executioner holding a large sword (illustration 3.10). Dacian and another figure, of indeterminate gender, look

3.10 St George is beheaded. Fol. 161v.

on from within a building in the background.
(21) The final scene is of a golden reliquary, which presumably contains relics of St George. It is displayed on an arcaded structure, with four male religious of two different orders in the background and three lay people kneeling in the foreground.

The Borbjerg retable (illustration 3.11), a sculpted altarpiece dated to *c.* 1480, is a product of the late medieval English alabaster industry that was probably centred on the area around Nottingham. English alabaster was widely distributed across most parts of Europe, both as ready-made 'off-the-peg' pieces and as specific commissions: this cycle is known by the name of the Danish village in West Jutland where it is located. It is quite likely that this altarpiece was ordered from a travelling alabaster merchant in order to honour the local patron saint, for the nearby town of Holstebro is dedicated to St George, and still holds an annual St George parade every February. The retable consists of five panels of alabaster and two terminal statues. These would originally have been displayed in a custom-made wooden framework that has been lost at some point in the retable's history. The current arrangement probably does not accurately reflect the original format, because of disruption caused by the dismantling and hiding of the panels during the Reformation, and it is possible that two further panels, probably the execution of St George and perhaps either the baptism of converts or another scene of torture, have been lost. The extant panels are currently arranged as follows:

(1) A standing figure of St George with the dragon under his feet.
(2) St George is tortured by three men. The torturers hold small implements that they are applying to the saint's limbs. This could be read as a scene of flaying, or perhaps as burning with torches; the loss of colour on the body of the saint makes it impossible to know which reading is intended. The Emperor Dacian and a second figure look on.
(3) This is a scene of the trial before Dacian, combined with the torture of the poison. Dacian is seated on a throne, with a decapitated male figure at his feet. St George stands in the centre of the composition, turning towards a man holding a golden chalice containing a red dragon: this identifies him as Athanasius, the magician who tries to poison St George. The saint's right hand is raised in a gesture of blessing over the chalice, which implies that he is depicted in the act of nullifying the poison. A fifth figure kneels in the foreground on the right side. He wears a robe similar to that of both Athanasius and the decapitated man: it is possible that they are three entirely separate people but, given the resemblance between the robes, it seems likely that we are shown Athanasius three times in this panel: trying to poison

Opposite: *3.11 The Borbjerg retable of the life of St George,* c. *1480.*

יהוה
Loven er given
ved Moses,
Hvo som æder mit Kjød og drikker mit Blod
han bliver i mig og jeg i ham.
Naaden og Sandheden
er vorden ved
Jesum Christum.

St George, then, having failed and then converted to Christianity, about to be executed by Dacian, and finally, beheaded.

(4) In the central, taller, panel St George is shown before a heathen temple. The temple structure is painted to resemble flames, and on the top is a grotesque idol holding a flesh-hook, an instrument used in medieval kitchens to test the readiness of meat cooking on a spit and often used as a weapon by demons in late medieval imagery. Alongside the demon stand three men, including Dacian in his gold crown. In the lower part of the temple, under an arch supported by twin pillars, stands a man who is presumably the heathen priest.

(5) This panel combines scenes of the resurrection of St George and the arming by the Virgin. St George kneels in full armour on a grassy hillock in the centre of the panel. The Virgin holds a large helm over the saint's head; this has been entirely hollowed out by undercutting, a feature that demonstrates the high quality of the sculpture. An angel holding the saint's spear and shield stands behind the Virgin, while a smaller angel kneels to attach his spurs. The saint's horse, wearing a red saddle and bridle, stands in the background. On the left, an angel holds a large sword in a scabbard figured with a blue floral pattern. The end of the sword is obscured as it enters an empty chest-tomb; the graveclothes are patterned with a blue trefoil motif, and a similar design is picked out in the gold area that indicates the lower part of the tomb.

(6) St George, fully armoured and mounted on his horse, plunges his lance into the breast of a fallen knight, who lies sprawled in the foreground on the right. This figure holds a shield in his left hand (device lost); he is mounted, but his horse has fallen beneath him. Behind the fallen knight is a tower with a portcullis, and three men armed with sticks emerge. It is unclear whether these men are allied with St George or with his antagonist, although the style of their helmets tends to suggest the latter: given the Danish tradition of St George fighting with the Danes against the Swedes they may be intended to be read as Swedish.

(7) St Michael, identifiable by his prominent red-feathered wings, stands with a dragon under his feet, thrusting a lance into its mouth. His position is a mirror image of St George at the other end of the cycle. The device on his shield seems to be a red cross: he is occasionally depicted carrying a shield with the 'cross of St George – for example, in a fourteenth-century stained glass image at Goodnestone (Kent) – and this presentation serves to underline the connections between them as soldiers of Christ.

The La Selle Retable (illustration 3.12) is another sculpted English alabaster altarpiece, dated slightly later than the Borbjerg

3.12 The La Selle Retable of the life of St George and the life of the Virgin Mary, c. 1485.

retable (*c.* 1485) and named after the small hamlet in Normandy where it is currently situated. It is a very unusual two-tiered arrangement with thirteen extant narrative panels, six drawn from the legend of St George (on the upper tier) and seven from the life of the Virgin Mary (on the lower tier, plus the central panel). These narrative scenes were originally augmented by twelve figures of saints, of which four small statuettes are extant. The history of this altarpiece is uncertain, but several unusual aspects of the iconography suggest that it was commissioned by a Norman patron. For example, the saint's red cross device is notably absent from the work, almost certainly because at this time the red cross was associated with the English enemy during the Hundred Years' War, and St George was not identified by the Normans as an 'English' saint.

The very existence of this altarpiece is strong evidence for the association that existed between St George and the Virgin Mary in the minds of late medieval people. It is particularly important to note the efforts made to link the stylistic forms and the iconographic themes depicted in each vertical pair of panels: the subjects of the two cycles have not been put together randomly, it would seem, but with considerable care and forethought. Hence, we see that the first panels in each vertical pairing are associated with birth, and resurrection as rebirth, the second pair with a public acceptance of a divine commission, and so forth. The third pair of panels includes a number of particularly interesting parallels, which are discussed further in Chapter Five. The absence of any mention of torture in the St George imagery, as noted in Chapter Two, is almost certainly due to the demands of melding the two narratives together: the Virgin Mary is never said to have suffered any form of *physical* torment, and the introduction of the subject of her *psychological* suffering, such as the Lamentation over the Dead Christ, would have been too far removed from the overall narrative scheme. For our current purposes the salient factor in this retable is the iconography of the resurrection and arming of St George by the Virgin, which occurs in the upper scheme; the narrative of the St George cycle is as follows:

(1) The resurrection of St George by the Virgin: the Virgin blesses St George and assists him to rise from a tomb, while three angels look on (illustration 3.13).
(2) The Virgin arms St George: assisted by an angel, she lowers a helm over the saint's head, while a second angel is placing spurs on his heels. Two further angels carry a lance (on the left) and shield (on the right: the edge of the shield is just visible behind the Virgin's back).
(3) The battle between St George and the dragon. Most features of this subject are quite typical, such as the praying figure of the princess whom St George is rescuing, and her crowned parents looking out from the tower.
(4) St George baptises three converts, who are presumably the rescued princess and her parents.
(5) St George debates with the Emperor Dacian, whose villainy is clearly underlined: he wears a dog-crested hat, is flanked by a cloven-hoofed idol, and is using a defeated enemy as a footstool. His legs are crossed: this pose also betrays his status as a malefactor, according to medieval iconographic tradition, as does the very obvious sword.
(6) The final panel of this sequence shows the saint's martyrdom. Dacian and the executioner both brandish swords, and bear the blackened faces of the villains of medieval drama. The central figure is probably Dacian's secretary; he also has a blackened face and carries a scroll. The saint's head lies on the ground in the bottom right corner, while his soul is borne away to heaven by two angels.

The iconography of the lower cycle and the central panel is concerned with both canonical and apocryphal stories of the Virgin Mary. The narrative is laid out thus:

3.13 The La Selle Retable: *detail of the resurrection and the arming of St George, and the combat with the dragon.*

(7) The Nativity of the Virgin. St Anne, the Virgin's mother, lies in a canopied bed whilst a midwife or serving-maid attends to her. A second assistant is holding the swaddled infant, whilst a third reaches out as if to take the baby and place her in the bed she has prepared.

(8) The Presentation of the Virgin, a subject derived directly from the Apocryphal Gospels, a group of non-canonical early Christian writings that contain information about the Virgin, the childhood of Christ and other 'dubious' legends. Here the Virgin is shown as a child ascending the fifteen steps of the Temple towards the priest who waits to receive her into her new home. Her parents, St Anne and St Joachim, are in attendance, along with two female bystanders who may represent the other virginal girls who lived in the Temple. The small figure of a bedesman occupies the area under the stairs, probably to draw attention to the Gradual Psalms that the Virgin is reputed to have recited as she mounted the steps of the Temple.

(9) The Annunciation, with the Virgin's signifying lilies wrapped around with a scroll that presumably bore the opening words of the *Ave Maria*. The figure of God the Father, holding an orb, stands behind the Angel Gabriel.

(10) The Nativity, or Adoration of Christ. The Virgin kneels in an attitude of prayer, while St Joseph stands in the background holding a crutched staff. The Christ Child lies on two sheaves of corn; these are placed in cruciform, as an archetype of the Crucifixion, and the ears of one sheaf form a halo effect behind his head. An angel flies overhead with a scroll. There are two midwives in attendance, and the conventional ox and ass occupy a small space below St Joseph, where they are enclosed within a strange architectural setting.
(11) A conventional Adoration of the Magi, with the offering of gifts to the infant Christ who sits enthroned on his mother's lap.
(12) The Presentation of Christ. Simeon the priest and the Virgin are holding the Christ Child on top of an altar whilst St Joseph carries the conventional basket of doves for an offering, and two female figures at the back look on. One is probably meant to represent the prophetess Anna, who foresaw the coming of Christ.
(13) The central panel of the retable shows a combination of two subjects: the Assumption of the Virgin and her Coronation by the Trinity. The Virgin is supported by a team of nine angels as she ascends to heaven, four on either side of her mandorla and one pushing at her feet. On the left, St Thomas kneels to receive her girdle, as tradition dictates. The four small figures of saints around the upper part of the central panel are SS Peter, James the Great, Mary Magdalen and probably Bridget of Sweden.

The latest medieval English cycle of the life of St George (illustration 3.15) occurs in the north window of the west aisle of St Neot's Church in the village of St Neot (Cornwall). However, it originally occupied the fifth window from the east end of the south aisle. The images are arranged in three rows of four images, reading from the top left. It dates from the early years of the sixteenth century and contains twelve scenes:

3.14 The St George window at St Neot: detail of the arming of St George.

(1) St George fights an enemy host labelled as the 'Gallicani', which probably translates as 'the Gauls'.
(2) He is beheaded before an altar bearing an image of the Virgin.
(3) St George is resurrected from a chest-tomb by the Virgin.
(4) He is armed by the Virgin and angels, one of whom holds a lance and shield while the other, kneeling, holds a sword and spurs (illustration 3.14).
(5) St George fights the dragon, watched by the princess, who kneels with her lamb, and her parents, who are in a tower of the city wall.
(6) The trial of St George before an enthroned king. This ruler cannot be the Emperor Dacian, who is distinguished by the

3.15 The St George window in the parish church of St Neot (Cornwall), early sixteenth century.

arched imperial crown that he wears in later scenes. However, this subject has been heavily restored, and it is possible that an inaccurate restoration is giving a misleading impression.
(7) The saint is assaulted by two torturers, apparently using rakes.
(8) St George is ridden as a horse by the emperor's son, who holds a whip above his head. One torturer stands in front of the saint and strikes him with a club; a second stands behind and thrusts a spear into his leg.
(9) St George is hung from a gibbet with a millstone tied to his feet while the emperor looks on.

(10) A torturer throws the saint headfirst into a cauldron of molten lead, as the emperor looks on.
(11) St George's feet are tied to a horse, and he is dragged through the city. One man rides on the horse while a second holds its bridle.
(12) St George, wearing armour, is about to be decapitated by an executioner wielding a sword. The emperor stands on one side and an official on the other.

Despite their apparent chronological proximity, these four cycles show considerable variation in their iconography. One of the most obvious differences is the choice of subjects, for several episodes that commonly occur in literary versions of the saint's legend appear in only one or two of these cycles. For example, the casting down of the idol in the temple occurs only at Borbjerg and the imprisonment occurs only at Stamford. Some anomalies may well occur because of losses: at Borbjerg, a cycle that has been seriously affected by dismantling, the absence of scenes of baptism and execution seems very unlikely to have been a design decision as these subjects are integral to the narrative of the legend. However, we should note the omission of the subject of the baptism of the rescued princess and her parents at St Neot; although several scenes in this cycle have been heavily, and probably incorrectly, restored, it is unlikely that it could have suffered the loss of an entire subject. The implication seems to be that the dragon story and its associated imagery was of little interest to the patron or designer of this particular window: there seems to be a desire to show St George as a believer who suffered for his faith, not a valiant Christian hero who overcomes the evil dragon and converts the heathen. A similar rationale may have informed the unusual treatment of the dragon episode in the Borbjerg retable: in the other cycles this subject is accorded a far higher status, with an entire panel devoted to it, but at Borbjerg there is a mere visual reference in a terminal figure.

This type of design variation is also evident in the treatment of torture: as observed in Chapter Two, at Stamford there is a strong emphasis on the physical torment of the saint, with nine of the twenty-one documented subjects concerned with some form of torture. This approach is echoed in the St Neot glass, where five of the twelve subjects are images of torture, but this is in clear contrast to the two alabaster cycles as torture only appears in two panels at Borbjerg, in the form of burning and poison, and seems to be entirely absent from the La Selle retable. At first glance it may seem that the difference in approach may be due to the difference in medium: Stamford and St Neot were both cycles in glass, Borbjerg and La Selle are both in alabaster, but the existence of alabaster panels of the torture of other saints gives the lie to this claim.

Rather, it seems most likely that the variation has arisen because of differences in the requirements of the patrons of these cycles: this possibility may also explain the presence of the second baptism, the second resurrection and the final subject of the reliquary of St George in the Stamford cycle, subjects that do not appear in the literary tradition.

Perhaps even more striking than the variations in the treatment of the subjects drawn from literary sources is the addition of extra scenes that do not appear in the written lives. The scene at the well, documented at Stamford, seems to have no analogues. It may reflect an error on the part of Dugdale or his limner Sedgwick, or a confusion of two different images: it seems likely that they made notes and sketches of interesting objects 'on the spot', and that Sedgwick later worked up the sketches into the illustrations found in the *Book of Monuments*. The time delay involved, which seems to have been no less than three weeks in the case of St George's Church, Stamford, will have certainly permitted the possibility of some errors creeping in. However, the other non-literary subject-matter occurring in these cycles, which relates to the resurrection and the arming of St George by the Virgin, occurs with a fair degree of consistency across the four cycles, and it is thus likely that we are looking at a narrative scheme that was either unique to late medieval English visual treatments of the legend of St George, or, more persuasively, reflects a lost English oral or written tradition concerned with this saint.

If we focus on the narrative of St George resurrected by the Virgin, armed as her knight and then going forth to kill the dragon, we find that this story occurs in all four of the English cycles. Only the St Neot glass tells the entire legend, but the correspondences between this narrative and the other three are sufficiently strong to allow us to conclude that we are looking at an otherwise lost legend of St George. The story seems to be that St George is a valiant Christian knight, identified by a red cross, who fights a heathen enemy (illustration 3.1). At St Neot the enemy are named as 'Gallicani', a term that can be glossed as 'the Gauls': it has been suggested that this story may have arisen during the Hundred Years' War, when France was the national enemy, as a variant of the story of St Mercurius/St George and the Emperor Julian. It is possible that the saint's enemies are also intended to be read as the Gauls at Stamford – indeed, the omission of scenes of the battle and subsequent execution at La Selle could have occurred because the work was commissioned by a Norman patron – but it is likely that the salient factors are that St George's assailants are both heathen and non-English. Alternative readings are also possible: as observed above, the saint's enemies in the Borbjerg retable may be intended to be read as Swedish.

Whoever his enemy is, St George is presumably overcome, for the next image at both Stamford and St Neot shows St George being beheaded before an altar bearing an image of the Virgin and Child (illustration 3.2). This narrative device simultaneously underlines both St George's devotion to the Virgin and his executioner's heathen beliefs, for only a heathen would pollute the ground before a Christian altar. The next two images in the sequence show the Virgin rewarding St George by resurrecting him and arming him as her champion: at La Selle and St Neot these two episodes are treated separately (illustrations 3.13 and 3.15), but at Borbjerg they are shown in the same panel, possibly to economise on space: the tomb recently vacated by the saint is visible in the background of the scene of the arming of St George. At Stamford the scene of the arming seems to be missing from the sequence, probably as a result of damage in advance of the recording of the cycle in 1642 (the deliberate omission of an arming scene would be especially strange in the context of a patron whose important position in the Order of the Garter implies that he will have been very interested in the role of the knight), but the resurrection of St George by the Virgin occurs in its correct place, immediately after the beheading.

At Stamford, La Selle and St Neot the story concludes with a scene of St George fighting the dragon; as noted above, the narrative scheme at Borbjerg has clearly been disrupted, but the presence of a small terminal image of St George and the dragon, rather than a full-size panel, may imply that the designers of this cycle were content to complete the legend in a rather less clear-cut way than their counterparts responsible for the other three cycles. We can read the motif of the dragon fight as emblematic of the saint acting as a Christian knight-errant: as we shall see in Chapter Five, the dragon fight is often symbolic of the Church overcoming heresy or other forms of 'evil', and this reading fits in well with the identification of St George as the Virgin's personal champion. It is perhaps useful to note that in the earlier version of the resurrection story, when St Mercurius/St George was resurrected in order to kill Julian the Apostate, no reference is made to the question of how the hero died initially. In the later version it is made clear that he died because of his devotion to the Virgin and that she resurrected him in tribute to his devotion, to be her champion generally rather than for any more specific assignment.

Further evidence for this lost tradition of St George and the Virgin Mary is found when we compare these four English cycles with a contemporaneous cycle in England – the Windsor cycle – which was probably carved by English craft workers but almost certainly designed by a Flemish sculptor. Given the dedication of St George's Chapel, Windsor Castle, it is unsurprising that there are several occurrences of imagery associated with St George within the woodwork of the building. For example, a scene of St George, mounted, spearing the dragon appears on a misericord on the south side of the quire, while the arming of St George by the Virgin appears on a desk front on the north side. In addition, there is a cycle of St George imagery on the carved wooden desk-ends on the south side of the quire, where the choirstalls were erected during the period 1477 to 1484, the closing years of the reign of Edward IV. Today there are a total of twenty subjects on double-faced desk-ends featuring imagery of the lives of St George and the Virgin Mary, of which sixteen are apparently original. Six of the extant medieval images relate only to the Virgin (the Annunciation, the Visitation, the Nativity, the Adoration of the Magi, the Assumption, and Christ in Judgement with the Virgin and St John the Evangelist), but ten subjects feature St George. The scheme of this cycle seems to be decorative rather than narrative, with the images placed in a random pattern rather than reflecting the chronology of the saint's legend, but the cycle is summarised here according to the logical narrative sequence:

(1) The subject that seems to begin the sequence is an image of the obeisance of St George before the Virgin and Child (illustration 3.16). The Virgin is seated on the left of the subject, with the infant Christ on her lap and a bunch of lilies behind her. St George kneels on one knee before them in the centre of the composition; he wears full armour but no helm is visible. His horse stands on the right of the scene and two angels appear in the background, one holding a small banner bearing a letter 'G'.
(2) The next subject shows the princess taking leave of her parents (illustration 3.17). The king stands in the centre of the composition facing his daughter. A lamb wearing a collar and lead is in the foreground, and the king is passing the end of the lead to the princess. The queen, who is wiping tears from her eyes, stands behind the king, and two other figures look on from the background.
(3) This subject shows St George mounted and in full armour, apparently talking with the princess, who stands on the left side, partly obscured by the horse's head (illustration 3.18). She still has her lamb, which looks out from underneath the horse. Presumably the saint is offering to slay the dragon.
(4) Here St George, mounted, spears the dragon in the lower part of the neck, while the princess looks on from the background. Her parents watch from a tower in the background and other spectators are visible in a distant town on the right.
(5) The next subject shows St George standing astride the dragon while the princess leads it towards the town, indicated by a tower on the left side (illustration 3.19).

3.16 to 3.21 *The St George cycle in the bench ends of St George's Chapel, Windsor Castle, 1477–84.*

3.16 *The obeisance of St George before the Virgin Mary.*

3.17 *The princess takes leave of her parents.*

3.18 *St George meets the princess.*

3.19 St George and the princess lead the dragon to the town.

3.20 St George is dismembered and boiled.

3.21 St George is dragged.

(6) The right side of this subject has been heavily damaged, with only a pair of shoes surviving to indicate where St George presumably stood. The king stands in a central position, facing towards the right side, and two further men stand behind him. The subject may well be St George demanding the conversion of the town to Christianity as recompense for slaying the dragon. Alternatively, it could be the king offering his daughter's hand to St George, which is a feature of some textual versions, but the absence of the princess from the scene would seem to make this unlikely.
(7) St George, wearing armour, appears to be seated on the edge of some kind of board. He is threatened by a group of five evildoers. This may well be a scene of the stripping of St George, as it seems that he is about to be divested of his armour and placed on the board.
(8) We now see St George wearing only a loincloth, his usual mode of apparel during torture scenes. He is lying on a board, which is possibly the board indicated in the previous scene, and is being dismembered; his body parts are boiled in a cauldron by a small figure with a spoon (illustration 3.20). Dacian and two further torturers look on.
(9) In the next subject St George is shown tied to a hurdle that is drawn by two horses; a rider is falling backwards from one of the horses (illustration 3.21). A further four torturers or bystanders look on from the background.
(10) The final subject of the St George imagery seems to be the poisoning. Dacian stands in the background, with a demon on his crown, his right hand raised, a bowl in his left hand. Four attendants stand around him. In the foreground St George stands over the legs of a prostrate man; it seems that the bowl contains poison that has been tested on this unfortunate character.

It appears that several subjects have been lost from this cycle. Logic dictates that there really should be an image of the execution of St George, with the saint's soul taken up to heaven. Equally, there is no scene of the baptism of the king, queen and princess, or of the trial of the saint before the emperor; both these subjects are virtually ubiquitous in extant medieval cycles of St George and their omission seems odd in a cycle of this size. However, the four carvings on the desk-ends of the returned stalls (the stalls which face East, towards the altar, rather than North, across the width of the quire), are all modern replacements; the subjects they originally contained are unknown, and it is possible that some of these 'missing' subjects were located here. Meanwhile, the number of unique subjects occurring in this cycle is quite remarkable. For example, there is no known analogue for the images of the princess taking leave of her parents and the threatening of the saint, and while the dismemberment of St George does appear in some textual versions of the life of the saint the standard visual representation is to show St George boiled entire (see illustration 3.7). The torture of being dragged is also textual, and appears in the St Neot cycle, but the motif of the figure falling from the horse is apparently unparalleled in written or visual sources on St George.

For our purposes, the most interesting factor about this cycle is the absence of imagery associated with the resurrection of St George by the Virgin. This may also be explained by the loss of the four images on the returned stalls, but it is perhaps more likely that this lacuna derives from the probability that the carvers responsible for the work were working under the direction of a Flemish designer: the overall impression of the imagery of the desk-ends is that they are outside the established English tradition of the life of St George. Whilst a scene of the arming does occur elsewhere in the quire it seems very unlikely that the whole narrative of battle, execution, resurrection and arming of the saint could have once occupied the desk-ends on the returned stalls, especially as this would demand that this group of carvings displayed a narrative coherence that is singularly lacking in the other desk-ends.

Despite the absence of the visual narrative that clearly identifies St George as the Virgin's knight – he is executed because of his faith in her, and then rewarded by resurrection and arming as her knight – we can identify the obeisance scene as an analogue of the subject of the arming of St George by the Virgin: he kneels before his patroness in a composition that is strongly reminiscent of feudal custom, where subordinates pledged allegiance to their superior in return for the granting of favours. There is also an instance of the Virgin knighting St George with a sword while a pair of angels holds his shield and horse, in a late fifteenth-century wall painting at Astbury church (Cheshire), where it is combined with an image of St George on foot, encountering the kneeling princess. If we compare this image with the armings found at La Selle or St Neot (illustrations 3.13 and 3.14), we see that the Virgin is not arming the saint, by placing a helm on his head, but is dubbing him a knight as an earthly monarch might do. However, for a late medieval spectator the distinction between the two treatments was probably not too obvious, for the presentation of arms and armour to a squire was considered to be the direct equivalent of being made a knight. It is noteworthy that the Virgin holds the Christ Child in the Astbury wall painting, a motif that also appears in the Windsor subject of the obeisance of St George: again, we are probably looking at little more than a variation on the theme of the arming of St George by the Virgin.

Although all extant imagery of the execution of St George before an image of the Virgin, and his resurrection by the Virgin is English,

3.22 Alabaster sculpture of the Virgin and Child, with predella of St George and the dragon, late fifteenth century.

we should note that at least part of this story occurs elsewhere in Europe. The arming of St George by the Virgin appears in isolation in the Valencia altarpiece (illustration 2.2), a German work probably created in the early fifteenth century for a Spanish guild devoted to St George. This version differs in some important ways from the English versions of the subject found at Borbjerg, La Selle and St Neot: rather than lowering a helm on to the saint's head the Virgin is touching the saint's sword. Meanwhile, an angel holds the helm, and Christ looks down from above and blesses the saint. This example, along with the image of the obeisance of St George before the Virgin at Windsor, may well imply that the motif of the arming was free-standing and was not necessarily associated with the English resurrection legend. Rather, there may have been a more generally recognised link between the Virgin and St George where he functioned as 'Our Lady's Knight', a link that the Valencia panel tends to suggest was known in late medieval Germany at least. We should, however, be careful to distinguish the specific image of St George armed by the Virgin from more general images of the saint armed as a knight: he is also shown armed by angels alone in several continental examples, such as a relief panel on the pedestal of the large sculpted St George group in the St Nicholas' Church, Stockholm (1489), and on the predella, or supporting area, of a Netherlandish altarpiece, *c.* 1525, at Vreden. The subject of the saint armed by angels may originate in Reinbot von Durne's early thirteenth-century poem *Der Helige Georg*, which claims that an angel brought St George his armour and banner; the existence of this motif in addition to the subject of the saint armed by the Virgin demonstrates that the imagery of the arming of St George was not drawn from a single source, and that he need not always have been identified as the Virgin's knight rather than simply as a Christian warrior.

Despite this complication, there is clear evidence of the link between St George and the Virgin outside the English tradition. A late fifteenth-century alabaster statuette now in Krakov, Poland, which does not appear to be English work, shows the Virgin and Child alongside a crucifix draped with a dead serpent (illustration 3.22); on the predella of the composition is a relief carving of St George, mounted, spearing the dragon while the princess looks on. This work draws a clear comparison between the Devil, in the guise of the serpent in the Garden of Eden, and the dragon killed by St George: both are incarnations of evil, both are overcome by incarnations of goodness. The serpent is defeated by Christ, the son of a Virgin who was herself immaculately conceived so that no stain of sin should taint him; the latter is despatched by St George, the *miles Christianus* who was also the Virgin's champion. The fact that Christ is presented as a child is crucial in this reading of the iconography: far more emphasis is placed on the Virgin herself than on the infant in her arms. Late medieval theology held that it was the Virgin's conception of Christ that was the masterstroke in God's plan to redeem the world: the Devil did not suspect that it would be possible to create a being so perfect that his death would redeem the faults of all of humanity, and thus we see the Virgin's motherhood being placed on a par with the Crucifixion itself in this image. Just as a virginal mother was able to outwit the Devil, a knight (a virginal knight?) was able to overcome the Devil who stood in the guise of a dragon and threatened humanity which was all too vulnerable to his depredations.

It seems likely that the connection between St George and the Virgin suggested by this statuette and other images and texts may be an intimation of an association between the saint and the concept of chastity, for the virginal Queen of Heaven would surely require a virginal champion. The medieval Church was ambivalent about sexuality, recognising on the one hand that most people were subject to strong sexual desire, and that without procreation there would be an end to the human race, while simultaneously castigating the sexual act in all its forms. The Church encouraged

3.23 Master of Oberrheinischer, The Paradise Garden, *fifteenth century. (Stadelsches Kunstinstitut, Frankfurt-am-Main)*

other two saints is unclear. Whoever he is, the main puzzle in this work is why three *male* figures have been allowed to penetrate the *hortus conclusus*, which is essentially a female domain?

As we know, St George is clearly linked with the Virgin, while St Michael is often associated with St George, such as in the Borbjerg altarpiece (illustration 3.11): they both kill dragons and hence make useful companion pieces. Meanwhile, St Michael is himself strongly linked with the Virgin Mary, particularly in the iconography of the Last Judgement where he weighs the souls of men and women against their good deeds while the Virgin intercedes on behalf of the less righteous by throwing her rosary on to the scales. However, this kind of connection is insufficient reason to allow male figures into the sanctity of the *hortus conclusus*: the rationale behind this image seems to be somewhat more complicated. My own feeling is that both St George and St Michael (and, by extension, the third male figure) are being presented as virginal figures themselves, and are hence worthy of inclusion in this sacred virginal space. St Michael, as an angel (not to say archangel), has a strong claim to be a sexless figure, for angels are often understood to be ethereal rather than physical beings, composed of light rather than flesh and blood. We have already established that St George was likely to be understood as a chaste figure, as a consequence of his identification as the champion of the Virgin Mary, but further evidence for this contention is found within the iconography of this image itself, and specifically in the presentation of the dragon. Close examination of this toy-like beast reveals that there is a curious display of the dragon's pudendum, with an orifice clearly visible. An important late medieval theme in the depiction of the battle between St George and the dragon concerns the identification of the dragon as female – this is discussed at some length in Chapter Five, but the salient factor to note at this stage is that the feminised dragon is strongly associated with female *sexuality*. The dragon in *The Paradise Garden* is not only female but is very obviously dead: it lies in the classic death position for small animals, on its back with all four legs in the air. This presentation indicates that St George has slain not only the dragon but also his own sexual urges: he has overcome the temptations of the flesh and made himself fit company for the Virgin and her female companions, just as a eunuch is permitted entry into a harem. There is no suggestion in St George's legend that he literally castrated himself, although this rather excessive means of curbing sexual desire was indeed known to medieval people and practised by (or on) a few unfortunate souls, such as the twelfth-century cleric, scholar and illicit lover Peter Abelard. The method for suppressing physical desire practised by St George seems to have been purely symbolic, but the killing of the female dragon was nevertheless an important aspect of his cult in the fifteenth century.

It is notable that in some post-medieval versions, such as Johnson's *The Most Famous History of the Seven Champions of Christendome* (1576–80), St George does marry the princess, a reversion to the 'original' narrative device found in the romances of pre-Christian heroes such as Perseus. Indeed, in this tradition St George and his wife Sabra go on to have three children, all sons. Such a development tends to underline the oddity of the late medieval image of St George as a virginal, or at least chaste, hero. This particular construction was very much a product of its time; with the Reformation and Counter-Reformation and their concomitant changes in attitudes to chastity and marriage – and perhaps especially the reformers' emphasis on the importance of the family and the father's role as the dominant figure within each microcosm of society – a valid exemplar of masculinity needed to be seen to take on the role of husband, and perhaps that of father too. The pre-Raphaelites' approach to the legend of St George reveals a similar post-medieval attitude, despite the name that was

4.1 Milemete treatise, *1326–7. St George arming Edward III. (Christ Church, Oxford, MS 92, fol. 3r.)*

It was not until the time of Edward III (reigned 1327–77) that royal devotion to St George really came to the fore. Edward clearly had a strong interest in St George even in the early years of his reign: illustration 4.1 shows an image of St George arming the young king. This manuscript, known as the Milemete treatise and dated to 1326–7, was made as a gift for Edward by Master Walter of Milemete, who held an important position in the Royal Household as King's Clerk. The work instructed the new monarch on both his responsibilities and the moral virtues that he should embody. St George and the king have a very similar presentation, both

4.2 Douce Hours, *1325–30. Thomas, Earl of Lancaster with St George. (The Bodleian Library, University of Oxford, MS Douce 231, fol. 1r)*

wearing armour covered by a tabard and epaulettes. The saint's tabard and epaulettes bear his red cross, while the king's are charged with lions, as is the shield presented to him. The implication seems to be that Edward should seek to emulate the chivalric values embodied in this soldier–saint. A second manuscript that also dates from the earliest years of Edward's reign again features St George as a prominent subject. The Douce Hours (fol. 1r, *c.* 1325–30) shows Thomas, Earl of Lancaster (d.1322) with St George (illustration 4.2). Lancaster was a leading figure in the opposition to Edward II, and was executed for treason following the battle of Boroughbridge.

Edward III unsuccessfully pressed the Pope to canonise Lancaster, and it has been suggested that the placement of an image of him at the head of a series of images of saints was intended to suggest his sanctity. The fact that this rather modest manuscript was not intended for royal use – it was apparently created for use in the diocese of Lincoln – seems to indicate that interest in the saint was by no means confined to Edward's immediate circle, but the king's own devotion was almost certainly a significant factor in the development of a wider cult. He owned a relic of the saint's blood, which was included in an inventory of royal relics made in 1331–2, and wall paintings dated to *c.* 1355–63 on the east wall of St Stephen's Chapel, Westminster, featured the king, his wife Philippa of Hainault and their ten children with St George as their patron saint. The paintings were destroyed *c.* 1800, but several copies had already been made of them, including four watercolours by Robert Smirke (illustration 4.3). The upper part of the image was a version of the Adoration of the Magi, with the royal family below. The figures are disposed in an arcaded framework, with a suggestion of screens or windows between each bay: this presentation gives the impression of individual chapels, but St George reaches through the partition to lead Edward and the other males of the royal family towards the high altar.

Perhaps the greatest testimony to Edward's devotion to St George was the founding of the Order of the Garter during the winter of 1347–8 and the establishment of St George's Chapel at Windsor Castle as the focal point of the Order (illustration 4.4). It is significant that St George's Chapel was actually a rededication and partial rebuilding of a royal chapel dedicated to St Edward the Confessor: this is a clear indication of the extent to which St George had usurped the role of this royal patron saint. Furthermore, the Order of the Garter was actually founded under the joint patronage of the Holy Trinity, the Virgin Mary and St Edward the Confessor as well as St George, but the other dedicatees were quickly relegated to a very minor role. The chapel itself was filled with imagery of the saint, much of which is now lost. The carved wooden desk-ends that feature a

*4.3 Robert Smirke's watercolour (*c. *1800) of a wall painting of St George with Edward III and family,* c. *1355–63, formerly in St Stephen's Chapel, Palace of Westminster. (Society of Antiquaries, London)*

4.4 Interior view of the quire of St George's Chapel, Windsor Castle. (Royal Collection, Windsor)

cycle of the saint's life (illustrations 3.16–3.21) and several misericords and desk fronts with subjects of the saint or his emblem are extant, but they were originally augmented by a statue of St George and the dragon, a painted figure of St George (paired with Edward the Confessor) on the roodscreen and a silver reliquary, containing three of the saint's bones, which had formerly belonged to the Bishop of Lincoln. Images of the martyrdom of St George were displayed on a small altar near the high altar, which itself was occupied by a large sculpted reredos of English alabaster. The subject of this altarpiece is unknown but, given the dedication of the chapel, it is very likely that it featured the life of St George. It was an emblem of devotion conceived on a grand scale, and was certainly considerably larger than the Borbjerg or La Selle retables (illustrations 3.11 and 3.12) created a century later: the panels were transported from Nottingham to London in no fewer than ten carts, drawn by a total of eighty horses. The framework which held the panels seems to have also contained a number of jewelled reliquaries that held treasures such as the Croes Neyd, a piece of the True Cross obtained by Edward I from the Welsh in 1283.

The first formal celebration of St George's Day at Windsor seems to have taken place in April 1349, soon after the institution of the Order of the Garter. It has been claimed that Edward was formerly in the habit of distributing small images of St George to his companions-in-arms, but following the English victory at the battle of Crecy (1346), when the king is said to have used the device of the garter, he decided to put his devotion to the soldier–saint on a more formal footing. It seems that the Order was not confined to men alone – women could be inducted under the title *Dame de la Confraternité de St George* – but the emphasis was clearly on masculine chivalric prowess, summed up in the insignia or 'jewel' depicting St George overcoming the dragon which was worn by all the knights as a badge of their membership. In fact, it has been suggested that the Order of the Garter was based on the concept of two finely balanced tournament teams, one led by the king, the other by the crown prince, in order to provide the ultimate chivalric encounter. Each team comprised twelve knights, in addition to their leaders Edward III and his son Edward 'the Black Prince': the arrangement of the Garter stalls in the quire of St George's Chapel at Windsor allows the knights to 'square up' to each other across the space before the high altar. Meanwhile, their leaders, father and son, sat at the west end of their respective teams in the positions of honour, in the 'returned' stalls, which face towards the high altar. They were thus aligned together, as befits the members of a royal dynasty, while also clearly associated with the knights on their own team. Illustration 4.4 shows a modern view of the quire at St George's Chapel, looking towards the high altar from the returned stalls. The individual stalls of the Garter knights are clearly visible under highly decorated wooden canopies. Each knight's stall is surmounted by a banner bearing the individual's personal device, while the back of each stall is decorated with a collection of 'stall-plates', metal badges that depict the devices of knights who formerly occupied this position.

The Order of the Garter was based on the concept of a brotherhood of chivalric knights with a marked emphasis on loyalty, both to the values of the Order and between the members themselves. It has been suggested that one of Edward's motives in establishing the Order was to unite his fractious nobles, and he was careful to bind these magnates to the throne as well as to each other. One example of the penalty paid by members who were deemed to be guilty of disloyalty is found some years after the foundation in the case of Sir John Fastolf (*c.* 1378–1459). A professional soldier who served under Henry IV's second son Thomas (later the Duke of Clarence) and subsequently rose to the position of councillor of France and governor of Anjou and Maine, Fastolf was thrown out of the Order in June 1429 because of a charge of cowardice. It was alleged that he had deserted his post at the battle of Pataye in order to avoid capture: Fastolf's previously glittering military record, which included capturing the Duke of Alençon at the battle of Verneuil and subduing Maine in 1425, was unable to save him from the consequences of such apparently ignominious behaviour.

Besides the Order itself, there are many other reflections of Edward's interest in St George as a figure of chivalry and knightly valour. The chronicler Thomas of Walsingham claimed that the king called on St George's aid at the siege of Calais in 1349; the resulting rout of the French will almost certainly have strengthened still further his devotion to the saint. Meanwhile, it has been suggested that imagery such as the Heydour glass of SS George, Edward the Confessor and Edmund, dated to *c.* 1360, mentioned above (p. 22), may well have been inspired by the success of Edward's military campaigns, particularly the battle of Poitiers (1356), when the huge ransom obtained for the release of the French king led to a period of considerable prosperity in England. It is known that the window's patron, Henry Scrope, was actively involved in this victory. Interestingly, Edward III is also known to have been devoted to the Virgin: he tended to commit himself to her care when danger threatened. For example, the foundation charter of the abbey of St Mary Graces in London states that it was established by the king as a thanksgiving to the Virgin for safe deliverance from a fierce storm at sea in the 1340s. He dedicated several other foundations to the Virgin too, and featured the Virgin and Child alongside St George on the great seal used during the later years of his reign. Given the clear links between the Virgin and St George discussed in Chapter Three it seems possible that St George was of interest to

Edward not only because he was a knight and a clearly powerful patron of soldiers, but specifically because he was identified in contemporary English tradition as the Virgin's champion.

St George's military associations also made him popular with Edward III's successors, most notably Henry V (reigned 1413–22). His departure for Normandy in 1415 was marked by an order to all English people to abstain from servile work, to attend church and to pray to St George for the safety of their king; Henry himself is also known to have made oblations to the saint before he left Westminster. A fifteenth-century poem of St George, quoted above (p. 70), refers to the tradition that St George was seen over the battlefield at Agincourt later that year, a ghostly manifestation in the style of Antioch, Jerusalem and Acre which inevitably presaged a great English victory. In the aftermath of Agincourt, the saint's feast day was elevated by Archbishop Chichele to the rank of a 'greater double' festival, which meant that it was to be celebrated like Christmas Day, Easter and major saint's days, with everyone taking a holiday from their normal work and attending church; the declaration contained the comment that the St George was considered as 'the special patron and protector of the English nation'. When Harfleur was captured Henry set up the banner of St George alongside the royal standards over the town gates and, under the terms of a statute drawn up in 1388 in relation to the campaign against the Scots, he declared that English soldiers must wear St George's cross, and that they had the exclusive right to do so. Some sources claim that St George miraculously appeared again during Henry's triumphal return to London from the French battlefields, a manifestation that serves to underline the strong links between the English successes and the king's patron saint.

A less supernatural, but equally singular, vision of St George is found in references to the festivities held at Windsor Castle in 1416 to mark the induction into the Order of the Garter of Sigismund, King of Hungary and Bohemia and Holy Roman Emperor from 1411 until his death in 1437. One of the first of a number of foreign rulers to be inducted into the Order by various English kings, in an apparent use of the foundation as a weapon of diplomacy, Sigismund brought with him the precious relic of the heart of St George in a silver reliquary, which was installed in a place of honour in St George's Chapel. The subsequent feasting included special references to St George: a series of 'sotylties' or 'soteltes' featuring imagery of the saint are recorded. These 'sotylties' were formerly understood as a kind of mime or *tableau vivant* but are now thought to have actually been a number of large, highly decorated cakes or raised pies. The subjects were, firstly, the arming of St George, with an angel fixing on his spurs, secondly, the combat with the dragon, and thirdly, St George with the princess leading the subdued dragon to the gates of city. This vision of the supreme art of the king's pastry-chefs is tantalising indeed.

Another important, but far more sober, reference to the links between Henry V and St George occurs in the dominant image of the folio devoted to imagery of the saint in the Bedford Hours (illustration 2.8). This image, created *c.* 1423 and hence shortly after the death of Henry, features a depiction of Henry's brother John, Duke of Bedford, kneeling before St George. In an apparently unique treatment, the saint is depicted wearing what seem to be the sovereign's robes of the Order of the Garter: a chronicler, writing the following year, described Bedford in his new role as regent, wearing a blue velvet robe with a red cross superimposed on a white cross, leading the English troops to victory at the battle of Verneuil. It has been plausibly argued that the Bedford Hours image is actually a deathbed portrait of Henry, with the newly dead king presented in the guise of his favourite saint entrusting his kingdom of France to the regency of his brother until his son, the infant Henry VI, should be old enough to rule both England and France in his own right. St George's right index finger points towards the knot fastening his mantle, which seems to lie over his heart, a gesture that is probably symbolic of the ties of loyalty binding the Garter knights both to each other and to their sovereign, as well as the bond between the regent and the English realm. Knots are often used in medieval art to symbolise an indissoluble bond of union or loyalty; indeed, a knot is used as one of the badges of the Order of the Garter. Although Bedford is known to have been interested in St George – for example, a cycle of the saint's legend occurs in the Salisbury Breviary (illustration 1.1 shows part of the legend), another manuscript commissioned by the duke – there is plenty of evidence that his personal patron was his name-saint St John the Evangelist, and this factor strongly supports the assertion that it is Henry V who is presented here in the guise of the saint. A sculpted figure of a standing St George and the dragon, dated to the late 1440s, appears in a prominent position in a niche of the reredos of Henry's chantry chapel at Westminster Abbey; this work was a clear influence on sculptures of the saint created for subsequent English kings (such as the image made for his son's chapel at Eton, discussed below), and provides further evidence of the links between Henry V and the saint.

Henry V's son Henry VI (reigned 1422–61 and 1470–1) seems to have inherited his father's reverence for St George, although it may well be more correct to say that this devotion was foisted upon him as part of the duties of an English king. When he was crowned at Westminster in 1429, at the age of eight, another 'sotyltie' of St George was created to grace the coronation feast. On this occasion the saint was clearly construed as an embodiment of England, and Henry's right to rule the country, rather than simply as a figure of chivalry, for he appeared with St Denis, representing France, on either side of the Virgin Mary. St George was shown in the act of presenting the new monarch to the Virgin; the whole scene was accompanied by a scroll held by the king himself and bearing an appropriate verse. St George was apparently invoked again when Henry went to be crowned in France in 1430. An anonymous fifteenth-century lyric, 'Speed Our King on his Journey', includes a section specifically about this saint:

> Seynt george, oure ladyes knight
> On whom alle englond hath byleve,
> Shew us thy helpe to god almyght,
> And kepe oure kyng from all myscheve.
> Thu art oure patronesse knyght y-preve
> To defend wyth fyght oure ladyes fe,
> Seynt george, by oure helpe yn all oure greve,
> Saluum fac regem domine.[2]

This long poem also invokes the aid of God the Father, Christ and the Holy Spirit, the Virgin Mary and a veritable slew of saints: St Anne, the mother of the Virgin; the eleven faithful Apostles; the four Evangelists; St Stephen, the first Christian martyr; SS Michael, John the Baptist, Mary Magdalen, Katherine, Helen and other unnamed saints and martyrs. Some specifically English saints are also called upon: St Oswald (a King of Northumbria who died at the battle at Maserfelth in AD 642, fighting against the heathen Penda, King of Mercia), St Erconwald (a seventh-century Bishop of London), St Thomas Becket (the Archbishop of Canterbury murdered at the behest of Henry II in 1170), and St Edward the Confessor. In an effort to ensure a safe passage for his king, the composer of this poem evidently wished to invoke as many heavenly helpers as possible, but St George stands out from this mêlée of holy figures: he is the only saint to be mentioned twice. The closing stanza of the lyric calls upon St George for a second time, and again invokes him in connection with the Virgin Mary:

> Swete seynt george, take to oure kyng heed,
> To hys lynage and to other lordes all yn fere,
> They mowe haue grace well to speed
> And couer hem alle vnder thy banere.
> To that gloryose gemme that shyneth so clere,
> Goddes moder and mayd of pyte,
> Devoutly seyth all that bene here,
> Saluum fac regem domine.

This invocation of St George is clear evidence of the extent to which his position as the patron saint of the monarch, and of England too, was being consolidated. During the course of the poem the Virgin Mary is explicitly said to be 'oure patronesse', in reference to the idea of England as the special realm of the Virgin, while her champion is described as a holy advocate 'on whom alle englond hath byleve'. Henry's magnificent foundation at Eton College was beautified by several images of St George, notably a large figure of the saint overcoming the dragon which is paired with a figure of St Edmund, high up on the buttresses of the east wall of the college ante-chapel.

Despite this apparent identification of Henry VI with St George, his Yorkist enemy and deposer Edward IV (reigned 1461–70, 1471–83) was also interested in the saint, a fact that indicates the extent to which St George was now identified as a patron of the English monarchy and the English nation, rather than of any one specific sovereign. In fact, it seems that Edward used the image of St George as a way of asserting the legitimacy of his claim to the throne, and it has been stated that he let it be known that he regularly prayed to the saint, in an effort to present himself as a 'conventional' English king. He is known to have attended a pageant in Bristol where the story of St George and the dragon was re-enacted in 1462, complete with the princess and her lamb and her parents watching the combat from a castle, while a window in the north-west transept at Canterbury Cathedral, *c.* 1482, shows Edward himself kneeling at a prie-dieu decorated with an image of St George, with Yorkist roses emblazoned on the cloths hanging behind him. The inscription accompanying this image makes explicit reference to the king's right to hold the English and French thrones, and also claims lordship of Scotland for him. In 1475 Edward began to rebuild St George's Chapel at Windsor, possibly in thanks for the saint's aid in the recovery of his crown after the temporary re-establishment of Henry VI, at an enormous cost of over £1,000 per year. The inclusion of the motif of the Yorkist rose, which appears in profusion around the chapel, demonstrates once more the extent to which this apparent interest in St George was a convenient vehicle for establishing a political and dynastic argument.

The accession of Henry VII (reigned 1485–1509) marked the end of the upheaval of the Wars of the Roses, but the advent of the Tudor dynasty also seems to have witnessed the apogee of the cult of St George as a saint of the monarchy. Again, the king's devotion was probably based on a need to legitimate his rule: as a minor Welsh lord with only tenuous links to the dynasty that gave rise to both the Yorkist and Lancastrian factions, his claim to the throne was far from persuasive. Following the battle of Bosworth Henry presented three standards, including the arms of St George, at St Paul's in London, and 6 yards of crimson velvet were used in the manufacture of a cross of St George for his coronation. Henry and his wife Elizabeth of York were depicted with St George and St Michael on an altarpiece, probably commissioned between 1503 and 1509 from 'Maynard', a

4.5 English School, The Family of Henry VII with St George and the Dragon. *(Royal Collection, Windsor)*

Flemish artist employed at court from around 1496 and recognised as 'the king's painter' from around 1505. The altarpiece itself is lost, but the panel of the royal family and the saints survives (illustration 4.5). Henry and Elizabeth each kneel at a prie-dieu, with their sons and daughters ranged behind them in a manner very reminiscent of the lost wall painting of Edward III and his family from St Stephen's Chapel (illustration 4.3). The king, queen and children (whose apparent ages are by no means realistic) are all dressed in identical robes, which underlines their solidarity as a family and the legitimacy of their ongoing dynastic claim to the English throne; the canopies above their heads also emphasise this presentation as they bear the Tudor rose and other family symbols. St Michael stands between the husband and wife: his function is not entirely clear – he is not accompanied by a dragon, as is usual in images where he is paired with St George (see illustration 3.11, for example) – but his pose is very reminiscent of that observed in late medieval images of the Last Judgement, where the angel–saint stands centrally, holding the scales on which souls are measured. Perhaps he is 'measuring' the values of the royal household here, and, presumably, not finding them wanting. Above St Michael a large, perhaps even over-large, figure of St George fights a flying dragon to rescue the princess who watches in the background, holding her lamb on a lead. The iconography of the combat differs in some respects from the standard late medieval depictions found in illustrations 3.4 and 5.20: no spectators are visible in the castles in the background, and it has been suggested that the architecture probably represents the royal palaces of Sheen and Richmond rather than a simple fantasy of 'Silene', the city named in most versions of the legend. Furthermore, the deployment of a dramatic *flying* dragon seems to be a sixteenth-century innovation: earlier dragons, though often winged, are almost invariably shown being trampled, whether by St George himself or by the hooves of his horse. It seems likely that the dragon may represent the discord of the Wars of the Roses: although St George, as a figure of Henry VII, is not shown triumphant, it is clear which of the protagonists will eventually win. The king's devotion to his patron saint also extended to the possession of a major relic: his will mentioned a portion of the leg of St George, which he had been given by his cousin Louis of France. A gold image of the saint, weighing 260 ounces, also features among Henry's bequests; this was destined to stand on the high altar at Windsor. Meanwhile,St George and the dragon feature twice on the tomb of Henry VII and Queen Elizabeth at Westminster Abbey: a relief carving in a gilt-bronze tondo (alongside St Anthony and his pig), and a sculpted group on the grate, or grille, surrounding the tomb. A further statue of St George and the dragon, which was probably polychromed, appears in the triforium level of Henry's chapel at Westminster.

Henry VII's son Henry VIII (reigned 1509–47) maintained the connection between St George and the monarchy, issuing coinage featuring the saint and depicting him in the metalwork of one of his crowns. It was during this reign that the emblem of the saint – the red cross on a white field – came to be recognised as a true flag of England and many sixteenth-century paintings of the English army feature this banner, sometimes as the sole standard flown. Henry VIII also seems to have borne the image of the saint on his own person on occasion, quite apart from his regalia of the Order of the Garter: a silvered and gilt suit of parade armour made for the king, dated 1510–20, features a large engraving of St George and the dragon on the breastplate, with a corresponding figure of St Barbara and her attribute of a tower on the backplate. A bard – a set of horse armour – also made for Henry was quite possibly specifically decorated to match the iconography of this suit. It features eight circular and oval panels devoted to the same pair of saints: four images of the martyrdom legend of St Barbara adorn the off side, whilst the corresponding panels on the near side feature images of the passion of St George. He is shown on trial before a heathen ruler, being boiled in a brazen bull, stretched between two wheels and, finally, about to be beheaded. The depiction of the subjects of boiling and stretching on wheels is remarkably close to those found in Jan

4.6 Engraving of Edward II's throne at St George's Hall, Windsor Castle.

4.7 Gérard Loyet, St George presenting Charles the Bold, *reliquary,* c. *1467–71. (Liège Cathedral)*

Borman's St George alterpiece of 1493 (illustration 2.5); the probable influence of this work can be explained by the fact that Paul van Vrelent, who is recorded as Henry VIII's 'harness-gilder', was of Flemish origin. He is generally credited with the decoration of both sets of armour – for king and steed – even though it is likely that both were actually manufactured by armourers outside England; it seems probable that Van Vrelent had some memory of Borman's work, or another source common to both artists, and incorporated these Flemish ideas into the depiction of the saint in what would otherwise seem to be a very English context.

St George's appeal to these medieval and post-medieval English kings seems to be based primarily on his status as a model of chivalry, and it is likely that the saint was viewed in a similar light elsewhere in Europe. It is sometimes claimed that the earliest known order of knighthood was the Constantinian Angelic Knights of St George, an apocryphal organisation that is said to have been founded by Constantine himself in AD 312. (The current Constantinian Order, the membership of which is restricted to Roman Catholics with proof of noble descent, dates from the second half of the sixteenth century.) However, several Spanish orders of chivalry were certainly founded under St George's patronage, with further examples in Burgundy, Austria, Germany, Holland and Genoa. One fifteenth-century pope is said to have founded an order of knights, giving it the magnificent appellation of the Pontifical Equestrian Order of St George. Various rulers, such as the Emperor Sigismund and James, a late fourteenth-century King of Portugal, are known to have invoked St George during ceremonies of knighting, and during the early 1380s King Pedro IV of Aragon established the Order of St George at Livadia in central Greece. Its membership was entirely drawn from the ranks of the nobility; here we find evidence of the other defining characteristics of the cult of St George as a patron saint of royalty, for he is almost invariably associated with the display of authority. For example, the Order of the Garter was not only concerned with chivalry and loyalty, but also with a display of the king's power and legitimacy: four knights of the Garter had the honour of holding a canopy over the king during the ceremony of anointing that formed part of the coronation. Meanwhile, the throne of Edward III (illustration 4.6), the founder of the Order of the Garter, was ornamented with a carving of St George overcoming the dragon. It has been plausibly suggested that this image was intended to evoke ideas of great rulers in history, who were often depicted on horseback. For example, a standardised type of equestrian statue – which probably represented Roman emperors such as Marcus Aurelius – was thought for several centuries to be an image of the Frankish king Charlemagne (reigned AD 768–814), who also assumed the title of Holy Roman Emperor (AD 800–14).

Charlemagne was hailed as a great conqueror – of the Lombards, the Saxons and the Avars – but was also recognised as a reformer of the judiciary and the Church, and as a promoter of commerce and agriculture throughout his imperial realm. He is also thought to have encouraged a revival in learning, and was thus considered by many later medieval commentators to have been an all-round performer, the consummate king.

Several other rulers linked themselves directly to St George. For example, a reliquary at Liège Cathedral shows Charles the Bold (or 'the Rash'), Duke of Burgundy 1467–71 (illustration 4.7). Charles, kneeling, holds a phial containing a relic of the finger of St Lambert, but rather than being accompanied by a figure of this local martyr–bishop he is shown being presented by St George. Both men are wearing armour, although the duke's ensemble is rather less ornate than that of his patron as a sign of deference. Charles married Margaret Plantagenet, the sister of Edward IV, in 1468 and it is interesting to conjecture that the inclusion of St George in this image may have been a reflection of his links with the English throne. Their heir, Mary of Burgundy, was offered in marriage to the Duke of Clarence, brother of Edward IV, in an effort to cement relations between Burgundy and England, but she ultimately became the first wife of Maximilian I, King of Germany (1486–1519) and Holy Roman Emperor (1493–1519). In 1508 Maximilian was depicted by the engraver Hans Burgkmair in the guise of St George, mounted on horseback and accompanied by the dead dragon and the rescued princess; only the arms borne by the knight reveals that this is Maximilian and not St George himself. A similar device is used in the depiction of St George in Albrecht Dürer's Baumgartner altarpiece, *c.* 1500 (illustration 4.8): the patron of the altarpiece, a Nuremberg patrician named Stefan Baumgartner, is shown in the guise of St George. This mode of presenting a ruler is strikingly similar to the motif used in the Bedford Hours (illustration 2.8), where John, Duke of Bedford, is apparently depicted accepting the role of regent from his dead brother, Henry V, in the guise of St George. It seems likely that in this latter image St George represents not only Henry himself and the English Crown, but also acts as an incarnation of the divine right of the ruler. This reading is also applicable to several post-medieval versions of the theme of 'the king as St George', such as an image of St George and the dragon created by Peter Paul Rubens for Charles I in 1629–30, and now in the Royal Collection at Buckingham Palace. The setting of this picture seems to be the banks of the Thames, as Lambeth Palace and Southwark Cathedral are discernible in the background. The saint bears a strong physical resemblance to Charles, a king for whom the question of authority was of supreme importance, while the princess seems to be modelled on his wife Henrietta Maria. It has been

4.8 Albrecht Dürer, The Baumgartner Altarpiece, *1502–4, detail of left wing: Stefan Baumgartner as St George, (Alte Pinakothek, Munich)*

suggested that, despite the overt martial content, this image can be read as an allegory of the king as peacemaker: the dragon represents the horrors of war which Charles had recently overcome by concluding a peace treaty with Spain.

Despite this accumulation of evidence for royal interest in the cult of St George as a symbol of chivalry and authority, it is clear that the monarchy of England and other parts of Europe did not have an exclusive claim to this saint. Whilst evidence of the devotion of 'lesser people' is much harder to interpret conclusively – as a result of the losses of altars, images and other tangible aspects of the cult, in addition to the simple lack of recording of many types of veneration – there are still strong indications that St George was a popular saint in many parts of England as well as elsewhere in Europe. Almost one hundred English wall paintings featuring the saint are known (over half are lost, and only known from antiquarian sources and similar records, and many of the remainder are barely legible). They date largely from the late fourteenth and fifteenth centuries and often depict St George in combat with the dragon (for example, illustration 4.9); as we have seen (p. 20) some much earlier wall paintings in Sussex seem to show St George appearing miraculously during the Crusades. Late medieval English images in glass (illustration 5.9), wood (illustration 5.24) or other materials are less common, almost certainly as a result of iconoclasm, but it is notable that St George is recorded as a painted decorative figure on seven church screens in Norfolk alone. There is little direct evidence about the motives for such commissions: the venerators who expressed their devotion to a particular saint by paying for the creation of wall paintings and other images within churches are almost always anonymous and have left us few clues about their wealth, status or personal concerns. We do not know, for example, who decided to commission the images of St George and the dragon found on church screens such as those at Filby (Norfolk) and Somerleyton (Suffolk) (illustrations 4.10 and 4.11). These works could have been created as the expression of a general interest in St George in these communities, or it could be that a small group of relatively wealthy devotees were imposing their reverence for the saint on their neighbours simply because they were the only people rich enough to be able to afford to pay for the beautification of the church.

St George is also found quite regularly among the saints featured in Books of Hours. These works, which combined litanies, prayers, the Penitential Psalms, calendars and similar accessory texts, also date largely from the late fourteenth century through to the early sixteenth century. They were created for literate or semi-literate lay people who wished to deepen their personal religious experience, or perhaps to impress others with a display of piety (or wealth). It seems that Books of Hours were personalised, rather than

4.9 Thomas Fisher's drawing of the fifteenth-century wall painting of St George and the dragon at the Guild Chapel, Stratford-upon-Avon (Warwickshire), drawn when the painting was first uncovered in 1804. (The Shakespeare Birthplace Trust, Stratford-upon-Avon)

4.10 Detail of roodscreen with St George and the Dragon, fifteenth century, Filby (Norfolk).

standardised, particularly in the choice of saints whose images, sometimes accompanied by a short text, were often included in these manuscripts in a special section known as 'suffrages'. Virtually all Books of Hours are highly decorative, and a depiction of the legend of St George was an obvious choice for a significant number of patrons. Illustration 5.26 is taken from a French Book of Hours, but the substance of the image – the combat between the saint and the dragon – is quite representative of manuscript illuminations of the story produced elsewhere. Dedications of churches and chapels to this saint are also indicative of an underlying interest in the cult, and it is known that by the end of the Middle Ages St George was a popular choice as the patron of parish churches – 193 churches in England were dedicated in his honour. Again, the name or names of the people who decided that this particular saint should be honoured in this way are invariably not recorded, but it is interesting to note that in a few cases the dedication of a church to St George seems to have superseded a dedication to St Gregory, a saint who had been formerly acclaimed as a patron of England.

The survival of pilgrim badges depicting St George, such as those shown in illustrations 4.12 and 4.13, suggests that St George was venerated by a wide social mix during the late medieval period, for these relatively cheap devotional objects would have been affordable to all but the poorest people. In the absence of a native tomb of the saint, a healing well or other natural geographical focus for the cult, it seems likely that pilgrim badges of St George would have been bought at Windsor, but people who undertook pilgrimages to the castle and its chapel in the late fifteenth century were probably less interested in the specific connection to the English monarchy than in

Opposite: *4.11 Detail of roodscreen with St George and the dragon, fifteenth century, Somerleyton (Suffolk).*

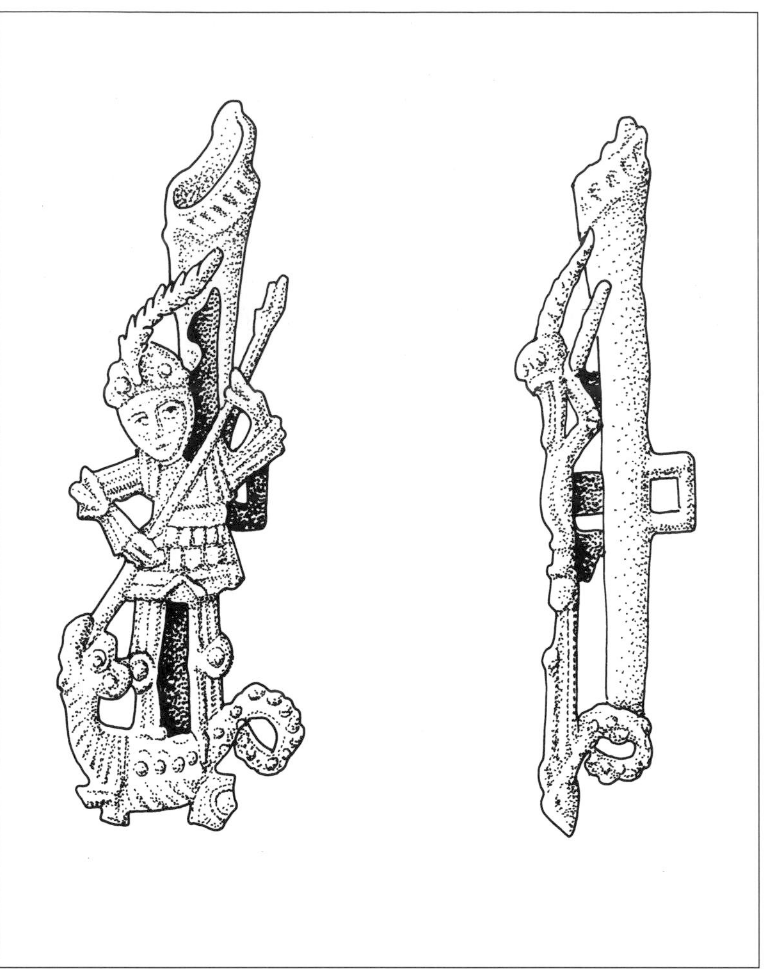

Above: 4.12 *Pewter plume holder in form of St George and the dragon, fifteenth century. (The Museum of London)*

Right: 4.13 *Pilgrim badge of St George and the dragon, fifteenth century. (Salisbury & South Wiltshire Museum)*

the veneration of treasures such as the Croes Neyd and the relics of two men acclaimed as saints, Sir John Schorne (a Buckinghamshire priest who conjured the Devil into a boot) and the 'martyred' Henry VI, whose body was translated from Chertsey in 1484. As we have seen, several relics of St George were housed at the chapel, including his skull, heart and unspecified bones, and these objects would almost certainly have claimed the attention of pilgrims. However, it is very difficult to know whether the survival of pilgrim badges reflects a genuine groundswell of middle- and lower-class interest in an individual saint, for pilgrims are known to have amassed the badges of shrines as a kind of hobby, just as some people today collect badges depicting the insignia of the countries and towns that they visit without necessarily feeling any real regard for each particular place. It is likely that a proportion of the unknown owners of these badges will have had a genuine attachment to St George, but in many cases it seems reasonable to assume that this was merely one devotion among many.

It is hard to quantify the real level of popular interest in St George during the late medieval period, mainly because the signs of ordinary people's interest are often elusive or difficult to analyse with any real sense of certainty. We have seen, for example, that St George was invoked against 'the night-mare' (p. 71), but we do not know how many people used this kind of charm, when exactly it was current, and in what precise geographical area. It is equally difficult to draw firm conclusions about claims that St George served as the patron saint of farmers, soldiers, sailors, armourers, horsemen, saddle-makers and archers: the derivation of his name (a 'tiller of the land') and the substance of the dragon legend (a heroic mounted warrior overcomes a water-dwelling monster) would suggest that he could have appealed to all these different groups, but it is impossible to know the extent to which real faith was placed in his powers to protect his devotees. References to St George's potency as a healer and protector of health also occur with some frequency. He was invoked against leprosy, syphilis, herpes and occasionally the plague, as well as snake-bite – his efficacy against all these conditions is thought to be linked to his overcoming of the scaly-skinned and poisonous dragon – but he was also called upon, rather obscurely, to aid the mentally ill and to guard against the malicious actions of witches. Believers would probably have taken recourse to St George's healing powers through prayer and perhaps pilgrimage (by the afflicted person or their representative) to a place associated with the saint. For example, St George was one of nine martyrs listed in an East Anglian Book of Hours *c.* 1480, now at the Fitzwilliam Museum in Cambridge, to whom prayers offered in times of trouble were bound to be successful: this list of saints seems to be an English equivalent of the Continental idea of the 'Fourteen Holy Helpers', a group of saints, again including St George, who were thought to be particularly efficacious when called upon for aid.

Healing wells dedicated to, or even discovered by, a saint were often visited by medieval people in search of a cure or a prophylactic remedy – Sir John Schorne had discovered a healing well at North Marston (Buckinghamshire), for example – but there is no evidence to suggest that any wells were associated with St George in England. By contrast, wells of St George are known abroad, such as the three *fontaines de St Georges* in Normandy, and there is an interesting record of a Welsh well associated with the saint. It is recorded that up until the late nineteenth century people would visit the village well at the hamlet of St George, or Llan Sain Siôr, in Denbighshire and sprinkle their horses with the water to both bless the animals and cure them of any sickness. The water was thought to be so efficacious that if a person owned several horses then only one would need to be treated, as the powerful effect would spread from one to another if they were housed together. As we have seen (p. 20), this community is one which claims to be the site of the battle between St George and the dragon but it is likely that the connection with the healing of horses predates this legend, for many place-names in the area (such as Tremeirchion and Kin Meirch) include the Welsh word for horse. This implies that the area has a long association with horses, quite possibly going back to a pre-Christian religion where horses were considered to be sacred animals.

Despite the problems associated with reconstructing the popular cult of St George in England, there are a few cases where it is possible to uncover a considerable amount about an individual's veneration. William Bruges (*c.* 1370–1450), the patron of the Stamford cycle of St George (illustrations 3.1–3.10), was strongly attached to the saint and spent a great deal of money honouring his patron. Admittedly, he was an important royal functionary, but it seems very likely that his devotion was only partly related to the model of reverence offered by his king. Henry V appointed Bruges in 1415 to the newly-created heraldic position of Garter King of Arms, the apogee of a career that had encompassed the roles of Chester Herald and Guyenne King of Arms. Bruges petitioned unsuccessfully to have the rights and responsibilities of his new role defined, but it is clear that he was generally recognised as the chief herald of all England. While he clearly held a rank considerably below that of the monarch, Bruges was just as strongly attached to St George as were Henry V and his successors. He was an extravagant patron of St George's Church in Stamford for almost thirty years: his work included rebuilding the chancel, leading the roof, glazing the windows, tiling the floor and installing new desks and pews in the chancel. His will stated that his body was to be buried in a prestigious place before the high altar, and he also bequeathed to the Lady Chapel of the church his painted stone images of the Virgin, the Trinity and St George, which had formerly been housed in the private chapel of his London residence. His interest in St George may derive to some extent from his association with the Order of the Garter: an image of Bruges and his patron saint, which appears in Bruges' Garter Book (illustration 4.14), shows the herald wearing a robe emblazoned with the devices of the English Crown, with two garters prominently displayed in the background. The presence of figures of the founder knights of the Order of the Garter, along with the patron and his wife, in the lower tier of the Stamford St George cycle, also indicate that Bruges was very proud of his position in the Order. However, the narrative of the life of St George, in the upper tier, tells a rather different story. As we have seen (pp. 55–7), the emphasis is clearly on images of torture, rather than chivalry, and it seems likely that the iconography was inspired to some extent by an *imitatio Christi* that encouraged the patron and other viewers to understand the Passion of St George as a mimesis of the Passion of Christ, and called on them to emulate the saint's forbearance under torture in their own struggle to live a Christian life.

This plurality of meaning is a fundamental aspect of the cult of

4.14 William Bruges' Garter Book, *fifteenth century, Bruges kneeling before St George. (British Library, London, MD Stowe 594, fol. 5v.)*

St George: he is far more than a soldier–saint who embodies the mores of the medieval chivalric code. For example, another image that shows St George presenting a devotee is Jan van Eyck's *The Madonna with Canon van der Paele* of 1436 (illustration 4.15). St George is depicted as a soldier–saint, but the reason for his inclusion in this work almost certainly has nothing to do with this status. The kneeling cleric is Canon *George* van der Paele: St George is simply his name-saint. The figure on the left is St Donatian, the patron saint of the church in Bruges to which van der Paele presented this picture, and the Virgin and Child occupy the conventional central position, which denotes that they are invoked and honoured by the gift of the image; despite his prominent position in the right foreground,

4.15 Jan van Eyck, The Madonna with Canon van der Paele, *1436. (Groeningemuseum, Bruges)*

St George is a very secondary character in this composition. It is interesting to note that the positioning of the figures of St George and the donor was reproduced very closely some thirty-five years later in the reliquary of Charles the Bold (illustration 4.7): the only changes are the placement of the saint's left hand and the addition of a dragon, whose tail curls around his left leg. It seems likely that the van Eyck picture provided an inspiration for the designer of the reliquary, although the political rationale linking St George with Charles the Bold was quite different from the simple coincidence of names that connected the saint with Canon van der Paele.

Alongside these signs of individual devotion to the saint stands a considerable body of evidence for corporate reverence for St George. This phenomenon seems to have something in common with the dynastic cult of the saint in the English monarchy, particularly the association of concepts of authority with the person of St George. The practices of English guilds of St George during the fifteenth century, in terms of both their membership and their annual festivals, suggest that these organisations were deeply concerned with the demonstration of a hierarchy of authority over their social inferiors, and drew on both the legend and the iconography of the saint to achieve quite specific ends.

Guilds, which are recorded throughout late medieval Europe, were religious and social groupings of individuals who paid membership fees and agreed to keep their patronal feast day together, usually with religious services in the guild chapel, or at the guild altar, and feasting. Guild membership was often open to both men and women, and members elected their own officials to oversee business transactions, arrangements for feasts and other dealings. Guilds often provided a pension or alms for members in penury, but an even more important function was the arrangement for masses to be offered asking for God's blessing on members who had died. These posthumous masses were perceived as a potent means of speeding the dead person's soul through the trials of Purgatory, and they are frequently mentioned in the wills of testators wealthy enough to leave monies specifically to pay for a mass or a series of masses to be said for them. The guild member enjoyed the privileged position of knowing that his or her name would be remembered not only in such 'personalised' masses but also in more general masses said for all deceased 'brethren and sustren' which were often performed by a priest specifically retained by the guild for this purpose: it was thought that the more masses offered in memory of a person, whether as an individual or as part of a group, the greater the effect would be. It has been observed that guilds seem to have had their origin in the secular imitation of monastic associations by people who wished on the one hand to accumulate the greatest possible amount of merit for the next world, and at the same time not to renounce the benefits of the present world; joining a guild was rather like taking out an insurance policy that promised treasures in Heaven in return for the payment of an annual premium.

Whilst membership of guilds devoted to St George in England was open to all ranks of society, it was often associated with the ruling elite in towns; this factor seems to have marked out guilds of St George from other guilds. Norwich, Chichester, Coventry, Reading, Leicester, Exeter and King's Lynn all had guilds of St George, and almost certainly York, Hull, Salisbury, Southwark and Louth too. There are also records of St George guilds in smaller places, such as Woodbridge (Suffolk), New Romney (Kent) and Aston (Warwickshire). The Chichester Guild, which was founded in or soon after 1368, gives us a potentially important insight into the socio-political rationale of the organisation, for local law stated that to be a freeman of this guild was one of the three qualifying conditions that had to be met before a man could claim the right to vote for members of Parliament for Chichester. A similar position prevailed at Exeter, where by 1531 every member of the 'Twenty-Four' who governed the city was expected to belong to the Fraternity of St George.

The phenomenon of a guild that was ostensibly formed for religious purposes assuming power and influence until it becomes the ruling body of the town does occur with other guilds, such as Holy Trinity, Wisbech; St Mary's, Lichfield; and Holy Cross, Stratford-upon-Avon, but it is difficult to establish the extent to which this was a conscious decision enacted through lawmaking and other formal means. The best-attested guild of St George, at Norwich, demonstrates just how close the ties could be between the civic authority and a guild. The Fraternity and Guild of St George in Norwich was founded in 1385 and granted a charter by Henry V in 1417. The reasons underlying the granting of the charter at this date are unknown, but it has been suggested that it was because of the presence of members of the Guild at Agincourt. Influential members of the Norwich Guild at this period included such men as Sir Thomas Erpingham and Sir John Fastolf (who was later to fall foul of the Order of the Garter's code of loyalty). It was certainly impossible for the Guild itself to be powerful enough to have acquired the charter as it had insufficient funds at this time to cover the considerable costs of the purchase. With the granting of the charter the Guild became a perpetual community with royal protection and with franchises and liberties similar to those enjoyed by other corporate bodies. The Guild retained its religious and charitable nature but now had a constitution, rights, including the right to hold property to the value of £10, and the power to plead and be impleaded. These rights were symbolised by the possession of a common seal, with an image of St George, which was kept in a chest with a charter and other guild evidences, probably at the 'St George Inn' at Fibridge, which the Guild owned and used for meetings. Through the terms of the charter, the prior of the Cathedral and the mayor and sheriffs of the city were given power to dismiss Guild members for misconduct, a very significant change to the way that the Guild was constituted, as the city hierarchy of Norwich was now firmly linked with the fortunes of the St George Guild.

Whilst the granting of the royal charter was undoubtedly important, of even greater significance for the fortunes of the Guild was an event in 1452 known as Yelverton's Mediation. The Guild had been associated with long-running opposition to the government of Norwich following the grant of a mayor and county administration in 1403/4, with particular problems arising during the period 1410–50. Given that membership of the Guild at this time included such luminaries as William de la Pole, Earl of Suffolk, we can see that opposition to the city government was far-reaching, and certainly not the stuff of simple mob protest. Under the terms of a resolution proposed by William Yelverton, King's Justice and Recorder of Norwich, the St George Guild seems to have absorbed the Guild of the Annunciation, known as Le Bachery. This had been the most important guild in the city, and had been trying to usurp the power of the civic government and important local industries. Doubtless in an effort to prevent St George's Guild remaining a focus for dissent against civic authority, it was decided that guild elections were to be held on the day following the celebration of St George's Day, and that the outgoing city mayor would automatically become alderman of the Guild for the following year. All city aldermen were to be brethren of the Guild, and common councillors of the city were offered that privilege if they desired it. Should any city alderman or common councillor be dismissed from office for misconduct, they would automatically be dismissed from the Guild also; if any brethren were evicted from the Guild, they would also be evicted from all the liberties and franchise of the city. As the most influential people in Norfolk and Norwich belonged to the Guild, the ruling body in Norwich would be brought into close contact with the nobility and aristocracy of both city and county. The agreement prohibited persons dwelling in the county from becoming brethren unless they were knights, squires or gentlemen by birth, or had some cause worthy of admission (the situation regarding women is unclear). It would seem that some attempt was made to restrict even the Norwich membership to the upper classes: in 1463 Thomas Antynghamm, a shoemaker, having been elected one of the common council of the city, was prevented from taking his oath whilst advice and counsel were sought in order to discover whether it would be to the dishonour of the Guild to receive a person of such a craft into the common council of the city and Guild.

The common council of the Guild consisted of the alderman (the outgoing mayor) and twenty brethren, plus subordinate officers as necessary. Those who ruled the city were to govern the Guild almost as if it were a department of the city administration. In future, it was decreed, the activities of the Guild were to be limited to social, charitable and religious works. Guild assemblies were then transferred from the public house at Fibridge to the city Guildhall; in 1486 the Corporation of Norwich gave the Guild the top chamber of the Guildhall in which to keep its property and to hold its councils.

The Guild worshipped in Norwich Cathedral where there was an altar or small chapel dedicated to St George, on the south side at the east end, below the high altar. It was probably very cramped, with most of the space occupied by the tomb of Bishop John Wakering (d.1425), a member and benefactor of the Guild. It is not known if the chapel and altar belonged exclusively to the Guild, but mass was said here daily by the Guild priest. The Guild had its own mass- and other vestments, also chapel and altar furniture, which are recorded in inventories. The list includes a ceremonial sword, banners, and a silver and gilt statue of an angel (a gift from Sir John Fastolf), which contained a relic of St George, said to be his arm. Two further relics of the saint are also claimed, apparently stained cloths from the martyrdom of St George; it is not known if the Guild had any documents to authenticate these relics. There was also an image of St George, recorded in 1444/5 and 1461/2. A bell in the Cathedral, known as St George's bell, tolled for the use of the Guild.

We know that the Guild took part in a great annual procession of guilds and crafts on the feast of Corpus Christi, and that there was a guild feast at Christmas, but the most important date in its calendar was undoubtedly St George's Day (23 April). Indeed, the celebration of this day was a highlight of the year for the whole city. Sadly, there seem to be no visual records of these festivals, but the documentary evidence at Norwich does at least allow us some sense of the splendour and pageantry associated with the marking of St George's Day.

St George's Day is known to have been kept with solemn ceremonies and festivities at Leicester, Norwich, London, York, Chester, Reading, Chichester and Worcester, amongst other places. In most areas we know little about what actually went on, but in Norwich and Leicester at least the chief ceremony of the celebration of St George's Day was a procession or 'Riding' in which people dressed as St George and the princess he is said to have rescued paraded in company with a dragon. The procession was often followed by a re-enactment of the story of the combat between St George and the dragon, and the whole event seems to have been the focus of much festivity. At Lostwithiel (Cornwall), for example, in the reign of Henry VIII, an annual parade along the main street was arranged by the Guild of St George. One of its members represented St George himself: he rode on horseback, was attended by mounted followers, and was furnished with armour, a crown, a sceptre and a sword.

The documents of the Norwich Guild provide a considerable amount of detail about the Riding and the ceremonies attached to it. The feast was always kept on 23 April, unless this date fell in Easter Week or Holy Week, when the Guild assembly chose another day, usually in May. The assembly also chose players to take the various roles of 'the George', 'the Lady', the dragon, henchmen, banner and torch carriers, and so forth. The ceremonies began on the eve of the feast with evensong, which the alderman and all the brethren were expected to attend. The feast day proper began with a breakfast of wine, bread and cheese, refreshments which were also provided by the Guild during the main focus of the day's events. This was the Riding, a grand procession, apparently beginning at the Cathedral; the Riding is not mentioned in ordinances of 1389, but was certainly in practice before 1420. Its splendour contributed much honour to the city, and the Guild books contain many orders relating to it. Like civic processions in Norwich, it was headed by man carrying an ancient wooden, gilded sword with a dragon's head carved on the handle, traditionally said to have been presented by Henry V at the granting of the Guild's charter.

The George followed behind. The fee paid to the George varied from 20*d* up to 10*s* in the sixteenth century. The same costume was not worn each year: there are records of gifts of money or food to different lenders, and purchases of materials are also recorded. The George wore armour, originally beaten with silver, and a brightly coloured gown, frequently fur trimmed; the colour varied year to year. Jewels and chains were often borrowed to decorate his outfit. The George always rode, and the armour on the horse was decorated with laces and ribbons. In later years attendants probably carried the George's armour and weapons. The inclusion of the Lady, sometimes referred to as 'the Margaret', seems to be later, as it is first mentioned in an account roll of 1532. The Lady seems to be the virginal princess rescued from the dragon in St George's legend, but it is likely that the name Margaret is derived from St Margaret, another saint with a dragon with whom St George is sometimes paired. The Lady also rode, and her costume seems to have been similar to the George's gown. Two henchmen attended the George, and there was one for the Lady; again, the colour of the costumes varied year to year.

Throughout the procession the George was supposed to be in conflict with the dragon, known later as 'the Snap' or 'Old Snap', an arresting creation carried by a man walking inside it. The dragon was constructed from hoops of iron and, apparently, of wood which were nailed together: the 1583 St George's Guild accounts yield payments of 8*d* 'to Henry Radoe for A hoope of yron for the dragon and for naylles for ye same';[3] 6*s* 'to A Couper for putting in hoopes to sett it owt in the bellye'; 3*s* 6*d* 'to A Carpenter for amending the Dragon and for the stuff [which] wherwith it was doone'; and 6s 8*d* 'for payntyng of ytt'. Covered with canvas to which cloth wings were attached, this spectacular puppet was repainted and equipped with 'ffur and tayles' in 1622, and the 4*s* 6*d* spent in 1626 'for the Dragon paynting & mending the Broken plotes' suggests that it also boasted accessory scales. The fee paid to the dragon actor was much lower than that paid to the George:[4] never more than 12*d*, except in 1429 when 2*s* 4*d* was paid for 'playing in the dragon with gunpowder'. This rather worrying experiment seems not to have been repeated!

The last Civic Snap, which was made in 1795, is still in existence (illustration 4.16). It measures some 5 feet high and 15 feet long (1.5 metres × 4.6 metres); the carrier's legs were hidden by a large canvas skirt and the articulated jaw could be controlled from within. It is painted with a pattern of green, red and yellow scales on its body and wings, with a thin red tail and a reddish fur trim along the backbone. It may well resemble earlier, medieval versions of the dragon, but, given the fact that no expense was spared on regularly changing the George's costume, it seems quite likely that the dragon may have varied from year to year, in its decoration if not in its basic

4.16 The Civic Snap, c. *1795.*

form. Furthermore, a photograph taken in 1887 of the St George Guild at Costessey (illustration 4.17), just outside Norwich, shows a rather different dragon with a much smaller neck and head and a thicker tail: this suggests that a fair degree of variation was possible without deviating from the underlying idea of a hooped shape carried by one man who also controlled the snapping jaws. The head of the Costessey Snap has survived (illustration 4.18); it has been suggested that this rather dog-like creation was possibly made for a civic dragon in Norwich pre-dating the current Snap.

A cross, the banner, or standard, of St George's Guild and other ornaments were also carried in the procession, as well as a stoop containing holy water. Banners bearing the arms of St George, or his painted image, trimmed with fringes and silk tassels are also recorded. Inventories also mention banners for minstrels, which were probably used to decorate trumpets and similar instruments. Four poor men were paid 2*d* each to carry torches; it is recorded in the processional records of the Corpus Christi Guild at Leicester that such torches were decorated with flowers, and it is quite possible that this was also the case in the Norwich Riding. Other candles, tapers and so forth were carried, as was wax to be offered at the Cathedral during the feast. The city waits attended with their

4.17 *The St George Guild, Costessey (Norfolk), 1887.*

instruments, and cantors, or chanting clerks, from the Cathedral church were employed to accompany the procession.

Every city alderman, and also those who had been sheriffs and were not aldermen any longer, had to send a priest to the procession. Twelve of these priests wore red copes, and twelve wore white; they were paid 4*d* each which also covered their attendance at a requiem mass the following day. Then came the mayor in his robes of office, and the city aldermen in scarlet gowns with scarlet and white damask hoods. The commoners of the Guild followed on. They had to wear a livery of gowns and hoods of red, later varied to red and white in 1473, and in 1485 to mulberry. The Guild officials wore their robes of office. Significantly, all the brethren rode on horseback. Throughout the procession the bells of the Cathedral were rung, and the thought of the bells combining with the waits' music, the cantors' singing, the colourful robes, as well as the fighting between the George and the Snap, evokes a truly dramatic event.

Though the route or time taken are not recorded, it was customary to ride to a wood outside the city, which was probably St William's Wood by Thorpe St Andrew, the place recognised as the site of the martyrdom of St William of Norwich, a child said to have been crucified by Jews in 1144. According to an order made in

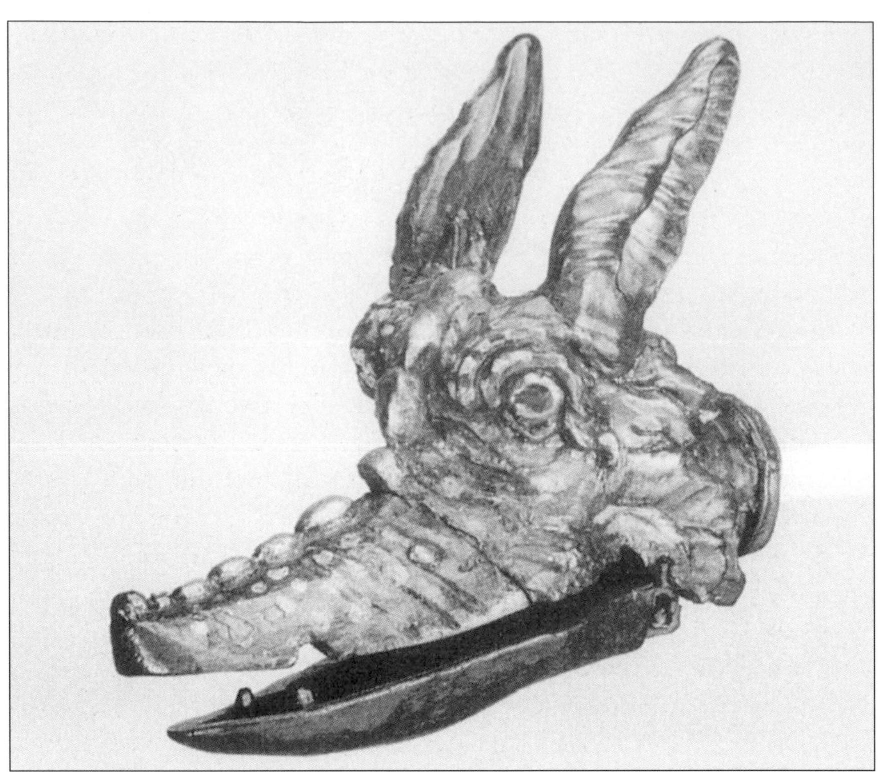

4.18 The head of the Costessey Snap.

1408, the legendary fight between St George and the dragon was re-enacted here. The procession then returned to the Cathedral, which was newly strewn with rushes to receive it; Guild members would then offer up wax to be burned at the high altar during a feast in honour of the Trinity, the Virgin Mary and St George, then a mass was held in honour of St George, the king, and the whole Guild.

Following the mass, the feast, or jantaculum, was held. The feast is not mentioned in the 1389 ordinances, but it was probably customary by 1417 when Henry V granted the Guild the right to hold a feast. Before 1473 the feast was held in the hall of the Dominican friars, but the venue was then changed to the hall of the Bishop's Palace whenever possible. Sadly, no details survive of what food was served, but an indenture of 1535 shows that access was allowed to the kitchens, pantries and other facilities for eight days before and six days after the feast, so we can assume that the meal provided was little short of spectacular. The Bishop's Palace was made available to the Guild with the proviso that no person of honour or dignity needed the hall: but it was only with special permission of the bishop that any such person could force the Guild to vacate the building, and this tends to emphasise the importance of the Guild feast. We do not have much evidence about the tableware used during the feast, but we do know that some of the vessels were pewter and bore the arms of St George; there are records of these being leased to other guilds for their own feasts. Guild brethren living at a distance from Norwich were not expected to attend the feast or ceremonies, but they could send for their share of the meat and were expected to supply an offering of wax to be presented in the Cathedral. At the conclusion of the feast, the brethren returned to the Cathedral, to pray for the souls of Henry V, thought of as the founder of the Guild, all benefactors and departed brethren.

The next day, the procession assembled again. The entire fraternity was expected to attend an early requiem mass in honour of the founder of the Guild, benefactors, departed brethren and sustren and all Christian souls. The St George bell tolled in the Cathedral in memory of the departed. The twenty-four priests provided by the aldermen were required to be present at these ceremonies. By 1471 this requiem mass had become 'rudely and dishonestly kept by persons and children standing about in temporal clothing',[5] so the Guild assembly ordered ten secular priests who were not brethren of the Guild to be present. They were paid 4*d* each from obit money: offerings were collected at all these services. The requiem mass was followed by what amounts to the Annual General Meeting of the Guild, which saw the elections of the masters, twenty brethren for common council, and other officers including the feastmakers for the following year, who would perhaps have been expected to start their planning whilst the events of that year's feast were still fresh in their minds.

As we know, the St George Guild at Norwich also took part in the annual procession of the Corpus Christi Guild, and it is interesting to compare these two types of processions. The processions of the Corpus Christi Guilds at Leicester and Coventry are quite well documented, and they serve as useful comparative examples. At Leicester, the annual procession of the members in their gowns, carrying their torches and bearing aloft the Eucharistic Host, and their feasting together afterwards took place from at least 1343, taking a route to and from St Martin's Church. A canopy was carried on staffs above the Host, serving to protect it from the elements as well as drawing attention to it. In addition to the Guild priests, the clergy of the various churches and the ecclesiastics belonging to the religious houses in Leicester would join the procession attired in their rich copes, and would intone a processional chant as they made their way slowly and solemnly along the streets. It is likely that the mayor and his brethren, attired in their robes and attended by the town officials and the waits, would also take their places in the procession; this is certainly attested to at Coventry.

The Coventry records of the Corpus Christi Guild also show that many characters from the Bible and the legends of the church were represented, such as the Virgin Mary, the Angel Gabriel, Herod, and the apostles. Other guilds also took part in the Corpus Christi procession, so it is likely that St Margaret and St Katherine represented their respective guilds, and quite possibly St George took part as well, whether with or without his dragon. There seems to have been a strong presence of banners and pensells from the various Coventry guilds too. The procession terminated at the Guildhall, where a feast was held. The cost of the dinner appears from the constitution of the Guild to have been paid by a contribution from each person (this is in contrast to the Norwich St George Guild where the feastmakers were expected to bear the costs of the meal themselves). After dinner the loving cup or mazor bowl was passed round, of which all, without distinction, partook.

The records of the Corpus Christi Guild at Coventry make it clear that many other religious guilds took part in the procession. This extension of festivities seems not to have been a feature of the Ridings of St George, and the implication is that the ceremonial of the Ridings was clearly focused on the membership of the St George Guild itself. As we have seen at Norwich, whilst membership of a guild of St George was not restricted to particular social classes, it was perhaps skewed towards the upper echelons of society, and there was a quite distinct link between civic government of Norwich and the government of the St George Guild. The contract between town and guild is equally apparent at Leicester. Here few facts about the St George Guild survive: the dates of foundation and suppression are unknown, but there is ample proof of its existence, and of the interest attaching to it, during parts of the fifteenth and sixteenth centuries. There is no record of where its income was derived from. It could have been purely religious, like the Corpus Christi Guild, or it could have combined secular business with religious advantages, like the St George Guild at Norwich, but we can infer that the Leicester Guild probably had little or no real property. A document of 1499 demonstrates that the income of the Guild was insufficient to cover its outgoings, and this could explain why the Leicester Riding was not always held.

In theory, the 'Riding of the George' was an annual festival. The mayor and corporation took their places in the procession, and to it all the inhabitants were summoned by a constable or other official. They were apparently bound to do so, for an Act of Common Hall in 1467 ordered them, upon due summons being made, 'to attend upon the mayor to ride against the King [that is, to meet the king], or for riding the George, or any other thing that shall be to the pleasure of the mayor and worship for the town'.[6] Absence occurred a penalty in money which went to the coffers of the Guild, as demonstrated in guild ordinances. During the reign of Edward IV a shilling fine was levied on the mayor's brethren, with commoners paying *6d*. The festival was held between St George's Day and Whitsunday. A document of 1523 shows that if the master of the Guild failed to ensure that the Riding took place within the limit of these dates, the mayor would levy a heavy fine of £5. By contrast, if the mayor was negligent over the matter he had to pay 26*s* 8*d*, and the mayor's chamberlains 6*s* 8*d*, all to be paid to the Guild; and there was also the return of a proportion of the fines that had been levied on the masters of the Guild since the last time the George was ridden, at rate of 26*s* 8*d*.

As at Norwich, the Leicester Riding was not always held on 23 April; the date was fixed by the Master of the Guild and proclaimed at the High Cross and other central places. In the early sixteenth century it seems to have lapsed for a time, for in 1523 the mayor ordered that the Master of the Guild 'should cause the George to be ridden, according to the old ancient custom, that is to say, between St George's Day and Whit-Sunday, unless there be reasonable cause'.[7] The saint himself was certainly represented in the pageant, and there must also have been a dragon, for in the Chamberlain's Accounts for 1536 there is an entry showing that 4*s* were paid in that year for 'dressing' it. Meanwhile, there is evidence of equal overlap between the city corporation and the Guild of St Christopher and St George who organised the Riding at York. In 1503 Sir William Todd, a former mayor of the city, bequeathed a helmet to the Guild for use during the Riding, and following the dissolution of the Guild under the terms of a 1547 Act of Parliament which suppressed fraternities, guilds and processions, the civic authorities decided to revive the celebrations of St George's Day in 1554. The festivities included a play, procession, mass and a sermon before a chapel of St George.

The impact of the 1547 suppression of the guilds on other Ridings is less clear. We do not know when the Leicester Riding ended, and although the George and Margaret in Norwich were suppressed in 1552 the Dragon was to continue to 'show himself for pastime' until 1732 when the St George Guild, which was by then known as 'the Company of St George', was finally dissolved and formally merged with the corporation of the city. The Ridings may then have ceased to be held on an official basis, but processions featuring the dragon certainly took place much later: the current Civic Snap was made in 1795. There is also evidence for Ridings of St George at Stratford-upon-Avon during the immediate post-medieval period at least: records suggest that several Ridings were organised in the late sixteenth century as a means of raising money for bridge repairs.

There seem to be two notable features about the Ridings of St George which distinguish them from the processions organised by other guilds. The first factor is that they seem to have been focused on the membership of the guilds of St George, which were clearly identified with urban government, with little of the dilution seen in the Coventry Corpus Christi procession, for example, where many guilds took part. The second factor is that the Ridings were mainly concerned with spectacle and revelry: no other feasts and processions involving just one guild seem to have been as spectacular. It would seem that, whilst the celebration of the feast day of St George had a quasi-spiritual basis, it was actually exploited by the urban elite as an opportunity to exert their authority over their fellow citizens. This is perhaps particularly apparent in Leicester, where the entire populace was required to attend and witness the procession. This was not a case of turning out to see the carnival because it was fun; it was more about having fun because you were told to. The fact that St George was identified as the patron saint of England must have contributed to the idea that his feast day should be marked in a communal way, but it must be borne in mind that the guilds of St George, and their restricted membership, were in sole charge of organising this celebration. The nature of this military saint, and his identification as a mounted knight rather than a mere foot soldier, ensured that the Ridings glorified a heroic noble, an aristocrat if you will, who was certainly someone to be identified with the elite that the Norwich Guild sought to enrol. We should particularly note the visual effect of placing all the Guild brethren in the Norwich Riding on horseback: they were literally and metaphorically placing themselves above the rest of the citizenry.

It is recognised that there was a strong aspect of social control within late medieval guilds. The ordinances of the Guild of St Anne at Lawrence Jewry, London, clearly try to control the behaviour of members and stipulate fines and even ejection from the Guild for misdemeanours such as adultery and being 'rebel of his tongue'.[8] But the Ridings seem to try to extend this control beyond guild members to the wider society, invoking St George as a figure of authority. Furthermore, the legend of St George makes it clear that the saint rescues not just a princess but also an entire town or city, which was suffering the effects of the dragon's pestilential breath. This aspect of the story is often reflected in the iconography of the dragon fight. For example, in a watercolour made of a now largely-lost wall painting of this subject from the Guild Chapel at Stratford-upon-Avon (illustration 4.9), an image which is placed in a very visible position next to the door, we see that the combat explicitly occurs *outside* the town; exactly analogous treatments occur in the Stamford cycle (illustration 3.4) and the Salisbury Breviary (illustration 1.1). In the latter image and in the Windsor cycle (illustration 3.19) we also see the princess and St George leading the dragon towards the town before the final *coup de grâce*. Likewise, in the Norwich Riding the George fights and defeats a dragon in a wood outside the town, reflecting this tradition of the saviour of the urban centre overcoming the ravening beast. The dragon is a frightening symbol of the chaos and disorder found in the natural, uncivilised wilderness, firmly put in its proper place by the triumphant hero of ordered city life. The world is decidedly *not* turned upside-down in the Ridings: the

Christian nobleman always prevails against the evil dragon, and the urban patricians defeat the forces that would overthrow their civilisation. It may be significant that Edward IV is recorded as having witnessed a pageant of St George at Bristol in 1462 which is described in terms directly evoking the typical format of the visual imagery of the fight between the saint and the dragon: not only is the authority of the town demonstrated to its inhabitants, it is also demonstrated to the king himself.

On a more practical level, we should consider the opportunity that the Ridings provided for a display of largesse. Large amounts of money were spent on producing a visual spectacle that varied from year to year. There may even have been some provision of 'corporate hospitality': we do not know exactly who received the wine, bread and cheese provided as refreshment during the Norwich Riding, but it is almost certain that the poor people employed as torch carriers and so forth would have received a share, and there may even have been some wider distribution. The feast does seem to have been a closed affair, but it is reasonable to suggest that any meal which took eight days to prepare would produce a sizeable quantity of leftovers to be distributed as alms, doubtless at the gates of the Bishop's Palace. Assuming the role of lord or lady bountiful has been a common way for members of the ruling classes to try to exert their authority over humbler folk, and it is certainly possible to interpret the Ridings of St George in this way, as an annual pageant of an urban and noble elite quite literally 'lording it' over their lesser neighbours.

In 1536 the development of the Reformation led to Henry VIII ordering the abrogation of nearly all religious holidays. The feasts of the apostles, the Virgin Mary and St George were specifically excluded from this order: all others were banned. The exemption of St George is rather surprising in this context: unlike the other named figures he is certainly not a Biblical character, and hence acceptable to the reformers who tried to excise all the accretions of myth and superstition from the tenets of the Church. The fact that St George was recognised as the patron saint of England will undoubtedly have contributed to the protection of his feast day, but in 1552 the Bishop of London declared that St George's Day was no longer to be observed. There is clear evidence to suggest that this edict was not generally obeyed, and the manner in which the feast day was kept will surely have been a factor in this resistance to official proscription. The Ridings were a convenient way of celebrating civic pride and allowing the urban patriciate to assert the status quo: the failure of the Reformation to suppress the Ridings is perhaps indicative of the extent to which this civic ritual ultimately fulfilled the secular, rather than spiritual, needs of specific groups within English society who took St George as their patron saint.

CHAPTER FIVE

THE DRAGON MYTH: LIGHT VERSUS DARK

The late medieval cult of St George clearly encompassed many different meanings and was able to serve the varied agendas of a range of patrons and devotees, but the sheer weight of evidence indicates that the single most significant presentation of the saint during this period was as a dragon-slayer. Although, as we saw in Chapter One, the story of the fight with the dragon was a late addition to the saint's legend, its popularity as both a visual and literary motif suggests that it was a very successful development. The inherent drama of the encounter between the good Christian knight and the evil monster ensured that St George remained a hugely popular figure well beyond the time when the Reformation had officially put paid to the cult of saints – most particularly non-Biblical saints – in Protestant states: the persistence of versions of the 'Riding of St George' even into the nineteenth century (illustrations 4.16 and 4.17) is ample testament to this.

The legend of St George and the dragon is a mainstay of English culture, featuring in many children's stories and used on coinage, commercial insignia and so forth. As a consequence, it is tempting to believe that this story is inviolable and unchanging, that our current understanding of it – as a rather exotic, but obviously invented, fantasy of the knight-errant – is the way that it has always been understood, and that the legend is too sacred, too complete in itself, to have ever been allowed to change or develop. Yet, as with so many of these notions of our heroic past, this conception of the dragon legend is not sustained by the evidence. This chapter considers the probable reasons why the story was added to the legend of St George, and then discusses some of the rather surprising ways in which the narrative, particularly its visual conception, has subsequently developed.

The origin of the concept of the dragon is shrouded in mystery. It is sometimes suggested that a belief in dragons arose from a combination of credulity and overactive imaginations, helped along by chance discoveries of dinosaur skeletons and the popularity of travellers' tales of monsters which were actually based on encounters with large and fearsome crocodiles. However, we should remember that throughout the medieval period 'dragons' were periodically sighted flying over European towns or infesting watercourses. In 1233 the Bishop of Hereford was one of many people who witnessed four red suns appearing in the sky in company with the natural sun, an event that presaged the beginning of a new round of difficulties between the king, Henry III, and his barons; the appearance of two dragons fighting in the sky off the coast of southern England a few weeks later was also understood to be an omen of civil strife. A fierce dragon is said to have terrorised many parts of England in April 1395, while another specimen was 'seen' by by a number of people in a river at Lucerne in May 1499. In August 1614 a dragon was allegedly slaughtering both men and cattle in a wood known as St Leonard's Forest near Horsham (Sussex), while in the mid-seventeenth century a similar creature is said to have terrorised herds of livestock at Evreux in Normandy. Whatever we make of these accounts, it is clear that these dragons were all too real for at least some people who were contemporaries to the events described. Our modern reading of dragon imagery and dragon legends tends to stress the allegories of heresy and evil which we see encoded in these monsters, but we must not overlook the simple fact that many of our forebears believed that dragons were literal creatures of flesh and blood with real powers to spread pestilence, to contaminate water supplies and to threaten life and limb. As late as 1725, Henry Bourne, a Newcastle curate, wrote that the custom of lighting bonfires on Midsummer Eve was derived from the desire to frighten dragons away: the monsters 'being incited to lust through the heat of the season, did frequently, as they flew through the Air, Spermatize in the Wells and Fountains'.[1] This apparent belief in the veracity of these creatures seems to have been widely shared. During the sixteenth and seventeenth centuries a well-documented vogue existed in England for 'Jenny Hannivers', figures assembled from the body parts of real animals (often dead lizards embellished with bat wings, sea horse tails, and so forth) which purported to be the preserved bodies of small dragons, basilisks, and similar beasts. These monstrous confections were even illustrated in some studies of natural history compiled at the time, which tends to suggest that a considerable range of people were taken in by the deception.

During the medieval period itself, belief in dragons seems to have been widespread. There are occasional references to the use of the monsters as a means of transport: they could be broken to the bit rather like a horse, although it appears that domestication was rather more complicated for dragons, with magical rites forming an essential component of the process. Such tales may have derived from the mythology which was associated with the historically authentic Alexander the Great (356–323 BC), who was credited with many bizarre habits. These included either travelling on the back of a griffin (a composite creature with the head and wings of an eagle and the body of a lion), or being carried in a wicker basket that was hoisted aloft by either two or four of the creatures. They were said to have been tied to the corners with chains and tempted to take wing by the simple expedient of waving pieces of meat at them held up on long spears. Alternatively, according to a medieval understanding based ultimately on a description of the wonders of the east found in Philostratus' *Life of Apollonius of Tyre* (*c*. 220 CE), dragons could be robbed of the precious gemstone 'dracontias', which they were thought to harbour inside their skulls. This trophy, which was used to detect poison and was hence a popular addition to the armoury of any ruler, had to be removed while the dragon was still alive, as the magical properties of the stone would otherwise be diminished. One theory proposed that a dragon could be lulled to sleep with the aid of charms and herbs, but retrieving the dracontias itself was obviously a job for a hero of the first order.

Other parts of dragons were much in demand throughout the Middle Ages for the preparation of love potions and medicines: dragon's blood could cure kidney stones and blindness, although the undiluted blood was thought to be a fatal poison. Meanwhile, the fat of a dragon, mixed with honey and oil, was used as a salve for weak eyes. A similar concoction, using the eyes of a dragon that had been kept until they grew stale, could be employed as a cure for night terrors; another preparation for the same problem, to be rubbed into the body night and morning, utilised the tongue, intestines and gall of a dragon as well as the eyes. These choice pieces were boiled in wine and oil, then cooled overnight. Alternatively, parts of a dragon's body were thought to be very efficacious in sorcery: a dragon head buried in the foundations of a house would ensure good fortune, while dragon fat could be made into an amulet that, when tied appropriately to the upper arm, could ensure victory in lawsuits. A preparation made from the head and tail of a dragon and various parts of a lion, a dog and racehorse was thought to confer invincibility. Despite these generally beneficial aspects of dragons' body parts, their urine was thought to be poisonous. 'St Anthony's fire', the medieval name for the contagious skin disease erysipelas, which is contracted by eating rye that has suffered fungal contamination, was sometimes attributed to putrefaction caused by dragon's urine coming into contact with the skin.

Writings about dragons in medieval bestiaries also indicate the extent to which these creatures were thought of as real animals. Bartholomew Anglicus was one of many bestiary writers who defined dragons as a form of snake; for him they were the 'most greatest of all serpents'.[2] Bartholomew discussed dragons in connection with elephants, another common approach, for they were considered to be mortal enemies. If an elephant was unfortunate enough to come across a dragon it was almost inevitable that both would die, for the dragon would wrap itself around the elephant's legs and body in an attempt to suffocate it. The elephant, thus impeded and fighting for its last breath, would surely trip and fall, crushing the dragon to death with its weight in the process. Bestiaries generally agreed that, despite a dragon's sharp teeth and pestilential breath, it was the creature's tail that formed its most deadly weapon as it was used as a club to beat victims to death as well as a means to crush them.

Much attention was also paid to the sexual behaviour of dragons, for it was believed that the bizarre habits then attributed to vipers were also adopted by their larger cousins. Pliny the Elder (lived AD 23–79) and many later natural historians claimed that vipers lacked any genitalia: insemination was achieved as a result of the male spitting semen into the female's mouth. In her sexual frenzy, or perhaps in her indignation at such an assault, the female invariably bit off the male's head. However, the female did not survive intact for much longer herself: lacking an obvious route out of their mother's womb, the progeny of the viper would bite their way out through her side and she would thus die of her injuries. It has been claimed that medieval people believed this rather gruesome and entirely fictitious practice of vipers was also found among dragons, but images of dragons with their progeny (for example, illustrations 5.26 and 5.27) tend to suggest that these beliefs were not generally accepted.

The dragon is a monster that seems to be common to virtually all cultures, although there is a sharp distinction between the generally beneficent dragons of the East and the largely negative views that dragons, or at least live specimens of the species, attracted in the West. The earliest records of dragon belief seem to derive from Mesopotamia in the ninth century BC, but later sources of information, which seem to have been particularly important influences on the later development of dragon-lore, were the Sumerian myth of Zu, a dragon or serpent of water and chaos (*c.* 4500 BC), and the creation epic of the Babylonian civilisation, which flourished between 1750 BC and 539 BC. This story related that at the beginning of time two elemental forces existed: Apsu, a male spirit of fresh water, and Tiamat, a dragon-like female spirit of salt water who was also associated with primeval chaos. The coupling of these two entities produced a vast and ill-assorted brood of gods, some of whom grew up to antagonise their father so much that he threatened to kill them. One of the young gods then murdered Apsu in a pre-emptive strike, whereupon the enraged Tiamat turned upon her offspring. To aid her vengeful fight she spawned a group of monsters – serpents, dragons and composite beasts such as the centaur and the scorpion-man – in preparation for a great battle. One of Tiamat's first brood, Marduk, emerged as

appetite for sacrificial offerings attributed to the statue of Bel was actually because of the greed of Bel's seventy attendant priests and their families, then he proved that the dragon, far from being a mighty god, was powerless in the face of determined opposition. He told the king that he would kill the dragon without the use of a sword or staff, then boiled together a mixture of pitch, fat and hair and formed it into cakes. He fed the cakes to the fire-breathing dragon, who promptly exploded. Daniel was thrown into a lion-pit for his pains (but miraculously survived), but his patent method of dragon-destruction became popular much later with heroes in legends from Scotland, Poland and other parts of Europe.

A third important Biblical source of dragon-lore occurs in the description of the Apocalypse that St John the Divine recounts in his Revelation. Dragons also figure in earlier references to the end of the world, in both the Old Testament and Apocryphal writings, but John's version is perhaps the most vivid. A red dragon with seven crowned heads and ten horns appears in the sky and sweeps a third of the stars from the sky with his tail. A war breaks out between the dragon and St Michael, both supported by angels, the good and the fallen: the heavenly army eventually vanquishes the dragon's legions and cast the monster down upon the earth. The dragon, who is then named as Satan, causes a huge flood, whereupon the beast of the Apocalypse arises from the sea. The dragon gives this monster his power and authority, but is himself chained up by an angel and sealed into an abyss for a thousand years. This identification of the Devil with a dragon is vitally important in the evolution of the creature in medieval thought, for the dragon is often presented in opposition to the saint as a heroic figure of Christ. The derivation of this idea is closely linked to the tradition of the serpent in the Garden of Eden: the terms 'serpent' and 'dragon' are often interchangeable, and a dragon is sometimes defined as a 'winged serpent'. Some images of the temptation of Adam and Eve make the link explicit: illustration 5.1 shows a winged serpent with an angelic face, a striking combination of the ideas of Satan as a fallen angel, a dragon and the tempter in the Garden of Eden. A fifteenth-century alabaster image that also draws on these ideas makes a specific allusion to the legend of St George and the dragon (illustration 3.22): in the main area a figure of the Virgin and Child stand alongside a crucifix that is draped with a dead snake, while St George fights the dragon in the predella below. This carving encapsulates a number of related ideas: the snake and the dragon both represent aspects of the Devil, and both are shown being defeated by the incarnation of 'Good'; firstly, through the willing sacrifice of the son of a Virgin and secondly, in the form of a clearly Christian knight. Christ himself is also identified as a dragon-slayer on occasion: an Islamic tradition claims that Christ will overcome

5.1 The Temptation, *fifteenth century, possibly French. (Library of Congress, Rare Books Collection, MS 139)*

the Anti-Christ at the gate of Lydda in the last days, a choice of location which is particularly interesting in the light of Lydda's associations with Perseus and St George's own dragon fights.

Paolo Uccello's famous, and somewhat unsettling, version of the combat between St George and the dragon (illustration 5.2) seems to be a conscious evocation of the knight as a representative of Christ. It is notable that this depiction places the dragon in front of the mouth of a rocky cave, which tends to imply that this is the lair of the monster; there is no sign of the marsh or lake that is conventionally ascribed to the beast in late medieval treatments of the legend. The cave itself may well stand for the mouth of Hell: the craggy edges of the rocky cavern are certainly reminiscent of teeth, and there is a strong impression that the dragon has emerged from a yawning abyss. The corkscrew curl of the creature's tail is undoubtedly serpentine, and thus inspires thoughts of the tempter in the Garden of Eden, while the curled storm clouds behind St George may put us in mind of a wrathful God, sending forth his envoy to visit retribution on the great enemy. Commentators on this image have often remarked on the clear deviation from the

5.2 Paolo Uccello, St George and the Dragon, c. *1455–60. (National Gallery, London)*

standard legend of the combat: the princess should hold the dragon on the leash made from her girdle after the battle, not during it (the fact that the princess is clearly wearing a girdle is also rather odd). However, these apparent problems can be resolved if we reinterpret this image in the light of the identification of St George as a figure of Christ, for the princess can be read as a figure of the Virgin Mary, or perhaps the Church, and the dragon is a clear representation of the Devil. Thus, the Virgin Mary has trapped the Devil by giving birth to the Saviour while still a virgin, or, alternatively, the Church has trapped the Devil by obeying the law of God and refusing to be tempted into sin. This trapping of the Devil allows Christ to administer divine retribution for all misdeeds, and, ultimately, to save his own people.

A similar drama is played out in an earlier work by Uccello, a panel painting dated some fifteen or twenty years earlier (illustration 5.3), but by comparing the two works we can see that the artist has made several significant alterations. Firstly, the cave occupies a far more prominent position in the later picture; the toothed effect is also much more pronounced. In the earlier depiction the cave was not clearly associated with the dragon, but the placement of the creature immediately in front of it in the second image makes the connection very obvious. Secondly, the princess's role in the first image is that of a spectator, simply standing in prayer. However, the

5.3 Paolo Uccello, St George and the Dragon, c. *1439–40. (Musée Jacquemart-André, Paris)*

later version shows the princess acutely involved in the action as she holds the dragon on a leash. A third significant difference is found in the treatment of the background: in the earlier treatment the conventional walled town is visible – admittedly, spectators watch from outside the town rather than inside, but they are certainly still present – while in the latter the city is so far away as to be virtually invisible. A city wall is just about discernible – to the left of St George's lance, beneath the tip of the dragon's left wing – but no spectators can be seen. This is in total contravention of the accepted practice, particularly for a version of the subject created on this scale; the presence of the threatening swirl of cloud is also a new departure. Finally, a significant change has also occurred in the presentation of the knight. In the first image he is clearly identified as St George, as he wears a red cross tabard, but in the latter there is no sign of his conventional device. While this need not imply that the saint is anyone other than St George, it is certainly an interesting omission: could the artist perhaps be subtly indicating that this St George is rather more than he appears?

As we saw in Chapter One, St George is by no means the only saint credited with overcoming a dragon, and it is likely that the legends of Christian figures such as SS Michael, Theodore, Margaret and Marcellus and other saintly dragon-fighters will have influenced the development of St George's own story. The iconography of St Michael suggests that he is the closest counterpart to St George: although there is no rescued female figure it is abundantly clear that the confrontation between the saint and the dragon is a physical contest rather than a battle of wills. Illustration 5.4 shows St Michael brandishing his sword at the already wounded dragon as they both fly over Mont-St-Michel: there is no question of subduing the monster with the sign of the cross in the way that St Margaret did. Significantly, in an early written version of his dragon legend, dating from the twelfth century, St George is said to have defeated the monster by making the sign of the cross, but this tradition quickly gave way to a full-scale battle between the two foes where the emphasis is on brute force and knightly skill rather than supernatural intervention. The abandonment of this topos diverts St George's story away from the model provided by St Margaret and some other less energetic dragon-slaying saints, and in consequence his actions resonate more clearly with the legend of St Michael.

These two knightly soldier–saints make a useful pairing: a good example is the Borbjerg retable (illustration 3.11), where efforts were evidently made to standardise their representations in the terminal statues (they both have red cross devices on their shields, and both trample their dragons to form a virtual mirror image of one another). However, the two saints are not strictly comparable. Like St Margaret, St Michael faced not a 'real' dragon, but a

Enedicite do
minum os
angeli eius
potentes virtute qui facitis
verbum eius ad audiendu
vocem sermonum eius ps.
Benedic anima mea do
mino et omnia que intra

creature that is explicitly said to be the Devil in the guise of a dragon; St George's foe can sometimes seem to be a representation of the Devil, but it is arguable that it more frequently presented as a physical creature of flesh and blood. Furthermore, as the imagery of *The Paradise Garden* (illustration 3.23) demonstrates, St Michael's foe is often a demon rather than an actual dragon, but St George seems only ever to fight dragons or, occasionally, humans. We should perhaps note in this context that the iconography of St George attacking a fallen human figure (for example, illustration 1.5) was not entirely superseded by the imagery of the dragon fight: the fragmentary tomb brass at Elsing (Norfolk) of the military leader Sir Hugh Hastings (d.1347) depicts an equestrian St George spearing a rather demonic figure that lies on the ground (illustration 5.5). The figure is certainly more human than animal.

The iconography of both St George and St Michael draws on the

5.5 Detail of the brass of Sir Hugh Hastings (d.1347) in Elsing church (Norfolk).

Opposite: *5.4 The Limbourg Brothers,* Les Tres Riches Heures du Duc du Berry, *1409–15, fol. 195: St Michael defeating the dragon above Mont-St-Michel. (Musée Condé, Chantilly, MS 65/1283, fol. 195)*

traditional identification of the dragon as an aggressive, death-dealing creature. These ideas also lie behind the heraldic significance of dragons: they were widely used in both Mediterranean countries and northern Europe on battle standards and similar insignia as emblems of the power and might of the army and its leader, and also to induce fear in the enemy hosts. The origin of this motif seems to be the use of the device by armies in the Eastern world, such as the Parthians and the Dacians: this type of imagery was adopted during the later period of the Roman Empire, notably in the form of the *draco*, the dragon-shaped banners that functioned as the standard of a cohort of men (the eagle standard was used to denote the larger body of soldiers which formed a Legion). This iconography intersects with the cult of St George because the dragon can be understood as a representative of pre-Christian religions that are overcome by the *miles Christianus*, the knight of Christ. The Christian soldier defeats the purple dragon of the Imperial standard just as Christ overcomes the heathen empire itself.

A similar reading relates to the suppression of pre-Christian religion within the British Isles. The long-standing Celtic fondness for dragons has meant that they appear as decorations on many artefacts, especially in the form of the Uroboros, or the tail-swallower, which functions as an evocation of eternity and the ongoing cycle of birth, fertility, death and rebirth. This generally positive manifestation of the dragon is quite separate from the negative overtones of the creature in the hero-dragon paradigm, but the victory of St George over the dragon is sometimes interpreted as an icon of the victory of the Roman Church over both the native religious cults and the pre-existing Celtic form of Christian worship. The combat between St George and the dragon was certainly used by some late medieval people as an analogy for the ongoing battles of the Roman Church against heretical movements. In 1418 Emperor Sigismund established the chivalric Order of the Vanquished Dragon to celebrate the extermination of heresy. The Bohemian heretic Jan Hus had been burned at the stake three years earlier, the same year that Sigismund himself was inducted into the Order of the Garter, and it is surely no coincidence that he chose a defeated dragon as the emblem of his new institution.

Later commentators also exploited the iconography of the dragon fight in order to support an argument about religious differences. Peter Gottland's engraving of 1552 (illustration 5.6) creates an allegory about the Roman Catholic and Protestant Churches. The figure of St George is replaced by the infant Christ, who is depicted killing a dragon that wears a papal tiara on one of its heads. This clearly identifies it as a figure of both the Roman Church in general and the Pope in particular. Meanwhile, the rescued princess in the background of this image represents the 'true', or reformed, Church. The allegory

5.6 Peter Gottland, St George and the Dragon – Allegory of the Triumph of the New Faith over the Old, *1552.*

plays, perhaps unconsciously, on the iconography of St George in the early Greek Church where the saint was a form of Christ, rescuing the princess Ecclesia (the Church) from the clutches of the Devil.

The many-headed monster depicted by Gottland emphasises another important aspect of dragons: the sheer variety of forms in which they are depicted. A glance through the images of St George fighting the dragon in this book will give some sense of the permutations. They can be large or small, winged or unwinged, with two legs, four legs or no legs at all, with one head, two and sometimes more. Dragons can resemble lizards (illustration 5.7), bears (illustration 5.8) or even dogs (the dragonlet in illustration 5.27), but an elongated, serpentine neck is a very common attribute; a long tail – useful for squeezing the life out of elephants and other enemies – is another motif that appears frequently. Dragons often seem to owe something of their form to several different creatures, and we can perhaps interpret this composite quality to the artists' desire to make the dragon appear as frightening as possible by combining the worst aspects of other recognisably dangerous animals. Yet the physical attributes of some specific dragons go well

5.7 Pere Nissart and Rafael Moger, St George and the Dragon, *1468–70. (Diocesan Museum, Majorca)*

beyond the realms of the familiarly fearsome, such as the specimen fought by St George in illustration 5.9. This animal possesses a secondary head in the end of its tail, in emulation of a mythical creature known as the amphisbaena. This snake-like oddity formed itself into a hoop by inserting the head at one end of its body into the mouth of the head at the other end, then bowled along at a quite considerable speed. The Classical natural historian Pliny maintained that the creature's primary purpose in having two heads was to be better able to discharge its venom; the ability to make itself into a

5.8 Swiss stained glass of St George and the dragon, fifteenth century. (Victoria & Albert Museum, London)

wheel was merely a convenient secondary function. The peregrinations that the amphisbaena is alleged to have undertaken were purely for nefarious purposes, of course, and it thus formed a very suitable model for the wicked dragon who was to be laid low by St George. The dragon in illustration 5.9, while clearly influenced by the legend of the amphisbaena, does not look as if it would get very far by forming itself into a hoop, as the rather plump body shape would unbalance the narrow tail. It seems clear that the artist has another purpose in mind, and it is likely that the design was chosen in order to highlight the mythical ability of the dragon to suffocate its enemies by entwining itself around them. Standing figures of

5.9 Glass panel of St George, c. 1505, formerly at 18 Highcross Street, Leicester. (Newarke Houses Museum, Leicester)

St George are often depicted with a trampled and speared dragon that wraps its tail around one of the saint's legs, and by giving this particular dragon a secondary head in the tail the artist emphasises just how hard the saint has had to fight to overcome the creature. Furthermore, the dragon's close relationship to snakes, and hence the serpent in the Garden of Eden, is clearly established by the device of placing a head on an obviously serpentine tail.

This most famous snake, the creature who tempts Eve to taste of the fruit of the Tree of Knowledge, thereby precipitating the Fall, the expulsion of Adam and Eve from the Garden of Eden and the penalty of suffering and death paid by all people, is deeply implicated in the construction of the dragon in a number of images of the conflict with St George. One of the most important aspects of the medieval understanding of the serpent is that it is consistently presented as a composite creature, very often in the form of a snake with a human head. This treatment cannot be derived from the Biblical description of the episode, for, although the tempter is clearly endowed with human speech, it is never said to be anything other than a serpent. One variation on this form is the so-called 'pre-Lapsarian serpent', a lizard-like creature with (usually four) short legs and, in general, a human face: this is thought to be a visual reference to God's subsequent curse that the creature should crawl in the dust on its belly, which tends to imply that it would lose the use of any legs that it may have had.

Furthermore, the human face or head is often clearly that of a woman. This humanising and feminising characteristic may well derive from, or at least have a common root with, the concept of Lilith. This character, who was probably based on a Babylonian storm demon, is named as Adam's first wife in some Jewish traditions, a woman who was created equal with her husband rather than fashioned on a rib taken from his side. She is envisaged as a snake with a woman's head, and is sometimes directly identified as the creature who gave Eve forbidden knowledge and thereby gained revenge on both her husband and God himself. Illustration 5.10 shows a typical visual treatment of the Fall from the end of the fifteenth century, by the German artist Lucas Cranach the Elder. The serpent is represented with not only the head of a woman but also a voluptuous torso, belly and hips that merge into a gently tapering tail, rather like a land-bound equivalent of a mermaid. Eve hands an apple to Adam, whose modesty is already protected by a carefully positioned small branch growing from the main trunk of the tree. Eve herself is turned towards her husband in a pose that highlights the similarities between her own body and that of the serpent, another common artistic device which seems to relate to the concept that Eve, as the first to fall, was particularly guilty; in some versions of the subject,

5.10 Lucas Cranach, The Fall of Man, *late fifteenth century.*

Eve's face and the serpent's face are mirror images of one another, a presentation that definitely singles out woman as the culpable sex. Cranach's version takes a slightly different approach, however, for he has underlined both the feminine and sexual elements of the composition by placing the apple very close to the breasts of the serpent: the similarity of shape and size is unmistakable. St Michael, who approaches on the left to warn of God's impending judgement, is something of a bit-part player in this image: the focus is clearly on the sensual group on the right. It is very common for the serpent to be represented as female in late medieval images of the Temptation. She is often gendered by obvious breasts and long hair, but occasionally she will wear a wimple or ornate headdress. This type of presentation is probably a reference to the idea that sexually experienced women are dangerous and untrustworthy: the serpent's covered hair forms a strong contrast to Eve's long, loose hair, a motif that often signifies a state of feminine innocence.

A rather different version of the Fall is found in the fifteenth-century French miniature shown in illustration 5.1. Eve is once more defined as the guiltier of the two people, but the presentation of the serpent is quite unlike the sexualised, voluptuous woman depicted by Cranach. In this version, the tempter is rather androgynous: there maybe a suspicion of a breast as the serpent leans around the trunk of the tree, but the hairstyle is far less obviously female than the long loose hair or ornamented headdresses found in contemporary visual treatments. In fact, the presentation of the serpent is rather reminiscent of an angel, a creature who tends to be understood as somewhat asexual (St Michael and, in general, the Angel Gabriel are obvious exceptions to this trend). It could be that the artist is seeking to invoke the fallen angel Lucifer rather than Lilith. The 'true' identity of the serpent is never made clear in textual sources, so an identification of the creature as a form of the Devil is quite permissible. It would certainly be reasonable to suppose that the supreme trickster could assume the guise of his former, angelic incarnation in order to tempt the unwary: as usual, the bestial tail betrays his true identity. The wings also contribute to the angelic impression of the serpent, but they must surely also put the spectator in mind of a dragon. As we have seen, dragons were not always thought of as winged but this was a very common way of depicting the creature; the combination of a pair of wings and a serpentine tail is almost irresistible to anyone on the lookout for dragons. If we return to the image of *The Paradise Garden* (illustration 3.23), discussed in Chapter Three, we can perhaps see the entire train of meaning at work. The serpent in the Garden of Eden is often female, sometimes it is winged, it is certainly evil; dragons are serpents, they are often winged, they are certainly evil. A feminised dragon, as we seem to have lying dead beside St George in *The Paradise Garden*, would seem to be a logical progression.

Dragons with a 'gendering' orifice similar to the beast in *The Paradise Garden* occur in at least forty images in the late medieval iconography of St George, and some of these treatments are reproduced here. Illustrations 4.11, 5.21 and 5.24 show the combat of St George with a gendered dragon, for example, while illustrations 4.8 and 5.13 (both by Albrecht Dürer) depict the victorious St George standing over or holding his defeated enemy, a dragon who seems to display a gendered pudendum. There is a wide variety of depictions of the orifice itself: some are almond-shaped (for example, illustration 5.9), some are more rounded (illustration 5.12), while others are slit-shaped, whether placed across the base of the tail (illustration 5.13) or orientated to lie along the line of the tail (illustration 5.14; strictly, the orifice in this image is an elongated almond shape).

It is difficult to decode these images with real confidence, and

5.11 Israhel van Meckenem, after Franz van Brugge, St George and the dragon, *c. 1500.*

5.12 The Master of the Calvary, St George kneeling on the dragon, *fifteenth century.*

5.13 Albrecht Dürer, St George on foot, c. *1500.*

5.14 Israhel van Meckenem, St George and the Dragon, c. *1500.*

although several factors point to the identification of the dragons as female we should also consider two other possibilities. The first consideration is that the 'orifice' is actually intended to be read as a wound, the site of a piercing made by St George's lance or spear. This idea must not be ruled out altogether, but the overwhelming body of evidence suggests that the iconography of the combat demands that the dragon is wounded in the mouth or, less frequently, in the throat. Indeed, this very group of 'gendered' dragons are all depicted being stabbed in the mouth or throat or else display clear signs of a wound to this area. I have yet to discover a medieval image that shows the dragon being attacked by St George in any other part of the body, but, given the vast numbers of treatments of the subject of the combat, we should not overlook the possibility that somewhere a depiction does exist of the saint stabbing the dragon in the genital region. However, such an image would undoubtedly be highly suggestive of a sexualised discourse. We must also bear in mind the contemporary medieval idea, outlined above, that the dragon's power lies in its tail rather than its teeth: the mouth is by no means the most dangerous part of the creature. It is notable that the only other dragon-slayers who direct their attention to the mouth tend to kill their monstrous enemy by feeding it explosive or corrosive matter – the apocryphal story of Daniel and the dragon, mentioned above, is a prime example – so the consistent presentation of St George as a man who stabs a dragon in the mouth is surely indicative of some underlying meaning. (In general, dragon-slayers turn their attention to other parts of the monster's body. Some attack the creature's eyes – this seems to be a well-established method for despatching crocodiles, as the eyes appear to be the only vulnerable part – while others try to wound the beast in the belly. One example of this latter strategy is the northern European hero Sigurd the Vulsung, who killed a dragon by hiding in a pit and stabbing the creature's underside as it walked overhead.) St George's fixation with attacking the dragon's mouth may well be related to the long-established popular connection made between the mouth and the female genitals: wounding in the mouth, perhaps particularly by means of a rather phallic lance, is likely to be sexually suggestive.

A second interpretation of the orifice is that it represents an anus. This argument does have rather more merit than the contention that a wound is being depicted, for the grotesque contortionist creature that displays its anus is a staple of the range of drolleries that appear in medieval carvings – and, to a lesser extent, other formats – much to the discomfort of some people in later, more prudish times. These carvings invariably depict humans or humanised creatures, which make direct comparison with the defiantly bestial dragon rather difficult, but a closer analogy can be drawn with some of the more fantastical animals that appear in contemporary bestiaries and other works of 'natural history'. One good example is the 'Bonnacon', a monster that had a particularly unpleasant weapon to employ against any hunter foolish enough to pursue it. The creature, it is claimed, would void the contents of its bowels in the general direction of its enemies: its excrement could cover an area of several acres and it was noxious enough to cause trees to burst into flames spontaneously. Interestingly, the Bonnacon may have had some links to the dragon, for it is claimed that the Tarasque, the dragon killed by St Martha at Aix-en-Provence, was the product of a coupling between Leviathan (whose progeny were legion) and a Bonnacon. Indeed, some images of St George's dragon probably do show the animal's anus: one good example is seen in illustration 5.11, where the clenched appearance of the musculature around the orifice is very striking. This is in stark contrast to the relaxed or unmuscled depiction of the orifice in many other images,

5.15 Israhel van Meckenem, St George and the Dragon, *fifteenth century.*

5.16 The Master of the Calvary, St George and the dragon, *fifteenth century.*

even some created by the same artist (illustrations 5.14 and 5.15), and it seems very unlikely that such clearly dissimilar depictions are intended to be read in the same way. Even if powerful evidence comes to light that the 'gendered dragon' is actually displaying an anus – for example, if a depiction of a dragon with a 'relaxed' orifice also shows defecated material, or if an accompanying text makes explicit reference to the dragon's anus – this will not necessarily undermine a sexualised reading of these images, for we should not overlook the possibility of the artist wishing to depict the dragon as a homosexual creature. Given the general taboo on homosexual activity found in the late medieval Church such a presentation would tend to define the animal as base; this reading still holds true even if we overlook any sexualised agenda, for the display of the anus is surely a bestial, sub-human act.

To return to the main contention, that these dragons are actually displaying female genitalia, it is important to recognise that no one today knows what such a creature's pudendum is actually *supposed* to look like. As a reptile, the dragon's genitalia should, in theory, be hidden inside a cloaca, the cavity in the pelvic region into which the alimentary canal and the genital and urinary ducts open in all vertebrates other than the higher mammals. It is difficult to interpret the extent to which this type of information would have been available to natural historians and the compilers of bestiaries, far less the designers, artists and patrons of these images that apparently depict gendered dragons. However, there is clear evidence that at least some people thought that dragons had humanised genitalia. For example, illustration 5.17 depicts a male dragon that evidently has a scrotum hanging down underneath its tail: this is a very important finding, which goes some way towards supporting the identification of a dragon with a definite orifice as female, for it is obvious that the artist of this work was not seeking to represent a 'realistic' reptile with its genitalia hidden inside a cloaca. Another pair of very interesting images depict a dragon with a humanised penis as well as a scrotum containing two clearly defined testicles. Illustrations 5.18 and 5.19 are so similar that it is almost certain that they have been produced from the same design; the probable dates of the works suggest that the manuscript illumination was the first to be created,

5.17 Grimani Breviary, *St George and the dragon, fol. 538v (1480–1520). (Bibliotheca Marciana, Venice, MS. lzt. I. 99, fol. 538v).*

5.18 Master of Jean Chevrot, St George and the dragon *in a Flemish Book of Hours, (c. 1450) (Pierpont Morgan Library, New York, MS 421, fol. 23v).*

5.19 St George and the Dragon, *pipeclay relief, (c. 1430–40).*

but it is by no means certain that they are not both derived from a third, prototype, image. This dragon evidently possesses male genitals, but it also seems to have an orifice immediately behind: it is perhaps slightly easier to detect on the sculpted image. This may suggest that the dragon's anus is also being shown, but an alternative, and equally valid, reading indicates that the dragon is actually a hermaphrodite beast, that is, an animal that possesses both male and female genitalia. Hermaphrodite animals were certainly recognised in medieval natural history – the hyena is the most celebrated example of a creature that was understood to possess both types of sexual organ – and it is by no means impossible that the originator of this version of the combat between St George and the dragon was seeking to highlight the depravity of the monster, or even its simple oddity, by depicting it as a hermaphrodite.

At this stage it is important to clarify just how unusual the presentation of the dragon as a sexualised animal actually is. There are literally hundreds, possibly thousands, of images of St George and the dragon extant from the medieval period, and those that appear to show genitalia constitute a tiny fraction of this number. The overwhelming majority of dragons are either shown in an attitude that obscures this area of their anatomy (for example, illustration 5.7), or they are depicted with the genital region visible but unmarked (illustration 5.20), in a way that is reminiscent of a doll's complete absence of genitalia. However, the group of images which seem to depict a dragon with an orifice are sufficiently numerous to allow us to infer that they have not arisen by chance. In particular, we should note that German and Netherlandish artists active around the time of the Reformation were particularly interested in this treatment of the dragon: Albrecht Dürer (illustrations 4.8 and 5.13), Martin Schongauer (illustration 5.21), Israhel van Meckenem (illustrations 5.11, 5.14 and 5.15) and the anonymous Master of the Calvary (illustrations 5.12 and 5.16) were all important artists and engravers who elected to make use of this motif in some of their depictions of St George, and it seems reasonable to suggest that they may have been drawn to the idea because it was widely accepted that femaleness, especially sexualised femaleness, was often a concomitant of evil and depraved creatures.

Illustration 5.22 depicts a good example of the iconographic link between female sexuality and depravity, for it shows the Papal Ass. This particular version was produced by the workshop of Lucas Cranach for use in a Reformist pamphlet of 1523, but the monster was a feature of pamphleteering by both sides during the Reformation and was invoked in political polemic in Italy as well as Germany from the end of the fifteenth century. The beast itself was said to have been dragged from the River Tiber in 1496, and was first pictured, in 1497, on a relief on the north door of the cathedral at

5.20 Master of the Retable of St George, St George and the Dragon, c. *1470. (National Gallery, Prague)*

5.21 Martin Schongauer,
St George and the Dragon, c. *1470.*

Como. It seems that the Papal Ass was originally conceived as an allegory of the faults of the city of Rome. However, once it had been engraved on copper by the goldsmith Wenzel of Olmutz, around the year 1500, it became widely accepted as emblematic of the hierarchy of the Roman Church and all its associated problems. In 1523 the German reformer Philipp Melanchthon interpreted the Papal Ass in terms that are deeply indicative of the revulsion with which semi-human sexualised monsters were viewed. The whole creature was an allegory of the institution of the papacy, he claimed, while the ass head stood for the Pope himself. The Church should not have a mortal at its head, and the ass head was thus as fitting as the Pope as head of the Church. The right hand, which is an elephant's foot, signifies the spiritual power of the Pope, which he uses to crush all consciences; the right hand usually signifies the soul, and it should be ruled by Christ, not an ass's head. The humanised left hand signifies the secular power of the Pope, something acquired only by human means. The right foot is the hoof of an ox; this signifies the servants of the Pope's spiritual powers who oppress the souls of all people in the Church, the preachers, confessors and theologians. The left foot is an eagle's or griffin's claw; this signifies the servants of the Pope's secular power, the canon lawyers. The female belly and breasts signify the

5.22 The Papal Ass, from M. Luther, Abbildung des papstums *(1545), fol. 1. (British Library, London)*

cardinals, bishops, priests and monks who lead whorish lives, just as the Papal Ass stands in its shaming nakedness. Martin Luther, an ally of Melanchthon and a close friend of the artist Lucas Cranach, wrote in his *Depiction of the Papacy* (1545) that 'what God himself holds of the papacy is shown by this terrible picture. Everyone should therefore shudder as he takes it to heart.'[3]

For our purposes, the salient aspect of the Papal Ass is the female gendering, which is achieved by the inclusion of breasts and a rounded belly. As the figure was used by Reformers to stand for everything that was wrong with the Church, this feminisation of the monster is deeply meaningful: femaleness, and specifically a depraved, sexualised femaleness, is cast as a wicked state of

5.24 St George and the d 0ragon, *polychromed English oak sculpture, mid- to late fifteenth century. (Herbert Museum and Art Gallery, Coventry)*

'retrocopulation'). It may be that St George has forced the dragon into this position, but it seems more likely that the message of the imagery is that the depraved creature is offering herself to him sexually as a way of trying to save her own life. We should not overlook the phallic nature of the weaponry St George uses, particularly the way that it often functions as a pointer to the orifice itself (for example, illustrations 5.21 and 5.25).

A rare example of an apparently feminised dragon that has adopted a different position is found in the scene of the combat within the La Selle retable (illustration 3.12 and 3.13).

5.25 The Danube Master, St George and the dragon, *relief sculpture, 1500–20. (Konopište Castle)*

Unfortunately, the panel in question is a modern replacement, but comparisons with antiquarian photographs indicate that the dragon itself is a very good likeness. For reasons that seem to derive from the overall iconography of the work – specifically, the wish to contrast the dragon with the Virgin Annunciate in the panel below – the monster is placed in an upright position that is apparently unparalleled in other depictions of the subject. However, the dragon clearly displays an orifice in the genital region which is further highlighted by the proximity of the horse's hoof acting as a pseudo-phallic pointer. As we have seen, the stabbing action of the lance into the dragon's mouth found in this sculpture is absolutely typical of the subject of the combat, and the popularly acknowledged link between the mouth and the vulva implies that St George is making a sexual statement towards the dragon.

The presence of external female genitalia in these images defines the dragon in a quite specific way, both as an obscene creature and also, crucially, in her relationship to St George. A complex paradigm is set up of an act of penetration by the aggressive male which overthrows the sexuality of the female (he refuses to have actual coition with her) and at the same time sublimates his own sexual desires. This reading is entirely congruent with our understanding of St George as a figure of chastity and helps to explain the rationale behind the presence of St George in *The Paradise Garden* (illustration 3.23): he is presented as a man who has overthrown his own sexual urges, which are symbolised by the dead sexualised dragon. *The Paradise Garden* and the La Selle panel also display similar ideas about the serpent in the Garden of Eden – the intricate working of the La Selle dragon's tail certainly points to this – but wider misogynistic themes are also called into play. St George is presented as the antithesis of the dragon: human to beast, good to bad, male to female. But given the quite specific overtones of sexuality, we can argue that St George is presented as chaste in opposition to the dragon's obvious sexuality. Within the panel, the dragon (female, sexual, evil, bestial) is placed, both literally and figuratively, in opposition not only to St George (male, chaste, good, human), but also to the rescued Virgin princess (female, chaste, good, human) and, at La Selle, the Virgin Mary (female, chaste, good, human). The dragon and the Virgin seem to be intended to embody the polar opposites inherent in late medieval attitudes to women, the nadir and the epitome: the evil, sexual, bestial creature and the good, virginal, saintly creature.

There is one further way of gendering a dragon as female, less clear cut than the presence of obvious breasts, dugs or genitalia, and perhaps ultimately less successful. Illustration 5.26 shows a miniature from *Les Belles Heures*, a French Book of Hours created *c.* 1408, while illustration 5.27 is a mid- to late fifteenth-century engraving by a Dutch artist known as 'Master Zwolle' (he is often identified as Jan van den Mijnnesten, *c.* 1440–1504). Both images feature an adult dragon along with one or more dragonlets. This presentation of dragons as parental figures seems to be very rare in the iconography of St George, possibly because it is a much less successful means of gendering a dragon than the use of breasts or genitalia. There seem to be two main reasons for this. Firstly, it is possible for the dragon to be interpreted as a father rather than a mother, although the acknowledged propensity for most male animals to leave as fast as possible once procreation has occurred and ideas about the fierceness of female animals defending their young – the tigress with her cubs, for example – make this quite unlikely. The second problem is that baby animals tend to have an inherent appeal, even baby monsters. These infant dragons are really rather sweet, and the danger is that the viewer identifies with the wrong protagonist in this combat. In fact, the dragon seems to be almost justified in her predation on humans, for she obviously has a family to support.

5.26 Les Belles Heures du Jean, Duc de Berry, *St George and the dragon, 1408–9. (Metropolitan Musuem of Art, New York, Ms 54.1.1, fol. 167)*

An English version of the subject of St George in combat with a mother dragon and her offspring, a fifteenth-century wall painting at St Gregory's Church, Pottergate, Norwich, contrives to make the dragon seem rather less empathetic: she is certainly presented as rather fiercer than her continental colleagues, perhaps because the

5.27 Jan van den Mijnnesten/ Master Zwolle, St George, *c. 1500.*

artist has made an effort to push the viewer to categorise the mother dragon as the worst type because she is bringing yet more evil into the world with her terrible spawn. This is reminiscent of the role played by Grendel's mother in *Beowulf*: her awfulness is made all the more terrifying by the fact that she has been able to reproduce, to make more wickedness. Furthermore, there is an implication that the dragon may have other progeny elsewhere, which clearly undermines the analogy between St George killing the dragon and Christ's ultimate overthrow of the Devil.

Illustration 5.28, a treatment of St George and the dragon *c.* 1515 by the German artist Leonard Beck, depicts another

5.28 Leonard Beck (1480-1542), St George and the dragon, *c. 1515. (Kunsthistorisches Museum, Vienna)*

interesting variation on the theme of the monstrous mother. In the foreground St George, mounted, is about to cut off the dragon's head with his sword. The creature is already wounded through the throat with a broken lance, and the remainder of the weapon lies behind the dragon's tail, closely aligned with a clearly drawn, oval orifice which lies horizontally across the base of the tail. A dragonlet, with a wound in its chest, lies prone alongside the adult, surrounded by skulls and bones. The princess and her lamb watch from a rocky outcrop, and in the background we see the city, perched high on a promontory overlooking verdant fields and woodland. In the middle distance St George and the princess make their way back towards the city; the horse looks round towards the lamb which the princess still leads, in a variant of the more usual subject of the subdued dragon being led on her girdle. Whilst this latter aspect of the image is of some interest, the most important elements are undoubtedly the presence of the dragonlet and a clear orifice on the pudendum of the adult dragon. The first of these motifs offers positive proof that the dragon is a parent, whilst the second strongly suggests that the monster is female. The juxtaposition of offspring and orifice carries the clear implication that the dragon is a mother, that she has spawned a terrible brood who must also be killed if the heroic knight is to win ultimate victory. The fact that the adult dragon is placed in the classic position for a 'female-gendered' dragon – on her back, beneath the hooves of the saint's horse, with her pudendum clearly visible – demonstrates that it is very likely that other dragons who are depicted in this pose were intended to be understood as sexualised, female monsters.

As we have seen, the image of the female dragon was in evidence throughout the fifteenth century, and into the sixteenth century, in a wide variety of media. Furthermore, there seems to be no distinction drawn between the art forms created for public display and those more obviously suited to private consumption. Thus, we find feminised dragons in public sculpture, such as the wooden statue from Coventry (illustration 5.24), which would have been visible to all, educated and uneducated alike, as well as in manuscript images (illustration 5.29), which would have been seen by a literate, moneyed elite. One particularly intriguing use of the motif suggests that it was actually a stock motif at one time: a late fifteenth-century English translation of the *Golden Legend* includes a woodcut image of St George and an obviously feminised dragon (illustration 5.30). There is no reference to a female dragon in the text – the creature is referred to as 'he' throughout – so there is no obvious reason for the patron or designer of the book to have stipulated the use of this depiction. Indeed, the fact that the illustration is a woodcut suggests very strongly that the design was not specifically created for this book: it is far more likely to have been a 'house' image, used whenever a depiction of St George was needed to illustrate or decorate the text.

The only textual reference to a female dragon that I have come across in relation to St George is rather later than many of these depictions. It occurs in Alexander Barclay's *Life of St George* of 1515, which is a translation of a slightly earlier Latin version; the earlier work seems to make no mention of the gender of the dragon. There seem to be no sexual references in this work, and no mention of the dragon's breasts, dugs, offspring or genitalia, but the dragon is definitely referred to as female. This work, or its own source, may well have influenced Edmund Spenser, for (as we shall see in the next chapter) the Redcrosse Knight fights the obviously female Error Monster. However, it is likely that a manuscript narrative that specifically related to St George overcoming a female dragon would have circulated throughout much of Europe during the fifteenth century. One of the most interesting aspects of the gendered dragon is that it does not appear to be constrained geographically: there are extant examples from England, Germany, the Netherlands, Italy and

5.29 Masters of Otto van Moerdrecht, St George and the dragon, *1430–40.*

France, encompassing a wide variety of media. It should be emphasised at this point that all these gendered dragons are chance finds, so there are almost certainly more examples out there. The images reproduced here are all Northern European work, but this should not be taken to mean that the motif does not occur elsewhere. Rather, the apparently limited geographical spread is a consequence of the areas that I have been able to investigate so far: a much fuller picture will undoubtedly emerge in time. We should also bear in mind the media employed in the production of these works, for we are looking at accidents of survival rather than decisions of manufacture; mass-produced engravings are more likely to survive by sheer force of numbers than a more fragile medium like glass.

There is also more to be said about the actual application of the image. For example, it is notable that the woodcut that illustrates the sole extant edition of Barclay's *Life of St George* – a printing made by Richard Pynson in 1515 – does not feature a gendered dragon (illustration 5.31). This is a complete inversion of the practice found in the 1498 *Golden Legend*, where a gendered dragon (illustration 5.30) illustrates a text with no mention of such a creature. These two examples demonstrate not only the extent to which such images were used as simple decoration, in that they each bear very little relationship to the text they accompany, but also confirm our suspicion that the motif of the female dragon is sometimes just one of a number of stock images of St George. However, a very different approach is found in Albrecht Dürer's Baumgartner altarpiece. The image of the saint in this work (illustration 4.8) is actually a depiction of the work's patron, Stefan Baumgartner, and the fact that he is presented with a dead female dragon is surely no accident. It seems very likely that the artist and patron will have made a joint decision about this aspect of the iconography, and the appearance of the motif in a prestigious work like this as well as mass-produced woodcuts speaks volumes about the extent to which the topos had permeated the cult of St George during the early sixteenth century.

5.30 St George and the dragon woodcut used in an English version of the Golden Legend, *1498. (Leicester University Library)*

While it is obvious that simple misogyny informs the construction of the feminised dragon, we must be careful not to see St George's monster simply as female. Rather, she stands for a specific type of femininity that is sexual and bestial, everything that is worst about women to the late medieval mind. In these images a chaste woman (the virginal princess) is rescued by an embodiment of chastity (St George), who saves her from an embodiment of sexual evil (the dragon). This demonstrates the extent to which it is possible to manipulate iconography and hagiography to make a specific point, or to suit a specific audience. St George is a very good example of a saint whose cult has embodied several quite separate meanings according to time and place: as we have seen, ideas of chivalry and national pride are very important, but the emphasis on torture in his cult, discussed in Chapter Two, seems to have functioned as a means of aiding religious meditation, or perhaps evoking empathy in the viewer. Given the apparent construction of George as a virgin martyr and figure of chastity, it is clear that the female-gendered, sexual dragon fits very neatly into his iconography as an antithetical figure.

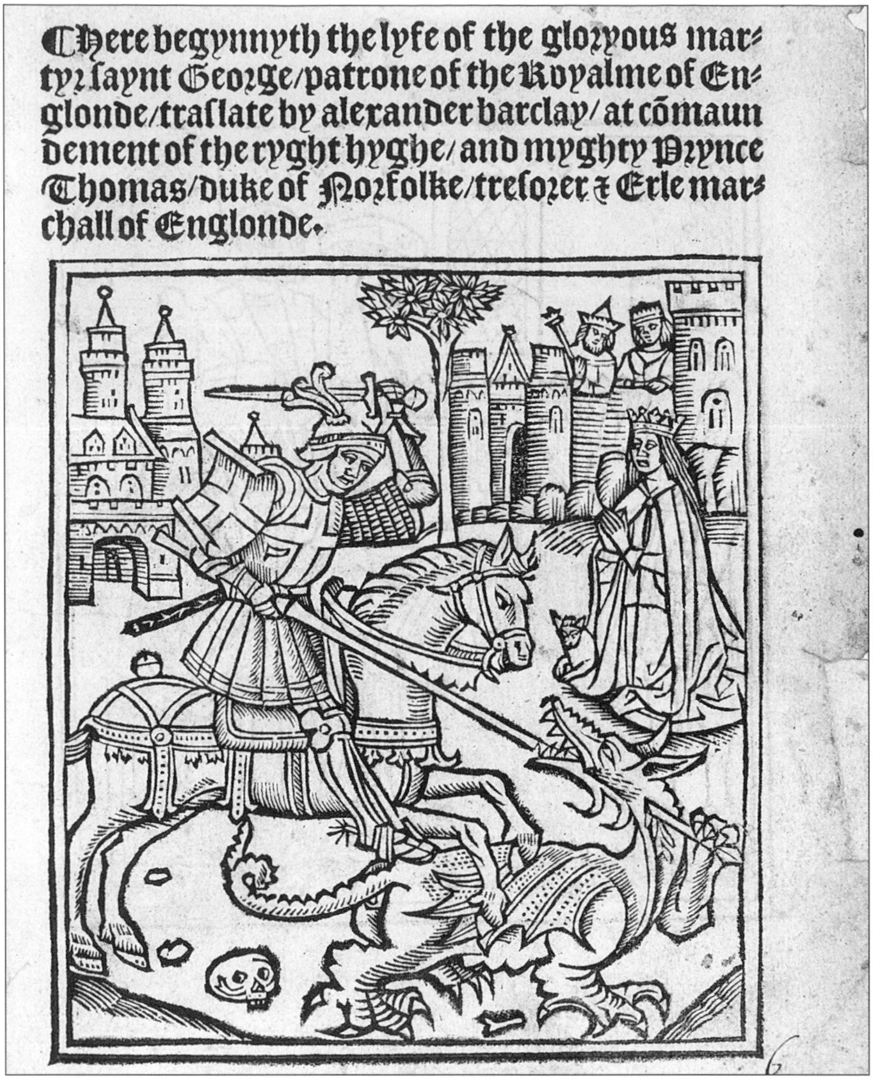

¶ Here begynnyth the lyfe of the gloꝛyous mar-
tyꝛ saynt Geoꝛge/patrone of the Royalme of En-
glonde/traslate by alexander barclay/ at cõmaun
dement of the ryght hyghe/ and myghty Pꝛynce
Thomas/duke of Noꝛfolke/tresoꝛer ⁊ Erle mar-
chall of Englonde.

5.31 St George and the dragon woodcut, frontispiece used in Richard Pynson's printing of Alexander Barclay's Life of St George, *1515. (Trinity College, Cambridge)*

However, we must not overlook the fact that the vast majority of medieval images of St George and the dragon feature a monster that is clearly not gendered; it is important that we do not attempt to generalise too far on the basis of these few works. That said, these feminised dragons do point toward a minor but nevertheless powerful theme in the iconography of St George.

Our overall conclusion concerning the motif of the combat between the saint and the dragon should perhaps be that it was a long-lived, dramatic and memorable topos that was surprisingly malleable. It could be presented as a full-blown narrative, complete in itself, but was equally useful as a single image. It played on the deep-seated fears of uneducated people, spoke to their need to assert control over the natural world, and also served as a tool of religious propaganda and sexual politics. As such, it can perhaps be read as a cipher for the ultimate purpose of a saint cult both in late medieval England and much further beyond.

CHAPTER SIX

POST-MEDIEVAL THEMES IN THE CULT OF ST GEORGE

Despite the official sanctions enacted as a result of the Reformation and Counter-Reformation against 'superstitious beliefs' – a term that included the cults of non-Biblical saints and certainly should have encompassed the highly dubious figure of St George – the patron saint of the English has continued to be recognised as a significant force, by some sections of society at least, in the nation's conception of itself. We have already seen that the Ridings, or pageants, of St George were still taking place in some form well into the nineteenth century (illustrations 4.16 and 4.17), and this popular veneration of the saint has been accompanied by more formal records of academic and sub-academic investigation into his history and devotion as well as many retellings of the dragon legend. The ongoing relevance of particular aspects of the saint's cult, such as his status as an icon of chivalric virtue, have ensured that St George has retained the interest of writers and artists across the centuries. He has appealed most notably to polemicists; the close identification that has sprung up between St George and the English nation has meant that he has often been used as a convenient embodiment of 'Englishness' by both native and foreign commentators. Some of the evidence for the survival of St George as a popular icon is linked quite closely to his legend: the numerous recastings of his story which have circulated over the last five centuries provide ample indication of the level of continuing interest in the cult, but of even greater importance is the written and visual evidence which suggests that the legend of the saint has been reinterpreted by writers, artists and patrons who seem to have been in pursuit of their own particular agendas.

One significant work that appeared in the time when the late medieval period was resolving itself into what we now think of as the early modern era was Richard Johnson's *The Most Famous History of the Seven Champions of Christendome* (1576–80). This work, which seems to represent the apogee (or perhaps the nadir) of the romanticisation of the legend of St George, went through many editions from its first publication through to the early twentieth century. The narrative inspired several imitations, such as the chapbook *The Life and Death of St George, the Noble Champion of England* (seven editions between 1750 and 1820), and the poems *The Birth of St George* and *St George and the Dragon* (published in Bishop Percy's *Reliques of Ancient English Poetry*, another very popular work which went through many editions following its initial publication in 1765). Johnson's version of the legend of St George has been alluded to on several occasions earlier in this book, particularly in relation to the adaptation of the basic story of the combat with the dragon to allow a strong claim to be made for the saint to be recognised as a true-born Englishman and also to show the hero marrying the rescued princess. However, Johnson's account is of such inherent interest as an example of the extent to which writers have been prepared to change and embellish a well-known narrative that we should now review a (highly summarised) account of the story of St George's role as one of the Seven Champions:

> St George is born in Coventry, the son of Lord Albert, the 'High Steward' of the city. The infant is found to have birthmarks of a dragon on his breast, a 'bloody crosse' on his right hand and a golden garter on his left leg. His mother dies shortly after giving birth, and he is stolen by an enchantress, Kalyb, who feeds on newborn children. She is intrigued by his birthmarks and so decides to spare his life; every day she becomes fonder of the child until her only wish is to keep him with her forever. But as St George grows to manhood he desires to seek adventure, and asks to be set free. Kalyb takes him to a dungeon where she keeps six champions of Christendom prisoner under an enchantment, and promises that he will be the greatest of them all if only he will stay with her. St George refuses. Kalyb then takes him to her stables and shows him seven beautiful horses. The strongest and swiftest is called Bayard; she offers the horse to St George if he will promise to stay with her, but again he refuses. Then Kalyb takes him to her armoury and promises him magic armour that no weapon can pierce and the great sword Ascalon if only he will stay, but still he refuses. Finally, desperate for love of the youth, Kalyb offers him her magic wand, the source of all her power. He takes the wand and promptly uses it to open a cleft in a rock, forces the enchantress inside and frees the other champions of Christendom. They all escape together and travel in company until they come to a place where seven roads meet, at which point they decide to go their separate ways.
>
> Each champion goes on to have many exciting adventures; St George journeys to Egypt, where he rescues Sabra, the sultan's

daughter, from a dragon. (Interestingly, Johnson makes it clear that the dragon is killed by a blow to the breast, rather than through the mouth or neck, a clear alteration of the typical medieval narrative motif.) Sabra's father had promised her hand in marriage to whomsoever should save her, but Almindor, the 'Black King of Morocco', who was one of her other suitors, dissuades him from permitting the union by arguing (with some justice, it would seem) that St George would insist on converting her to Christianity. The Sultan then commands St George to take a letter to the King of Persia: inevitably, the letter instructs that the bearer should be put to death, and St George is chained up in a dungeon where ravenous lions are set on him. He manages to free himself and kill the lions with his bare hands, then steals a horse and rides back to Egypt, pausing only to kill a giant and rescue another woman in peril along the way. He eventually enters the realm of a wizard named Ormandine, who is holding St David, one of the other champions of Christendom, captive under an enchantment. The power of the spell can only be broken if a hero from the North draws a magic sword from a stone. St George duly accomplishes this task and frees his friend, then continues on to Egypt. Seven years have elapsed by the time he arrives back at the Sultan's court, and he finds that Sabra has already been married to the evil Almindor, although she has managed to preserve her virginity with the aid of a magic golden chain.

St George secretly visits Sabra; she recognises her true love when he shows her the betrothal ring that she had given him and they elope together to Greece. Once there, they meet up with the other six champions of Christendom and are challenged to fight the massed ranks of the 'Paynim' lands. Every champion then returns to his own country and raises an army; battle is then joined, and the kingdoms of Persia, Egypt and Morocco are conquered. St George is chosen to rule over all these lands, but once peace and prosperity are assured he appoints a regent for each land and returns home to Coventry with his new wife Sabra. They have a long marriage, which is blessed with three fine sons, one of whom grows up to become the monster-slayer Guy of Warwick. In general their lives are happy, although Sabra does contrive to need rescuing for a second time when she is threatened with burning at the stake after murdering a would-be adulterous suitor. At length she dies as the result of a fall into a thorny plant when out riding; St George then goes on a pilgrimage to Jerusalem. He returns to England to fight a second dragon, who is terrorising a town, and in the battle both dragon and knight are killed, in a close parallel of the death of Beowulf.

It is clear from this précis that this particular version of the story was subject to a great many influences, notably Arthurian romances, and that it entirely omits the important medieval motifs of the torture and martyrdom of the saint. Much of the narrative seems to be derived from a late medieval English poem known as *Sir Bevys of Hampton*, but it is important to add that Bayard, the name of the horse offered to St George by the enchantress Kalyb, is the same name used for the faithful and courageous horse of the knight Renaud in a medieval French legend of Charlemagne and the hero Roland. Likewise, the name of the enchantress herself may be a borrowing: 'Kalyb' is rather reminiscent of 'Caliban', the unwilling slave of Prospero in Shakespeare's play *The Tempest*. Caliban's mother, Sycorax, is thought to be a cognate of the mythical Circe, an allegory of a seductive aspect of nature which enslaves men, and the correspondences with Johnson's Kalyb are quite striking. Furthermore, in *The Tempest* we are told that Prospero rescued the spirit Ariel from imprisonment within a cloven pine, a punishment that Sycorax had meted out: in *The Most Famous History of the Seven Champions of Christendome* St George cleaves open a rock and imprisons Kalyb within. Given the disparity between the dates of these two works – *The Most Famous History of the Seven Champions of Christendome* was first published *c.* 1597, *The Tempest* in 1623 – it is possible that Johnson was a direct influence on Shakespeare, but it is more likely that both were drawing on a common source of legends about enchantresses and the punishments they use. The names 'Kalyb' and 'Caliban' also seem to carry overtones of otherness, evoking ideas of the Caribs of the New World and perhaps also Arabic terminology. The latter possibility would tend to indicate that the creators of these characters were seeking to exploit the anti-Turkish feelings which came to the fore during the Mediterranean wars of the late sixteenth century.

Edmund Spenser was another English author writing at the end of the sixteenth century who seems to have been attracted to the dramatic potential of the story of St George and the dragon. It is widely acknowledged that he drew inspiration from an Italian romantic epic poem, Ariosto's *Orlando Furioso*, which was first available in a complete form in 1532, and possibly also from a related work, *Orlando lnnamorato*, an unfinished poem by Bioardo published in 1487; indeed, it is claimed that Spenser aimed to outdo these poems in his own work *The Faerie Queene* (first published in 1589). The complicated story set out by Ariosto is again concerned with a conflict between Christians and Saracens this time located at the time of Charlemagne. The female protagonist, Angelique, is loved by many men, including the Christian hero Roland ('Orlando'), who eventually goes mad because his love is not returned. Another suitor, the pagan knight Roger ('Ruggiero') rescues her when she is chained up as a sacrifice to the Orc, a sea-monster (illustration 6.1). Roger rides on a hippogriff – the offspring of a griffin and a mare, with the head, wings and talons of an eagle, and the body and hind legs of a horse – and dazzles the monstrous Orc with a magic shield rather than killing it with a sword or lance, but in many other respects this episode is strongly reminiscent of the legends of St George and the dragon, Perseus and Andromeda, and other analogues of the hero–monster–princess formulation.

6.1 Jean Auguste Dominique Ingres, Roger delivers Angelique, *1819. (Louvre, Paris)*

Despite Spenser's debt to Ariosto's work, the Redcrosse Knight in Book One of Spenser's epic allegorical romance *The Faerie Queene* is more clearly modelled on St George than the pagan Roger: his device is identical with the saint's emblem, and the author also makes explicit comparisons between the two figures (for example, canto II, verses 11 and 12, and canto X, verse 61). In the first verse of canto I the Redcrosse Knight (a figure of the Anglican Church) is described, rather curiously, as an inexperienced soldier who nevertheless bears the scars of previous encounters on his armour and shield:

> Y cladd in mightie armes and siluer shielde,
> Wherein old dints of deepe wounds did remaine,
> The cruell markes of many a bloudy fielde;
> Yet armes till that time he did neuer wield[.]

He travels on horseback in company with a 'Ladie' (later named as 'Una', a figure of Truth and the True Religion), said to be of royal lineage, who has a lamb on a lead: she is clearly a form of the princess of the dragon-fight narrative. The dragon itself is also mentioned at this stage, though as a live danger rather than as a defeated enemy, and it seems that Spenser presents the Redcrosse Knight, at least initially, as the heir of St George rather than as a direct manifestation of the saint himself. Spenser's knight has inherited the trappings of the chivalric hero – the emblem of the cross, the scarred silver armour, the rescued sacrificial offering, the monstrous foe – but he has his own battles to fight. It has been suggested that Spenser has reinterpreted the original legend of St George in the light of romances of chivalric questing where the hero is guided by a heroine, a trope that occurs in Malory's version of the Arthurian epic, for example: this rationale may lie behind the presence of Una by the Redcrosse Knight's side at the beginning of the story, but it cannot itself explain the inconsistency of a novice knight who wears battle-scarred armour. Another important aspect of the Redcrosse Knight is that he is identified as the champion of 'Gloriana', the glorious queen of Faerieland. Gloriana is undoubtedly a form of Elizabeth I, but there is also a strong link between this motif and the role of St George as the champion of the Virgin Mary. Gloriana is described as 'Goddesse, heavenly bright . . . Great Lady of the greatest Isle' (Proem to Book One, verse 4): this epithet is equally applicable to the actual Queen of England and the Queen of Heaven who was thought (by the English at least) to have a special responsibility for the realm of England. Spenser later makes specific mention of the Redcrosse Knight as a virgin's champion (Book One, canto I, verse 49), and it seems very likely that this complex allegory refers to the Virgin Mary as well as the Virgin Queen, Elizabeth. The Redcrosse Knight fights three Saracen brothers, 'Sansfoy' ('faithlessness'), 'Sansloi' ('lawlessness') and 'Sansjoi' ('joylessness' or 'spiritual death'), an allegorical formulation that seems to owe something to the tradition of St George leading the Crusaders against the Saracens as well as his battles against pagans in literary works such as *The Most Famous History of the Seven Champions of Christendome* and visual imagery such as the Stamford glass (illustration 3.1) and the Borbjerg retable (illustration 3.11).

Interestingly, the Redcrosse Knight's first opponent is a female monster, half-snake and half-woman, a creature who was surely influenced by the female dragon in Alexander Barclay's *Life of St George* (1515) as well as the tradition of the female snake in the Garden of Eden. This foul fiend is named as the Error Monster; her femaleness is an essential aspect of her awfulness, for she is explicitly described as the mother of a spawn of a thousand serpents and monsters who suckle on her dugs, and later feed upon her 'cole black' blood as she lies dying. This latter, rather gruesome, motif does not appear in the iconography of St George, but the dragonlets who are occasionally depicted alongside their mother (illustrations 5.26, 5.27 and 5.28) were surely fed by the dugs seen in Altdorfer's interpretation of the dragon (illustration 5.23). Other links between Spenser's monster and the dragon fought by St George are also evident. For example, during an attack upon the Redcrosse Knight, the Error Monster is described as wrapping her tail around his body, in a rather exaggerated form of the iconographic motif of the tail wound about St George's leg (for example, illustration 5.9). In his turn, the knight attacks the monster by gripping her around the throat; St George invariably uses a lance rather than his hands, but the dragon's throat is certainly a close second to the mouth in the iconography of attacks upon the monster by St George. The Redcrosse Knight fights another monster, explicitly described as a dragon, later in the story and again there are several reminders of St George. During the three-day struggle the knight falters on several occasions and seems likely to die through loss of blood, but he is healed: firstly, by the water of life in a nearby fountain; secondly, by the fruit of the tree of life, again growing nearby; and thirdly, by a precious balm. This motif of healing is strongly resonant of the resurrections performed on St George in some versions of the narrative of his martyrdom, and it is notable that the first two healings draw on clear allegories of the Garden of Eden and the Eucharist. By contrast, the third healing is less easily explained, but it does seem significant that the balm is administered by Una: this may well be a reference to the English tradition of the resurrection of St George by the Virgin Mary. The dragon eventually dies, as we might expect, of an injury to the throat administered through the open jaws. Book One ends with the marriage of the Redcrosse Knight and Una, a motif that may well be influenced by the post-medieval version of the St George narrative used by Johnson in *The Most Famous History of the Seven Champions of Christendome*, where the saint is eventually married to the rescued princess. However, Spenser seems to use the marriage of his two characters in a more complex way, for it is thought to be an allegory of the Church of England as the home of the 'true' religion, the country having turned away from the Roman church for a second time during the reign of Elizabeth following the re-establishment of Catholicism under her sister Mary Tudor. Despite the apparently happy union between Una and her suitor, Spenser is quick to point out where the knight's true obligations lie. In the penultimate verse he returns to the service of the Faerie Queene: like St George, he is still strongly identified as the champion of the Virgin.

Gerrard de Malynes, a contemporary of Spenser, goes one stage beyond *The Faerie Queene* in his work *Saint George for England. Allegorically Described* (1601), for he uses the English patron saint as a figure of Elizabeth I herself. The preamble to this work states:

> For whereas under the person of the noble champion Saint George our saviour Christ was prefigured, delivering the Virgin (which did signify the sinful souls of Christians) from the dragon or devil's power: so her most excellent majesty by advancing the pure doctrine of Christ Jesus in all truth and sincerity, hath (as an instrument appointed by divine providence) been used to perform the part of a valiant champion, delivering an infinite number out of the devil's power . . .

The arresting image of the Virgin Queen as a knightly champion saving her people, presumably from the 'errors' of the Roman Church, is unfortunately not continued into the main body of the text. In fact, St George does not appear at all, despite the implications of the title of the work. The substance of the piece is actually a description of a dream in which a dragon threatens an island. The dragon is understood as a manifestation of political and social discord which inhabits an urban environment, an interesting development of the late medieval concept of St George as the champion of civic order discussed in Chapter Four. Sadly, the narrative ends before the dragon has been defeated, which may imply that Malynes hoped to be encouraged to write a sequel by politicians who were themselves seeking to reinforce the hierarchy of urban government.

Subsequent reworkings of the St George legend tend to be far more prosaic, and often add little to the basic narrative form. By contrast with the fabulous tale recounted by Johnson, who clearly thought that the telling of a good story was the paramount concern, and the many-layered allegories presented by Spenser and Malynes, versions of the tale from the seventeenth century onwards tend to be concerned with the establishment of St George as a simple figure of chivalry. Peter Heylyn, a religious historian who wrote in defence of the controversial policies of Archbishop Laud during the period of the English Civil War, formulated a life of St George which went through several editions in the early 1630s. He attempted to distinguish between the 'fictions of the Middle Ages' and the literal truths within the legend, and tried to contextualise Jacobus de Voragine's treatment of the story in the thirteenth-century *Golden Legend* by retelling the story of Perseus and Andromeda found in Ovid's *Metamorphoses*. His discussion of the dragon legend allows us an interesting insight into post-medieval beliefs about these monsters: he claims that the 'killing of dragons is both feasible and ordinary', and cites two English examples of dragon infestation, at Hook Norton in Oxfordshire and at an unspecified place in Sussex, in support of his argument. However, he is withering in his criticism of Johnson's *The Most Famous History of the Seven Champions of Christendome*, noting that the legends of all seven of the saints included in the story are equally misrepresented: the work 'must bee reckoned a discredit unto all'. Heylyn dismisses Johnson's contention that St George was a native of England, although he does mention Spenser's claim that the Redcrosse Knight was of English birth (Spenser not only wrote that he was 'borne of English blood' but also that he sprang from an 'ancient race of Saxon kings', a definition invoking a particular kind of pre-Conquest Englishness that was subsequently popular with commentators who bewailed the tyranny of the 'Norman Yoke').

Heylyn was also at pains to expound on the foundation of the Order of the Garter, and this connection between St George and the chivalric ideal is a common theme in post-medieval versions of his life. Thomas Lowick's rhyming life of St George, published in 1664 under the comprehensive title *The History of the Life and Martyrdom of St George, the Titular Patron of England, with his Conversion of Arabia by killing of a dreadful dragon and delivering*

6.2 *William Morris and Dante Gabriel Rossetti,* The Wedding of St George and the Princess, *glass panel, nineteenth century. (Victoria & Albert Museum, London)*

the king's daughter, was a simple retelling of the basic legend, dedicated to Charles II. Another account of St George which makes much of the links between the saint and the monarchy, specifically through his patronage of the Order of the Garter, was written by Thomas Dawson and published in 1714. The presentation of St George as a true medieval knight who embodies all the ideals of chivalric behaviour also underlies his appeal to the pre-Raphaelites, a group of English artists active during the second half of the nineteenth century, who sought to promote these virtues in a romanticised version of the medieval life. St George's legend was a popular subject for several members of the group: they tended to cast him in the same heroic mould as the figures from Arthurian legend whom they frequently depicted. Illustration 6.2 shows William Morris and Dante Gabriel Rossetti's glass panel of 'The Wedding of St George and the Princess', a subject of the wedding feast that formed part of a cycle of a post-medieval version of the legend of St George. Illustration 6.3 shows a second treatment of this theme by Dante Gabriel Rossetti. The usual title of this watercolour refers to the wedding of St George and the rescued princess, but it is apparent that the subject is actually the time after the wedding when the two lovers are spending time alone together, soothed by the music of angels. Despite the medievalising aspects of this image, such as the heraldic decoration of the chairs, both images are clearly dependent on a post-medieval version of the legend for, as we have seen, St George never marries the princess in

6.3 Dante Gabriel Rossetti (1828–82), The Wedding of St George and Princess Sabra, *(Tate Gallery, London)*

authentic medieval accounts of the story. Illustration 6.3 shows the princess cutting off a strand of her hair which she has looped through a ring on the top of the saint's helm, a visual allusion to the girdle that she placed around the neck of the dragon as a lead: the implication may be that she has, or plans to have, a similar degree of control over her new husband. The presence of the dead dragon, in the right foreground, makes an interesting parallel with the similar treatment of the monster in *The Paradise Garden* image of *c.* 1415 (illustration 3.23). The earlier depiction seems to tell us that St George has overcome his carnal urges and has hence been permitted entry into the enclosed garden of virginity, while the latter, pseudo-medieval image has lost this subtext about the sexuality of the saint: here the dragon is simply a vanquished foe with no particular symbolic meaning.

Besides his role as an incarnation of chivalry, St George can embody other quite specific agendas. For example, he can sometimes function as a simple emblem of the English nation, with no explicit reference to the dragon story or other parts of his legend. A series of poems and other texts appeared during the period from the mid-seventeenth to the early nineteenth centuries which compared the patron saints of different peoples, sometimes showing them in conversation together, with each patron saint standing as the emblem of their own people. An anonymous broadsheet, published in 1707 to mark the formal union of England with Scotland, utilises the motif of a dialogue between the patron saints of the two countries, celebrating the new status quo with references to patriotic emblems such as the rose and the thistle. Such texts can be fulsome in their praise of St George and 'his' country, but other writing, especially perhaps that which originates outside England, can be far less positive. One particularly scurrilous piece, an anonymous Irish satire dating from the eighteenth century, compares St George with St Patrick most unfavourably. The ostensible purpose of the poem is to debate the Union between Ireland and England: St Patrick typifies this unequal marriage of the two countries by drawing an analogy with a strongly flowing river that is subsumed into an overwhelming sea. In the poem St George is presented as a cold, arrogant soldier who will not listen to his 'brother',[1] St Patrick. Each saint is married, St George to 'Britannia' and St Patrick to 'Hibernia', but it is clear that only one of the wives is satisfied with her relationship. St George, for reasons not made clear, lives on the moon apart from Britannia, who languishes alone on Earth and dreams of cuckolding her husband with St Patrick. The latter, a sexually virile character, suggests that the two patron saints meet for negotiations on the planet Venus, but St George scorns the home of love, preferring instead the martial overtones of Mars. During the poem there is a reference to an obscure tradition, apparently known to Voltaire, that St George had been involved in a fight with St Denis: the French patron had cut off the English patron's nose, and the latter had retaliated by cutting off St Denis' ear; the Angel Gabriel then intervened and commanded them to restore each other. In this poem St Patrick also threatens St George's nose, but the English patron threatens 'a more mischievous part', making a reference to St Patrick's renowned sexual prowess.

A similarly partisan line occurs in an earlier anonymous tract entitled *A Comparison between St Andrew and St George*, which was probably composed in 1634. The Scottish saint is praised as a true apostle of Christ in contrast to the pseudo-historical St George, who is disparaged in no uncertain terms:

> The Red Crosse, in people or in priest,
> Was a foule marke upon a scotishe breist...
> St Andrew is for men, St George for clownes.

Whether written for or against him, these examples all invoke St George as a symbol of the English nation as a whole, but at least one political diatribe seems to have used patron saints as a mouthpiece of specific parts of society. *St George and St Denis. A dialogue*, published in 1821, uses a comparison of England and France to berate the target audience, apparently High Tories, about social issues such as charitable giving, and suggests that the role of St George as an emblem of discrete groups within a wider English community had not come to an end with the dawning of the early modern era. A Civil War ballad attributed to General George Monck, Duke of Albemarle (1608–70) – a trenchant monarchist until his capture by the Parliamentarians in 1664, whereupon he found it more tactful to support plans for a Commonwealth – is entitled *St George and the Dragon*. It attacks the Rump Parliament and presents the saint as the scourge of this unloved body of government, and certainly supports the contention that St George did not always operate as the patron of the entire nation. Interestingly, the dragon is not mentioned in this work, despite the promise of the title: it may be that the audience were expected to interpret the Rump itself as a manifestation of the evil monster. Another ballad, apparently of a similar date, is anonymous but entitled *The Second Part of St George for England*. It adopts a similar Royalist tone. The final stanza includes these lines:

> . . . So 'twas time for St George,
> That Rump to disgorge,
> And to send it from whence it first came.

The reference to 'disgorging' may suggest an attack on the throat, or 'gorge', of the enemy; this allegory seems to play on the iconography of St George wounding the dragon in the mouth or throat, but equally suggests the saint (as a form of Charles I himself) removing the power of speech from the Parliamentarians.

A far more specific analogy is invoked in an anonymous broadsheet *c.* 1851. The lengthy title of this tract is illuminating in itself: *The Doubly Great Exhibition!! The New St George and the Dragon and new Great Exhibition, or John Bull physicking popery-with a parliamentary pill! And the Rumish* [Romish?] *conversion of the Crystal Palace! – from – a great exhibition of the choicest of goods! into – a greater exhibition of the greatest of ills!* The image that accompanies the text shows John Bull, another well-known personification of part or all of the English nation, in the guise of St George. He is dressed as a Roman soldier rather than a medieval knight, but benefits from the additional protection of a stout pair of boots. He is mounted on a horse, which is labelled 'Parliament', and is shown overcoming a dragon who is clearly to be identified with Roman Catholicism. The monster has a human head that wears a papal tiara; its sinuous tail is crushing a number of naked human figures who are variously labelled as 'Ireland', 'Spain',

'Austria', and 'Italy' as an indication that the writer and artist believed that Catholic countries suffered as a result of their connection with the hierarchy of the papacy. The dragon holds in one paw a knife labelled a 'territorial carving knife', which underlines the evil intentions imputed to the monster. Meanwhile, St George is pushing a pill into the creature's mouth with the aid of his lance, an interesting variation on the well-established theme of the wound to the mouth or throat of the dragon. The pill itself is labelled, somewhat obscurely, 'Anti-papal scarlet fever pill': the significance of this is unclear, but it may be connected to the identification of the colour scarlet with the Roman Church, because of the hue of cardinals' robes; scarlet is also associated with sexual sins. This motif may also be a satirical comment on the patent medicines peddled by quack doctors. This image makes a very interesting comparison to Peter Gottland's engraving (illustration 5.6): both artists use the dragon as an allegory of the Roman Catholic Church, but the German version presents Christ, a universal figure, in the guise of St George rather than utilising an equivalent of the sharply nationalistic figure of John Bull. Furthermore, the martial overtones of the conflict are subverted in the German image by the depiction of Christ as an infant; the use of the swaggering and self-confident John Bull, by contrast, underlines the idea that England is strong enough to overcome her enemies easily.

The identification of St George with England was evidently a useful motif for satirists, but it is clear that the trope was recognised far more widely. The tradition established in Johnson's *The Most Famous History of the Seven Champions of Christendome*, and the various chapbooks and poems which followed it, identified St George as a native of Coventry, but several other regions of England also sought to claim him as their own. Sarah Anne Matson, writing under the pseudonym 'Guanon', published (in 1885) a detailed narrative of the life of St George which located him in Cornwall; the dragon was killed at St Michael's Mount and the saint's burial place is said to be on his family estate at Zennor. Matson's purpose in writing this story is unclear: she does not seem to assert her tale as 'truth', but equally makes no mention of other, more common, versions of the legend. By contrast, the anonymous 'Recorder of Avalon' who published *St George at Glastonbury* (1929) seems to have thought that St George was indeed born in Cornwall. This version of the story neatly brings together several different traditions, for St George is taken to Coventry by his mother whilst still a boy and subsequently travels to Glastonbury to seek healing for her. His prayers answered, St George becomes a knight errant and is entrusted with the sword Excalibur. Two centuries later, according to this account, this sword was borne by King Arthur, later still by Richard Couer-de-Lion during the Third Crusade. Richard then returned the sword to Glastonbury, where it was buried within the confines of the Abbey to safeguard it from Henry VIII's pillaging. The narrative set out in this work is clearly influenced by Arthurian motifs as well as the ideal of the chivalric Crusader, but its main rationale seems to lie in the need to claim the patron saint of England as a native hero. Indeed, the preface of the work is at pains to discuss the martyrdom legend: all is resolved through the assertion that 'St George the martyr' was an entirely different person, not to be confused with 'St George the dragon-slayer and true-born Englishman'.

As we have seen, retellings of the legend of St George and the dragon and studies of his significance, particularly in relation to chivalry, appeared fairly regularly through the late medieval and early modern period. However, it was not until the publication in 1888 of Sir E.A. Wallis Budge's book *The Martyrdom of St George of Cappadocia. Coptic Texts*, which included English translations of apocryphal Ethiopian traditions of the saint's life and martyrdom, that any real attempt was made to set the English cult in the wider context of the Eastern tradition. One reason for this omission would certainly have been the lack of material in translation, a problem rectified to some extent by Budge's own work, but another problem was that attention was focused in a different direction.

As noted in Chapter One, Edward Gibbon, in his hugely influential work *The History of the Decline and Fall of the Roman Empire* (published between 1776 and 1788), had propagated the idea that St George could be identified with the Arian Bishop George of Cappadocia; it has been claimed that Gibbon probably derived this idea from the opinions of a Dr Reynolds and a Dr John Pettingal. Ralph Waldo Emerson restated the thesis in *English Traits* (first published 1856), despite the fact that this argument had been refuted with some force in an essay by Dr Samuel Pegge presented to the Society of Antiquaries in 1777 and published ten years later in the journal *Archaeologia*. Other commentators also took up the fight to clear the English patron's name in works such as Dr Milner's 'Historical and Critical Inquiry into the Existence and Character of St George', which was presented to George, Earl of Leicester, in 1792, John Hogg's 'Supplemental Notes on St George the martyr and on George the Arian Bishop', published in the *Transactions of the Royal Society of Literature* for 1861, and the Reverend Herbert Thurston's article 'St George', published in *The Month* in April 1892.

Despite these efforts, the ill-founded identification of St George with a heretic bishop continued to sully the reputation of the saint for some time, although a few writers did contrive to avoid the dispute and investigate other aspects of the cult. Sabine Baring-Gould, a noted folklorist, included a chapter on the analogies between St George and heroes in other traditions, particularly Babylonian, Syrian and Egyptian myths, in his book *Curious Myths of the Middle Ages* (1888). John E. Matzke published two studies of the development of the legend of St George as a literary phenomenon in the *Proceedings of the Modern Language Association of America* in the period 1902–4. The highly focused academic approach demonstrated by these authors was balanced by a series of more-or-less scholarly books about St George and his cult in England which appeared during the period from the beginning of the twentieth century to the inter-war years. W. Fleming's *The Life of St George, Martyr, Patron of England* (1901), Elizabeth O. Gordon's *Saint George, Champion of Christendom and Patron Saint of England* (1907), Margaret H. Bulley's *St George for Merrie England* (1908) and Cornelia Steketee Hulst's *St George of Cappadocia in Legend and History* (1909) appeared in quick succession: of these works the latter is the most interesting, and includes an extended discussion of some versions of St George's legend from the Eastern tradition. A number of articles on St George were published in the *Analecta Bollandiana* in 1908–9; two were contributed by the French Bollandist Hippolyte Delehaye, who also included a chapter on St George in his *Les Légendes Grecques des Saints Militaires* (1909). Several German studies appeared, including M. Huber's *Zur Georgslegende* (1906), K. Krumbacher's *Der heilige Georg* (1911), J.B. Aufhauser's *Das Drachenwunder des Heiligen Georg in der griechischen und lateinischen Uberlieferung* (1911), an important study of the development of the dragon legend, and the same author's *Miracula S. Georgii* (1913). These publications were followed by Alice Brewster's *The Life of St George, the Patron Soldier–Saint of England* (1914); there was then a brief interlude before the appearance of G.J. Marcus' *Saint George of England* (1929) and Budge's second work on the saint, *The History of George of Lydda, The Patron Saint of England. A Study of the Cultus of St George of Ethiopia* (1930). In general, these works attempted to set the English patron saint in a wider context, but they often overlooked the evidence of the iconography of the saint, particularly the peculiarly English tradition of the resurrection of St George by the Virgin which had been published a few years earlier by M.R. James in *The Sculptures in the Lady Chapel at Ely* (1895). That said, the proliferation of studies of the cult published during such a short period of time demonstrates that there was a ready market for books on St George in England; the publication record tends to suggest that while there was interest in his cult elsewhere in Western Europe, the English were clearly claiming this saint as their own. It seems that this was a time when concepts such as chivalry and patriotism were extremely significant within English society, and interest in St George formed an important channel through which these ideas were both propagated and expressed.

As a martial saint, St George was a particularly useful tool for propagandists during wartime and it is notable that writers often used him as a figure of both Englishness and chivalry. Two publications of the Boer War period (*c.* 1881–1900) are most instructive. The Very Reverend C.W.B. Clarke, Dean and Rector of the Cathedral Church of St George at Cape Town, wrote an account of St George during this time which was virulently pro-English. The derivation of the saint's name is given as 'earthworker or boor (not Boer but Yeoman)': no reader could be left in any doubt of St George's racial credentials to be recognised as the English patron saint. A second work, M. Milles Deane's *St George and the Transvaal Dragon* (probably published in 1899 or 1900) identifies the Boers as the dragon who 'the sons of St George', that is, the English, are called upon to defeat, and speaks of 'this Africander Dragon and his Dragonettes'. This curious little book is very keen to extol soldierly virtues such as obedience and loyalty. It uses the German army as an example of the best sort of well-run military force, a sad irony in the light of events that were to take place during the next half-century. St George is also frequently invoked in the visual imagery of war. For example, in 1904 a memorial was erected to the forty-four former pupils of Clifton College, a public school on the outskirts of Bristol, who fell in the Boer War. Sculpted by Alfred Drury, the statue represents St George gazing out towards South Africa across the school grounds. The school ethos seems to have put great emphasis on virtues such as patriotism and chivalry, and the choice of St George for the monument is a reflection of this. In the years leading up to the outbreak of the First World War, a cataclysmic event that sounded the death knell for the British Empire, it seems that St George also functioned as a convenient personification of the best values of the Imperialists, especially in his incarnation as a chivalrous knight rescuing a damsel in distress. Earl Grey, the Governor-General of Canada from 1904 to 1911, is known to have asked his friends in England to send him banners of St George and the dragon so that he could decorate the walls of colleges with them and thereby proclaim and reinforce the aims and ideals of the Empire to all who saw them.

During the First World War St George was again used as an important rallying point. The commanding officer of a raid by Royal Marines on Zeebrugge on St George's Day 1918 is said to have led his men into battle with the cry 'Saint George for England! Let's twist the dragons' tails!' Another much recounted story relates that the saint appeared in the sky leading the English bowmen of

Agincourt in order to help the British army, much in the manner of the stories of the manifestations during the Crusades and at the battle of Agincourt itself. A British soldier, fighting forlornly in the trenches at an unspecified location, is said to have invoked St George using words that he had seen as a motto below an image of the saint reproduced on a plate in a restaurant: *Adsit Anglis Sanctus Georgius* (May Saint George be with the English), whereupon a long line of indeterminate shapes, suffused with light, appeared in front of the trench and set about the enemy with many loud cries in honour of St George. The account was derived from a work of fiction by Arthur Machen, 'The Bowman', which was published in the *Evening News* in September 1914, but it seems that it was quickly accepted as a factual event. A number of men claimed to have witnessed the apparition, and reports appeared of the discovery of the bodies of dead German soldiers which bore arrow wounds. It is said that a wounded Lancashire Fusilier claimed to have seen St George on a white horse, leading the British army in battle at Vitry-le-François. Later, St George seems to disappear from such accounts, and the shapeless forms surrounded by light are resolved into angels, particularly in association with an alleged manifestation at Mons. Visual images of the story of these holy visitations became a popular subject for wartime postcards and similar paraphernalia. The combat of St George and the dragon also played a role in the propaganda of the First World War, appearing on recruiting posters and cartoons, and also featuring prominently in memorial windows and sculptured tributes in the following few years, such as Adrian Jones's Great War memorial to the Cavalry of the Empire in Hyde Park, London. These signs of renewed interest in the saint prompted G.F. Raggett of the Royal Navy to publish a life of St George in 1919, with all profits devoted to a fund for the widows and orphans of the Dover Coast's Patrol Flotilla.

St George's contribution to the Second World War is generally less memorable, although the title of one book may suggest that he still had some importance as a rallying point for the English. Lord Elton's work *St George or the Dragon – towards a Christian democracy* (1942) was written about the struggle for victory during the darkest days of the war, when no one knew how much longer the conflict would last or what the eventual outcome would be. The English patron saint is evidently invoked as a heroic model, but he is used as a simple totem: like the English Civil War tract against the Rump Parliament, *St George and the Dragon*, there is no effort to allegorise the story of the hero and the monster in the text. A simple mention of the protagonists in the title seems to say all that needs to be said since both authors assume that the metaphor is too obvious to require any explanation.

Some efforts were made in late nineteenth- and early twentieth-century Britain to extend the ambit of influence of ideals of chivalrous conduct beyond the battlefield, notably to the youth of the country and the working classes through Christian Socialist organisations, the Boys' Brigade, the Cadet Corps and similar institutions. St George was frequently invoked as a role model, appearing on publicity material, for example, and even featuring on the cover of an album used to collect Sunday School attendance stamps. The most significant and successful of the organisations that utilised St George was the Boy Scouts, officially founded by Sir Robert (later Lord) Baden-Powell in 1908 but building on a number of initiatives that had taken place over the previous few years, notably his publications on the skills of scouting which appeared from 1884. Baden-Powell's major work, *Scouting for Boys* (first published in 1908) discussed chivalry as a fundamental concept of desirable behaviour for young men. One chapter of the book is devoted to 'The Chivalry of Knights'; this draws on the tradition of the knight-errant, which is claimed in the text, somewhat implausibly, to date back to the early sixth century, the date given by Baden-Powell for the time of King Arthur and the Knights of the Round Table. 'The Knight's Code', nine rules of behaviour which are presented as if formulated by King Arthur himself, are discussed at length in the book, in sections with titles such as 'Honour, 'Loyalty', 'Discipline', 'Humility', and 'Fair Play'. Many examples of chivalrous men are cited, and St George is declared to be the patron saint of both chivalry itself and Boy Scouts in particular.

Other works from the canon of Scouting literature also invoke St George. Around 1914 Alice Brewster published *The Life of St George, the Patron Soldier-Saint of England*, a work written explicitly for Boy Scouts. The writer claims to draw heavily on the work of Elizabeth O. Gordon's *Saint George, Champion of Christendom and Patron Saint of England* (1907), and presents the legend of Constantine and St George, the saint's date of birth (AD 207) and the story of the saint's inspirational role in the founding of King Arthur's Round Table as if they are undisputed facts.

St George was also explicitly invoked in the iconography of the early Scouting movement. One line drawing depicts a young man dressed in the regulation attire of long shorts, shirt with rolled sleeves, neckerchief and wide-brimmed hat, mounted on a horse and killing a dragon (quite correctly, he stabs it in the open mouth with a lance in the best medieval tradition). A comparable image (illustration 6.4) shows a similarly dressed Scout, rolling up his sleeves as if ready for action whilst gazing at a statue of St George and the dragon. The drapery around the image evokes national pride – the Union Flag and St George's cross – alongside the motto

6.4 A Boy Scout and St George, *early twentieth century. (The Scout Association)*

'Be Prepared' and the fleur-de-lis also associated with the Boy Scouts. The cover of the paperback edition of Baden-Powell's *The Young Knights of the Empire* (1916) shows a young man dressed in the armour of a knight, with a sword and dagger at his belt, holding a red shield bearing a device of the white fleur-de-lis associated with the Boy Scouts (illustration 6.5). In his right hand he carries a banner of a cross of St George, and he looks towards an imprisoned dragon. The bars of the dragon's cage are inscribed with mottoes such as 'Courtesy', 'Kindness', 'Obedience', 'Cheerfulness', 'Thrift', 'Purity', 'Honour God and the King', 'Obey the law of the Scouts', and 'Do a good turn to somebody every

6.5 The cover of Robert Baden-Powell's The Young Knights of the Empire, *1920. (The Scout Association)*

day'. The precise symbolism of the dragon is not explained, but it seems to represent the threat of profligacy, sexual depravity and socially subversive behaviour as well as more humdrum sins such as rudeness and unkindness. The traditional link between St George and the Scouting movement has been maintained up until the present day. The annual St George's Day parades of Scouts, Guides and associated organisations still take place in many parts of Britain, with colour parties carrying the British flag alongside their own banners as ranks of children and young adults process to their local parish church for a special service.

Besides the invocation of St George as a patron saint of both the English nation and specific groups within the nation, there have also been a number of modern organisations that have actively chosen to name themselves after the saint. Perhaps the most interesting of the associations that have taken St George as their tutelary saint is the Guild of St George, founded by the aesthete, writer and political thinker John Ruskin in 1871 with the principal aim of furthering and assisting agricultural society in England. One of the first goals of the organisation was to purchase land for agriculture 'which shall not be built upon but cultivated by Englishmen with their own hands';[2] another was to persuade members of the upper classes of English society that agriculture was an honourable occupation 'consistent with high thoughts and noble pleasures'. The list of objectives of the Guild includes not only the acquisition and cultivation of land, and the building of farms and houses for agricultural labourers alongside the repair of buildings in impoverished rural areas, but also the offer of financial grants and the erection of educational establishments. Besides the teaching of agricultural skills, there was also an intention to create museums of art and natural history 'for the cultivation of taste and intelligence among rural labourers and craftsmen', an undoubtedly well-intentioned project that seems, from a modern perspective, to have unfortunate overtones of mental eugenics. The Ruskin Museum at Meersbrook Park in Sheffield formed a lasting monument to the ambition to edify, but at the outset this aspect of the Guild's work was secondary: 'there were to be the schools of St George, the Museums of St George, and always first and foundationally the land of St George'. The creed of beliefs of the companions, or members, of the Guild, included the following:

> I will not kill or hurt or any living creature needlessly, nor destroy any beautiful thing, but will strive to save and comfort all gentle life, and guard and perfect all natural beauty upon the earth.

The sentiments expressed in this credo sum up a combination of interests – nature, art and chivalry – which were clearly important to Ruskin himself. It is likely that St George appealed to him as a figure of chivalry, although the choice of patron of the new organisation will almost certainly have also been influenced by the saint's links with agriculture, and perhaps also metalworking. Ruskin is known to have had a long-standing personal interest in the concept of chivalry. In *Sesame and Lilies* (1865), a work addressed primarily to women, he spoke of the ethic of courtly love: the female 'duty' to appear queen-like to the lover or husband, the male aspiration to serve and honour his lady. He claimed that a specific painting of St George and the dragon (from a cycle of the dragon legend by Vittore Carpaccio, *c.* 1505–7, at the Scuola di San Giorgio degli Schiavoni, Venice) represented a perfection of chivalry, reading into the image a moral lesson in the use of physical power for noble purposes. Ruskin was also a deeply patriotic man, actively promoting the idea that England should hold the premier position in world affairs. A lecture he gave at Oxford in February 1870 called upon the youth of England to serve their country by working in the colonies of the British Empire; his words were to inspire Cecil Rhodes and Alfred Milner (a future governor of South Africa) among many other imperialists. In *Fors Clavigera*, the series of open letters which he wrote to the working classes of the British nation between 1871 and 1884, Ruskin made it clear that he considered St George to be the essence of a Christian gentleman. The letters dealt directly with the problems of capitalism: he planned that the Guild of St George should evolve into a utopian rural society where the land would be worked for the greater good, where English people could flourish far from the corrupting influence of city life. This society would be by no means democratic, however: Ruskin envisaged a deeply hierarchical order in which landlords and tenants were clearly delineated. He planned that the members of the higher echelons should be equipped with the ability to work the land – although perhaps not necessarily to actually perform these tasks – with even greater skill than those of the lower orders, just as (he maintained) medieval knights had been more able fighters than the ordinary soldiers. In espousing such views Ruskin was clearly a product of his age, but the problematic aspects of his personal attitudes and the ways that they were expressed through the foundation of the Guild of St George can now be balanced by the positive work that the institution still undertakes today.

Another organisation invoking St George had an even more definite patriotic bent. The Royal Society of St George was founded in 1894 under royal patronage, aiming 'to encourage and strengthen the spirit of patriotism amongst all classes of the English people, and to foster and inspire our fellow-coutrymen with a jealous pride in all that concerns the welfare and greatness of their native land, or the land of their fathers'. In 1920 it boasted a membership exceeding 20,000 throughout the world, a number that included such luminaries as Rudyard Kipling, who gave an address entitled 'England and the English' at the St George's Day festival dinner that year. One of the Society's purposes was to foster patriotism through dissemination of the written word, publishing works such as Alice Brewster's pamphlet of 1914, *The Life of St George, the Patron Soldier–Saint of England*. Slightly earlier, *Saint George for England. The Life, Legend and Lore of Our*

Glorious Patron Saint, by 'H.O.F.', had been dedicated to the Society. A periodical magazine, *The English Race*, was also produced, which was published under the title *England* from 1939.

Other 'patriotic' organisations with an affiliation to St George also seem to have flourished in the first part of the twentieth century. One example, the Prestatyn Guild of St George, published a handbill bearing the emblem of the red cross some time before 1940. The tract bore the following message, with original punctuation preserved:

> ENGLISHMEN!
> DO YOU KNOW THAT :–
> Your ancestor ADAM was the first Aryan king of Sumeria;
> That he founded civilisation and overthrew barbarianism;
> Introduced Justice and Letters, and that Security whereby Men might live in Peace;
> Stamped out the blood sacrifices of the primitive barbarians and set up a pure religion based on the instinctive honesty of his race;
> Was the living original of the heroic myths of THOR, KING ARTHUR, and SAINT GEORGE of MERRIE ENGLAND;
> His blood, traditions and instincts are Your proud inheritance.
> Consider this, then pass it on.
>
> Send for more for your friends; 40 for 6d., 100 for 1/-, post free.
> A booklet on this subject, with historical notes and illustrations, is in preparation.

It is unclear whether the promised extended commentary on this bizarre ahistorical pronouncement ever materialised, but it is very likely that the underlying message of Aryan or English racial superiority was promulgated through other means too by this particular Guild of St George, so different from John Ruskin's foundation of the same name. Given that Prestatyn is not in England at all – it is a town on the coast of north Wales – the strong message of English patriotism, not to say jingoism, on this tract is rather surprising. It may be that it was the product of a colony of expatriates 'more English than the English', a self-declared outpost of the British Empire which sought to distance itself from the local Welsh community by asserting a particularly aggressive form of English nationalism.

'The League of St George', founded in 1975, seems to have inherited the mantle of embodying the worst excesses of the English psyche, particularly in relation to its stated belief that every nation should have a 'folk community' or 'folk state', a society made up exclusively of people who have a 'right', by reason of ancestry, to call themselves native to that place. The basic concepts of this organisation seem to owe a considerable amount to the apartheid system that was practised in South Africa until relatively recently, and can be understood to give unwitting support to Samuel Johnson's oft-quoted epithet that 'patriotism is the last refuge of a scoundrel'. The beliefs that the people who are invited to join the organisation are expected to subscribe to include morally suspect ideas such as the 'need' to protect blood and soil from 'pollution' and 'corruption', that 'racial solidarity' is to be encouraged, particularly between nations 'alike in blood, culture and sentiment', and that 'only members of the Folk should be automatically entitled to nationality and full citizenship in their own land'.[3] The League has stated that feminism is 'a left-wing cult' that 'destroys chivalry', a considerable departure from Gerrard de Malynes's evocation of Elizabeth I as a powerful chivalric knight in his allegory of St George. The organisation also appears to espouse homophobia and the repatriation of 'foreigners', and is opposed in principle to overseas aid in all but the most extreme circumstances. Interestingly, the organisation has also been ambivalent about Scottish and Welsh nationalism: despite its choice of patron saint, the League seems to consider itself British rather than English. The association of St George with this faction seems particularly unfortunate in the light of his own pedigree as a native-born Palestinian, or possibly Turkish, saint, and it is to be hoped that the majority of people will not be dissuaded from their interest in him and affection for him by such attempts to hijack his identity.

A particularly interesting evocation of St George which plays to some extent on this aspect of his cult dates from the early twentieth century. The children's novel *Where the Rainbow Ends*, by Mrs Clifford Mills, was first published in 1911. Despite its jingoistic and imperial overtones the book has a certain charm, and it is often reminiscent of the style of Edith Nesbitt's turn-of-the-century works for children which combine ordinary middle-class life with magical interventions. The frontispiece of the 1912 edition evokes a sense of blonde-haired and blue-eyed heroism and nobility, with the armour-clad saint surrounded by the four Aryan youngsters and their lion cub; in the story heroism and nobility are equated with white middle-class English children doing 'the right thing' by demonstrating integrity, courage, and above all, patriotism. The story was successfully adapted to become a stage play, with the script written by Mrs Mills in collaboration with 'John Ramsey'. This was a pseudonym of the actor Reginald Owen, who took the part of St George in the first production of the play (illustration 6.6), which premiered in London on 21 December 1911 and continued its run through the first months of 1912. The plot of the book and play is an interesting example of the way that

6.6 Scene from the stage play of Where the Rainbow Ends, *with Reginald Owen as St George, 21 December 1911. (Victoria & Albert Museum, London)*

St George and attitudes to him have sometimes been conceived in the modern era, and as such it will bear an extended summary.

The background of the story is that two children – Crispian, known as Cris, a naval cadet, and his sister Rosamund – are presumed to be orphans after their parents are lost at sea returning from India. They initially lived with kind Cousin Matthew, but on his death evil Uncle Joseph and Aunt Matilda have moved into Riversdale, Cousin Matthew's house, on the pretext of looking after the children. As the action begins Cris receives the dreadful news that he will not be allowed to join the Navy but will instead be set to work as an office boy in Uncle Joseph's business, and the children learn of their guardians' fiendish plans to sell off the beautiful house that Cousin Matthew had bequeathed to his wards. Furthermore, Uncle Matthew and Aunt Matilda are intractably opposed to Cris's pet, Cubby the British lion cub, who wears red, white and blue ribbons around his neck and needs regular doses of 'Colonial Mixture', which is formulated from 'equal parts of Canadian, Australian and New Zealand Iron, mixed with South African steel'. A blend of 'great traditions and virgin prowess', it is labelled 'Poison to Traitors'. The children are disconsolate at this turn of events, but Rosamund then remembers a book that Cousin Matthew had read to them, the 'Rainbow Book', which claimed that the 'Land Where All Lost Loved Ones Are Found' exists beyond the evil Dragon King's realm. A frantic search for the book ensues, before the library of the house is sold off to 'Schnapps', a man described as German with Jewish blood (interestingly, despite his evidently poor pedigree, according to the racist and jingoistic tone of the book, the character is used later as a device to underline Uncle Joseph's dreadful lack of patriotism by telling him off for sneering at St George's flag).

The book gives directions for reaching the 'Land Where All Lost Loved Ones Are Found', where the children hope to find their parents: the first task is to find Faith's Magic Carpet. Inevitably, it transpires to be the rather threadbare rug beneath their feet, and the children set about summoning the Genie, who is described as being 'of Ethiopian darkness, but not at all repulsive-looking'. He offers the children each two wishes. Cris decides to call upon the skills of his best friend from the Naval College, the wonderfully named 'Blunders', and his younger sister, Betty, who immediately appear in the room, eager to join the adventure. Rosamund, who is evidently a practical girl, wishes that Uncle Joseph, Aunt Matilda and Schnapps should start their dinner all over again, to give more time to allow for an undetected escape. She also wishes for an heroic knight to help them, and names St George. A grey-haired figure in a long cloak appears before them, much to the disappointment of the four children. The man tells them that he is indeed St George, and that he is one of Britain's 'unemployed ideals': he has been neglected by English people who have been blinded by gold-dust thrown into their eyes as a trick by the Dragon King. Nevertheless, Rosamund asks for his protection – 'I am an English maiden in danger, and I ask for your aid' – and an immediate transformation takes place. St George is now revealed as an armour-clad knight, 'golden-haired, blue-eyed, English of the English'.

Just as Uncle Joseph and Aunt Matilda enter the library, the four children, Cubby and St George all fly off on the magic carpet. However, a cowardly sneak, William the boot-boy – an enemy of Cris and Rosamund, and Cubby in particular – has been hiding behind the curtains. He had witnessed everything, including the Genie's warning that if anyone possessed so much as a thread of Faith's carpet they could use it to summon the fearsome Dragon King. William snatches a thread from the carpet as it rises into the air, and presents it, with the full story of what has gone on, to Uncle Joseph. The latter wastes no time in calling up the Dragon King, who arrives in a cloud of sulphurous smoke and denounces his arch-enemy, St George, as a champion of honour, the trait he most despises. The Dragon King, Uncle Joseph and Aunt Matilda then set off in pursuit of the fugitives, travelling by a devilish underground train.

Meanwhile, the children arrive at 'St George's Ground', a place that is described as 'like England in Maytime'. The flag of St George flies there as a symbol of the saint's power and protection. This place of safety, said to be a sunny, light green hilltop on which the original fight with the dragon had occurred, is surrounded by dark green forest, the Dragon Wood, a threatening place filled with evil spirits where the Dragon King rules. The children need to stay on St George's Ground through the night, as the Dragon Wood is safer during daylight, but once the boys have gone off to look for firewood young Betty is lured into the forest by a troupe of dancing elves. Finding her missing, Rosamund goes into the forest to look for her with Cubby. Their brothers follow on in turn, and an interesting interlude ensues where the boys meet up with a young Englishman known as 'the Slacker'. He has traded his noble birthright for the pleasures of an idle life, fishing, eating Dragon Fruit and watching the gnomes play cricket, protected from the wild beasts of the forest by the eerie Dragon Light, which, along with a Dragon Badge, signifies the protection of the Dragon King himself. The Slacker tries to tempt the young naval cadets to join him and forget about their quest, but has to admit that the ultimate price for defecting to the Dragon King will be metamorphosis into a blind, human-headed worm. Horrified, Cris and Blunders urge him to come with them, but he refuses to take on the obligations of a true Englishman: 'To fight, to work – perhaps to starve? Never. I'll stay here!' Soon after this distressing encounter the boys are reunited with their sisters and Cubby, and they all make their way to the edge of the Dragon Wood in search of Cris and Rosamund's lost parents.

Elsewhere in the wood, Uncle Joseph and Aunt Matilda have come to a bad end, as befits their evil characters. Pursued by hyenas, Uncle Joseph took refuge in a tree, leaving Aunt Matilda to be eaten by the ravenous beasts. Thinking that he is safe, he decides to slake his thirst by taking a swig from the bottle of Colonial Mixture which he has been cruelly withholding from the innocent Cubby. Alas, he overlooks the warning on the label, and promptly expires; his body is then also eaten by the hyenas. (This rather gruesome episode was excised from some versions of the story: in the stage play and the bowdlerized published editions he merely dislikes the taste of the mixture.)

The Dragon King, aware of all that has gone on, sends his flying dragons to capture the children and carry them to his castle on Thundercloud Mountain, where they are beyond St George's protection. The Dragon King passes judgement on the children: they are found guilty of having placed themselves under the protection of an Ideal – 'Ideals are dragons' greatest enemies, for where ideals are honoured our power is unknown.' Their choice of St George as a patron is particularly heinous, 'for he alone can build about your country, England, a sure, impregnable defence – the wall of patriotism'. The sentence passed on the hapless friends is death. However, the evil plan is thwarted by the simple expedient of constructing a flag of St George from Cris's white handkerchief and the red ribbon from Cubby's collar. The boys, thanks to their naval cadet training, are able to climb up the main tower of the castle and replace the dragon standard with St George's flag just as the execution party approaches. With this place of darkness now established as his own realm, St George appears in a flash of light and kills the Dragon King. As the castle crumbles and the Dragon Soldiers fall to their deaths down the side of the mountain the saint points out a path to the children which leads them to a golden beach. Once there, they are reunited with Cris and Rosamund's parents who are revealed to have been shipwrecked. This device carries strong, but perhaps unconscious, overtones of *The Tempest*, another story which is concerned with trials, findings and rightful lordship. St George comes home with the children and their parents on an English ship, to be restored to his rightful position and 'to live henceforth and forever in the hearts of the children of his race'. At the end of the stage version of the story he cries out to the audience:

> Rise, Youth of England, let your voices ring
> For God, for Britain, and for Britain's King.

All then stand to sing the National Anthem.

The play of *Where the Rainbow Ends* was phenomenally successful. It became an annual Christmas event, a rival to *Peter Pan*, and a production was staged every year up until the 1950s. It is thought that some 20 million people had seen the play by 1961. The novel went through several editions, which would certainly seem to imply a large readership, and it is perhaps surprising that the story is now almost entirely forgotten. The disappearance of this version of St George, with its clear message of patriotism and nobility, is regretted by some of the more right-wing commentators on his cult. One recent study of St George has held up *Where the Rainbow Ends* as 'a powerful and potent story . . . [whose] influence could only be for good'.[4] This writer seems to overlook the problems inherent in the fable – the racism, the imperialism, and the strongly negative presentation of William, the sole working-class character – and concentrates instead on the positive aspects, such as the encouragement of honour and integrity. Furthermore, the author suggests that those people who would wish to 'censor' the book 'plan to reduce the nation [England] to a rootless, idle and malleable rabble', a sad and ill-deserved indictment that goes some way towards explaining why a considerable number of English people seem to be ambivalent about the figure of St George as the heroic English knight representing them on the international stage.

A good contrast to this treatment of St George is provided by the cartoonist Steve Bell, a left-wing commentator of whom some enthusiasts of the saint would surely not approve, perhaps most particularly the supporters of organisations such as the League of St George. Bell has used the saint as an inspiration and model on a number of occasions, and says that he finds the story of St George and the dragon very useful as an easily recognisable paradigm of good and evil. Which character is identified as the representation of which trait is not always clear, however. Sometimes the dragon claims a long-overdue victory against the saint, and seems to make a mockery of the knight in the process. However, this should not necessarily be interpreted as an allegory of the overthrow of the English nation, the British government, or any similar trope: Bell informs me that he personally does not look upon St George as a figure of England and the English establishment, and considers John Bull and Britannia to be more apposite models when he wishes to make this kind of political observation. Instead, he finds that St George is far more meaningful as an inheritor of the tradition of dragon-slaying heroes. This understanding of the saint tends to suggest that Bell's use of St George is considerably closer to the probable roots of the cult, especially the influence of the stories of Apollo and Python, Perseus and Andromeda and similar heroic tales, than the overtly patriotic tone that is associated with the saint by some other modern commentators.

In one Bell cartoon (illustration 6.7) from May 2000, we see the right-wing leader of the opposition party in the British parliament, William Hague, presented in the guise of St George. He is depicted mounted on a horse which bears a strong resemblance to a leading member of his Shadow Cabinet, complete with a hangman's noose made into a tail to evoke the fundamentalist policies of his party. 'St William' wears a schoolboy's uniform – a reference to his relative youthfulness and lack of political experience – as well as a police helmet. This seems to be an allusion to Hague's apparent desire to present himself as a guardian of 'traditional' English values; the juxtaposition of the helmet and the cloak of the flag of St George evokes the idea of a child's dressing-up games, and thus the contention that Hague is adopting populist policies rather than a well-considered political theory. The specific use of the flag in this image also refers to Hague's attempts to appeal to a 'Little England' mentality, those reactionary sections of English society who lament the loss of the British Empire and feel that 'the English way of life' is threatened by a left-of-centre government. The dragon in this image represents this 'Liberal establishment'. Despite its fire-breathing antics, Bell's presentation of the monster clearly identifies it as a soft target for St William's attack. This may be a reference to the extent to which the current governing party has failed, despite their landslide election victory, to implement many of the

6.7 *Steve Bell,* Saint William taking on the Liberal Establishment, *published in the* Guardian, *19 May 2000.*

progressive reforms that people with left-wing sympathies had expected: the Liberal Establishment dragon is rather less fearsome and powerful than St William might like to pretend.

These various interpretations of St George have come together to some extent in the iconography of sports supporters. Anecdotal evidence suggests that St George's emblem, the red cross on a white field, is now used in preference to the Union Flag by many English fans, a development that is particularly noticeable in the crowds at international soccer matches but also manifests itself in rugby, cricket, tennis and other sporting events where an England team, or even an English individual, takes on the representatives of another nation. The re-establishment of St George's flag as a symbol of England may well be a concomitant of the recent moves towards political devolution for the Scottish and Welsh, for this has been accompanied by an increasing realisation in some quarters that 'Britain' and 'England' are not interchangeable terms and should no longer be considered as such. (It is arguable that the Scots and Welsh have always been very aware of the distinction,

6.8 St George and the dragon tableau, from the opening ceremony of the 'Euro 96' Championship.

and that it has only ever been the English, or some English people, who have misused the terminology.) A common sight at many international fixtures, increasing numbers of English football fans display the flag of St George, their faces painted with a clear symbol of nationality and national pride, although the extent to which such individuals will connect their decorations with St George himself is debatable. The saint himself was clearly invoked, however, in the opening pageant of the finals of the 'Euro 96' tournament, an international soccer competition that was held in England. In an apparently unconscious approximation of the late medieval Ridings, St George engaged in battle with a dragon (illustration 6.8). The tableau undoubtedly represented England defeating an enemy, a feat achieved off the pitch with rather less trouble than the English football team experienced on it, but it also sought to appeal to the spectators of all nationalities as an image of the universal hero, victorious over the trials and tribulations he encountered. There may even have been an element of the saint as an emblem of chivalry, a concept that would presumably seek to encourage a spirit of fair play among both players and supporters.

In May 1969 St George's feast was formally reduced by the Roman Catholic Church to the level of an optional local festival, although in England the day retained the status of a solemnity in recognition of the saint's special status as patron of the nation. However, apart from the observances of movements such as the Scouts and Guides, mentioned above, little attention is paid to the feast day in England. Despite the long association of St George with the English it was not until the eighteenth century that the saint was declared, by Pope Benedict IV, as the principal protector of England. It thus appears that St George enjoyed a semi-official relationship with the English for some four hundred years, and in some respects this description is applicable to the situation today. Small-scale campaigns, such as the St George's Day Association, have sought to encourage the observance of 23 April as a celebration of England and her patron saint, but even though some public buildings regularly display the emblem of St George, it is still quite rare to find English people displaying a flag, whether English or British, or wearing a rose on the day in question (the fact that native rosebushes are not generally in bloom in April may be a factor). This is a matter of regret to many patriots, but the increasing enthusiasm for the observance of the feast days of the patron saints of Wales, Scotland and, most particularly, Ireland does seem likely to spill over into the commemoration of the fourth patron saint of the British Isles. However, it seems clear that some re-evaluation of St George's role as an aggressively nationalist figure is required before his feast day will be celebrated more widely. If it can be conclusively demonstrated that patriotism need not be the preserve of right-wing groups, and that love of one's country need not be excluded from an internationalist outlook, it is likely that St George will once more be recognised as a valuable icon of heroism, honour and integrity both in England and abroad.

EPILOGUE

THE AFTERLIFE OF A HERO

In April 1999 I visited Crete, the most southerly island of the Greek archipelago, for a holiday with my family. I knew that St George was an important saint in the tradition of the Eastern Orthodox Churches, and, although I had not specifically planned to be in Greece for his feast day on 23 April, I hoped to be able to witness some kind of ceremony or celebration. As luck would have it, the area where we were staying in the north-east of the island was suffused with the cult of St George. A roadside shrine dedicated to him had been set only up a short walk from the centre of the village, and the locally-produced bottled water was extracted from a well of St George. Furthermore, a monastery under his patronage was situated on the side of a mountain a couple of miles inland, a quiet and beautiful place that was obviously well-used by people from the local area – the baptism of a baby was in progress during my first visit – even though the foundation was remote from any settlement.

I discovered that the situation of the monastery was no accident: a local legend stated that St George had been fleeing, on horseback, from an enemy army over the mountains and had made a death-defying leap from the summit of one rather high peak into the valley below. A tiny chapel had been erected in his honour on the point where he landed, and some time later a monastery had been founded further up the mountain, overlooking the sacred spot. As a medievalist I was disappointed to find that the original chapel had been recently rebuilt, but I decided that it would be appropriate to make a 'pilgrimage' up to the monastery on the morning of St George's Day to reflect on what I had learned about the western cult and perhaps to entreat the saint's assistance during my forthcoming doctoral examination. Having been warned that feast days that fell near Easter were sometimes moved around in the Orthodox tradition, I did not have any particular expectations of what I would find at the monastery and was quite prepared to be the only 'devotee' of the saint in attendance. It is, therefore, quite fair to say that I was amazed by the sight that met me as I drew closer to the buildings: several thousand people were thronging the road leading to the monastery and the open courtyard of the foundation, with more arriving by car and coach every moment. A large street market was in progress, selling all manner of toys and household goods (interestingly, very little food was on sale), and, naturally, some small icons of the patronal saint. As I made my way up towards the monastery complex I became aware of several people begging for alms, and a few others, all women, apparently undertaking some kind of penance, crawling on hands and knees to the chapel or shuffling up the road in a seated position, pulling themselves along with their arms. Some of the bystanders evidently found this sight as distressing as I did, but the penitents and their supporters seemed confident that this behaviour was both appropriate and necessary, and refused all offers of help.

Within the courtyard of the monastery several rituals were being performed simultaneously by a number of priests, some involving the intonation of blessings over large, circular loaves of bread which were stacked up in considerable quantities and brought forward a few at a time to the team of chanting clerics. The main ceremony was evidently taking place in the small church of the monastery: a huge crowd was gathered outside listening to the litany which was relayed on a public address system, some people repeatedly making the sign of the Cross at quite dizzying speed. A large and venerable icon of the saint was also on display, which many people genuflected before or kissed. At length the officiating priest and his entourage emerged from the church, resplendent in jewelled and embroidered vestments, and the church bell began to ring. This was the signal for sacks of bread to be distributed, great hunks of the round loaves that transpired to be a sweet confection flavoured with caraway. There was a mad scramble to secure pieces of this blessed bread, even though there seemed to be an ample supply, and many people made a private hoard in a bag, perhaps to take away and share with family and friends who had not been able to attend the festival themselves. Reproductions of an icon of the saint were also distributed, and again some people took several copies. Their task complete, the officiating priest and his assistants began to process towards the entrance of the monastery, pausing to clasp proffered hands and to bestow blessings. Their progress was accompanied not only by the pealing of the church bell, but also by the sound of a monk hammering on a large metal bar which was suspended under the roof of a cloister-like structure: the noise it produced was quite deafening. Meanwhile, the church had been opened to visitors, and several members of the local police force were on hand to control the movements of the crowd through the small building. When I eventually got inside I found that small votive offerings, likenesses in metal of a hand, an eye, or other body parts, had been hung in front of some of the icons either in supplication for aid or thanks for a cure effected. People were processing around the interior of the church, genuflecting, making the sign of the Cross, touching and kissing the icons, and some were also anointing themselves with holy water or oil from a chrismatory.

As I walked down the mountain away from the monastery complex I paused by the tiny chapel in the valley, which was curiously deserted in great contrast to the clamour and activity just a short distance away. I sat in the sunshine and watched as two people, a man and a woman, drove up to the chapel separately, got out of their cars and greeted one another. They were evidently friends, perhaps related, and talked animatedly as they walked over to the chapel. The woman waited outside while the man went in, genuflected and lit a candle. He emerged almost at once – the entire 'ceremony' had taken no more than five seconds – and resumed his conversation with his friend. They walked back to their cars, said goodbye and drove away. It occurred to me that this slight episode had been a perfect example of the way that the appearance of devotion is often more important than the substance. Whether or not the man and his friend felt real devotion for St George was irrelevant: for their purposes all that mattered was that they went through the motions of venerating the saint on his feast day to ensure his protection for the next year. This is very reminiscent of a belief that was widespread in late medieval England, that viewing an image of St Christopher was a sure safeguard against sudden death for the rest of the day. The placement of images of St Christopher on the north wall of English churches, directly opposite the doorway on the south side, is deeply significant: it meant that people could look upon the image simply by poking their head around the door without the bother of physically entering the building. Here too, the mechanical action of venerating the saint was more important than any feeling of reverence that underlay it. The apparent persistence of this type of attitude into the modern era raises some very interesting philosophical questions about the nature of 'devotion' and 'reverence', the extent to which belief needs to be bolstered by the substance of action, and even prompts us to ask what the true purpose of ritualised religious practice may be.

The Cretan celebration of St George's Day was instructive for a western medievalist in other ways too. This event was the closest that I am ever likely to come to the way that English people experienced the public ceremonial of religion during the late Middle Ages: the touching and kissing of images, penances such as Creeping to the Cross, and the use of votive images, holy water and oils are well documented as aspects of veneration at this time, but have all been virtually eradicated from modern rites. The only real difference from contemporary religious practice that a fifteenth-century English traveller may have noticed in late twentieth-century Crete would have been the absence of relics, but it is surely true to say that, despite the supernumeracy of preserved parts of St George's body, many places, both in England and throughout Europe, would have celebrated his feast day without recourse to the veneration of relics as not every site would have been fortunate enough to possess some.

The correspondences between the celebration of St George's Day in modern Crete and our understanding of practices of the late medieval English cult are also instructive as a sign of the extent to which our society has lost touch with our former traditions. The general English view of our patron saint tends to be a combination of misunderstanding and a simple lack of knowledge: our most familiar experience of the saint and his emblem are in the form of signs on public houses, commercial insignia and the flags flown on churches and some public buildings or paraded by Scouts and Guides on St George's Day, and it seems that few people have been motivated to look beyond this façade. A common though clearly misguided view of the saint is expounded by the broadcaster and commentator Jeremy Paxman in his recent book *The English: a portrait of a people* (1998). He defines the national protector as 'a vague, workaday saint of little spiritual or theological importance', a characterisation which is by no means sustained by the evidence of the English cult. The rise in right-wing organisations who have claimed St George as their particular patron, discussed in the previous chapter, has certainly not aided his public image in the wider community, but it is to be hoped that the advent of a more considered English nationalism, in the wake of increasing independence for Scotland and Wales, will lead to a reappraisal of the history and significance of the cult of the patron saint of England.

The wider importance of St George is also indicated by the obvious vitality of the Cretan cult. Furthermore, it is notable that the Eastern Orthodox understanding of the saint differs in several important respects from the Western tradition. For example, the iconography of the saint as a dragon-slayer is quite distinctive in the Greek Church, for St George is often accompanied by an auxiliary figure who is identified as a cup-bearer, a character who never appears in the Western iconography. Within the Coptic Christian sects of north-east Africa there are further variants, including the startling identification of St George as a bridegroom of Christ. This tradition, which dates from at least the fifth century, seems to identify a chaste same-sex marriage between the saint and the divinity as an equivalent of the 'mystic marriage' with Christ claimed by St Katherine of Alexandria and some other saintly women. Initial research into the topos has suggested that St George may have some claim to be considered as an icon of homosexual love. There is much in the wider cult of St George which lies beyond the scope of this book to explore and which awaits a full investigation, but there is undoubtedly yet more to learn about St George's role within the Roman Church too. For example, the saint is strongly associated with milk in Italy, where he is still invoked as a protector of dairies. The rationale behind this is somewhat obscure: it could be a development of St George's role as a patron of farmers or, alternatively, connected to the ancient belief that dragons suck milk from dairy cows (a misdemeanour of which hedgehogs are sometimes suspected too).

St George's cult flourishes today in many parts of the world, but it continues to develop, too. An Arabic epic poem of Girgis, or Mar Jiryis, which is apparently recited in Coptic churches dedicated to St George on his feast day and on the festival of the dedication of the church, is in many respects very traditional. The ancient themes are clearly visible: each year the dragon holds back the waters in the river at Beirut, and demands the sacrifice of a 'bride' before he will release the flow. Some variations occur – the dragon is stabbed in the eye rather than the mouth, and St George is invoked as a Roman hero rather than a native saint or even a Cappadocian – but it is evident that modern elements have crept into the story too, for the princess's finery of expensive clothes and jewels is augmented by several wrist watches.

As the preface to this book observed, definitive statements are often neither possible nor desirable within the historical disciplines. It is to be hoped that the commentary on St George and his cult offered in these pages will encourage the re-evaluation and further exploration of this many-faceted, and deeply meaningful, figure whose veneration has straddled seventeen centuries, countless countries and several varieties of religious belief.

TABLES

Details of all lives of St George referred to appear in the Bibliography

Table 1: Comparison of Literary Versions of St George's Legend[1] [for tortures and dragon story see Tables 2 and 3]

Work	Ælfric	*Golden Legend*	*South English Legendary*[2]	*Scottish Legendary*	Lydgate
Date	*c.* 1000	*c.* 1260	early 14th century	1400–1450	*c.* 1425
Birthplace	Cappadocia	Cappadocia	Cappadoce	Capadoce	Cappadoce
Status	rich noble	tribune[3]	holy man[4]	tribune	knight
Heathen ruler	Datian, emperor	Dacian, prefect	Dacian, prince	Dacyane, emperor	Dacyan, president
Heathen deity	Apolline	unnamed	---	Appollony	unnamed
St George 'recants'	yes	yes	---	yes	yes
Temple fire	yes	yes	---	yes	yes
Imprisonment	yes	---	yes	yes	---
Appearance of Christ	---	yes	---	---	yes
Magician converts	yes	yes	---	yes	yes
Ruler's wife converts	---	yes	---	yes	yes
Heavenly voice	---	yes	yes	yes	---
Beheading	unclear	yes	yes	yes	yes
Ruler killed by fire	yes	yes	---	yes	yes

Work	*Mirk's Festial*	*Speculum Sacerdotale*	Caxton	Mantuan	Barclay
Date	1400–50	15th century	1522	1505	1515
Birthplace	not stated	Capadoce	Capadoce	Cappadocia	Cappadocia
Status	not stated	tribune[3]	knight[3]	knight[3]	tribune[3]
Heathen ruler	Emperor Dyaclisian	Dacian, no status given	Dacyen, provost	Dacianus	unnamed king; Dacian is a judge
Heathen deity	unnamed	Appolini	unnamed	unnamed	unnamed
George 'recants'	---	unclear	yes	yes	yes
Temple fire	---	yes	yes	yes	yes
Imprisonment	yes	yes	yes	yes	yes
Appearance of Christ	yes	---	no, but angel heals St George	yes	no, but angel heals St George
Magician converts	yes[5]	yes	yes	yes	yes
Ruler's wife converts	---	---	yes	yes	yes
Heavenly voice	---	---	yes	no, but angels appear	no, but angels appear
Beheading	yes	yes	yes	yes	yes
Ruler killed by fire	yes	yes	yes	yes	Dacian dies, king's fate not stated

Table 2: Comparison of Tortures in Literary Versions of St George's Legend[1]

Work	Ælfric	*Golden Legend*	*South English Legendary*[2]	*Scottish Legendary*	Lydgate
millstone	---	---	---	---	---
lime kiln	---	---	---	---	---
scourged	yes	---	yes	---	yes
hooks/claws	yes	yes	---	---	---
burnt with torches	yes	yes	---	yes	yes
salted	yes	yes	yes	yes	yes
rack	---	yes	---	yes	---
wheel	yes	yes, with knives	yes	yes, with swords	yes
poison	yes	yes	---	yes	yes
boiled in molten lead	yes	yes	yes	yes	yes
beaten	---	---	---	---	yes
dragged	yes	yes	yes	---	yes

Work	*Mirk's Festial*	*Speculum Sacerdotale*	Caxton	Mantuan	Barclay
millstone	yes	---	---	---	---
lime kiln	yes	---	---	---	---
scourged	---	---	---	---	---
hooks/claws	on wheel	---	---	yes	yes
burnt with torch	---	yes	---	yes	yes
salted	---	yes	yes	yes	yes
rack	---	yes	---	yes	yes
wheel	yes, with hooks and swords	yes, with swords	yes	yes, with iron teeth	yes, with iron teeth
poison	yes	yes	yes	yes	yes
boiled in molten lead	---	yes	yes	---	---
beaten	yes	---	yes	---	---
dragged	---	yes	yes	dragged by bulls	dragged by wild bulls

Table 3: Comparison of Literary Versions of the Legend of St George and the Dragon[1]

Work	Ælfric	*Golden Legend*	*South English Legendary*[2]	*Scottish Legendary*	Lydgate
Comments	Does not appear	Baptism occurs before dragon killed	Unclear when baptism occurs	Baptism occurs before dragon killed	Baptism occurs after dragon killed
Country		Lybia	lyby	lyby	Lybye
Town		Silena	Gylona	sylena	Lysseene
Water		pond or lake	'gret water'	'locht'	---
Creature		dragon	'dragone'	'serpent fel'	'dragoun'
Foul breath		yes	yes	yes	unclear
Sacrifice		two sheep	two sheep	two sheep	two sheep
Lots drawn		yes	yes	yes	yes
Threat to burn king		yes	yes	yes	---
Grace period		one week	eight days	eight days	---
Bridal dress		---	---	yes	---
Wounds dragon		yes,[6] with lance	yes, with with spear	yes, with spear	yes, with spear
Girdling		yes	yes	yes	yes
Kills dragon		with sword	sword	sword	sword
Baptism[7]		20,000	20,000	over 20,000	unnumbered
Church dedication		Virgin and George[8]	Christ and George[9]	Virgin and George[10]	Virgin and George[10]
Healing spring		yes	---	yes	yes
Offer of marriage		---	---	---	---
Offer of money		yes	---	yes	---

Table 3: Comparison of Literary Versions of the Legend of St George and the Dragon[1] (continued)

Work	*Mirk's Festial*	*Speculum Sacerdotale*	Caxton	Mantuan	Barclay
Comments	Baptism occurs before dragon killed	Baptism occurs before dragon killed	Baptism occurs after dragon killed	Baptism occurs after dragon killed	Baptism occurs after dragon killed
Country	not stated	Libie	Lybye	Libie	Lybia
Town	not stated	Silena	Sylene	Silena	Sylena
Water	---	river or lake	'stagne' or pond	moat	dyche
Creature	dragon	edder or dragon	dragon	'monstro'	dragon[11]
Foul breath	---	yes	yes	yes	yes
Sacrifice	sheep and child	two sheep	two sheep	one person[12]	one person[12]
Lots drawn	---	yes	yes	yes	yes
Threat to burn king	---	yes	yes	---	unclear
Grace period	---	eight days	eight	---	yes, unnumbered
Bridal dress	---	---	yes	---	yes
Wounds dragon	with spear	with spear	with sword	with lance	with spear
Girdling	yes	yes	yes	---	---
Kills dragon	method unclear	sword	method unclear	method unclear	second spear[13]
Baptism[7]	20,000	20,000	15,000	unnumbered	unnumbered
Church dedication	---	Virgin and George[8]	Virgin and George[8]	not stated	Virgin[8]
Healing spring	---	yes	yes	yes	yes
Offer of marriage	---	---	---	---	yes
Offer of money	---	yes	yes	no, city offered	no, kingdom offered

NOTES TO TABLES

1. The layout used in these tables does not imply that the order of events is consistent between the different versions.
2. Two forms of the *South English Legendary* narrative exist, SELa and SELb. The martyrdom legend appears in SELa, the dragon legend in SELb.
3. This status is mentioned only in relation to the dragon story. When the legend gives an account of the martyrdom he is said to have laid aside military trappings.
4. St George is a holy man, not a soldier, but he arms himself with the Holy Spirit 'within and without' [l.10].
5. The poisoner is not identified as a magician, but simply as a man.
6. An alternative version is also given where the dragon is killed outright.
7. Numbers are given for the men baptised; women and children are mentioned but not numbered.
8. The only expression of a link between the Virgin and St George is through the joint dedication of the church; there are no references to the resurrection by the Virgin or the arming by the Virgin.
9. The final sentence of SELb, which relates to the founding of the church, is unfinished. It is possible that it could also have been dedicated to the Virgin, though it seems unlikely that she would be mentioned after St George.
10. In this version St George is identified as the Virgin's knight in addition to the joint dedication of the church; this may reflect a lost English tradition.
11. This dragon is explicitly referred to as female. See Chapter Five on the motif of the female dragon.
12. The sacrifice is made morning and evening.
13. A sword has already been used to wound the dragon.

NOTES

CHAPTER ONE

1. U.A. Fanthorpe, 'Not My Best Side (Uccello, S. George and the Dragon, The National Gallery)' in *Selected Poems* (London, 1986), p. 29.
2. *Gesta Francorum*, ed. R. Hill (London, 1962), p. 29.
3. M.H. Bulley, *St George for Merrie England* (London, 1908), pp. 21–2.
4. J. Lewis André, 'Saint George the Martyr in Legend, Ceremonial, Art, etc.', *Archaelological Journal* LVII (1900), p. 206.
5. *Calender of the patent rolls preserved in the Public Record Office. Edward III, A.D. 1327–1377*, vol. 9 (London, 1907), p. 127.
6. 'H.O.F.' *St George for England. The Life, Legend and Lore of Our Glorious Patron* (London, 1911), p. 30.

CHAPTER TWO

1. C.M. Kaufmann, 'The altar-piece of St George from Valencia', *Victoria and Albert Museum Yearbook* 2, 1970, pp. 65–100.
2. Abbé R. Berger, *Les Vitraux de la Cathédrale Notre-Dame de Clermont* (Clermont-Ferrand, 1968), p. 9.
3. '. . . *nihil prosit carnem habere virginem, si mente quis nupserit*'. Adversus Helvidium 20, in *Patrologia Latina* 23, 214, A, translated and discussed in D. Dumm, *The Theological Basis of Virginity According to St Jerome* (Latrobe, 1961), p. 108.

CHAPTER THREE

1. 'A Carol of St George' in R.T. Davies (ed.), *Medieval English Lyrics. A Critical Anthology* (London, 1963), p. 185.
2. D. Gordon, *Making and Meaning. The Wilton Diptych* (London, 1993), p. 58.
3. 'For the Night-Mare' in C. and K. Sisan (eds), *The Oxford Book of Medieval English Verse* (Oxford, 1973), p. 384.

CHAPTER FOUR

1. Jonathan Bengtson, 'Saint George and the Formation of English Nationalism', *Journal of Medieval and Early Modern Studies* 27:2 (Spring, 1997), p. 326. Bengston names his source as E.M. Thompson, ed. and trans., *Chronicon Adae de Usk, AD 1377–1404* (London, 1876), p. 26, but this seems to be an erroneous attribution.
2. 'Speed Our King on his Journey', in C. Brown (ed.), *Religious Lyrics of the Fifteenth Century* (Oxford, 1939), pp. 196–200.
3. David Galloway (ed.), *Norwich 1540–1642*, Records of Early English Drama, (Toronto, 1984), pp. 69–70, 169, 195.
4. Barbara D. Palmer, 'The Inhabitants of Hell: Devils', in Clifford Davidson and Thomas H. Seiler (eds), *The Iconography of Hell*, Early Drama, Art and Music Series, 17 (Kalamazoo, 1992), p. 4.
5. Mary Grace, *Records of the Guild of St George in Norwich, 1389–1547*, Norfolk Record Society, 9 (1937), p. 19.

6. Christina Hole, *English Folk Heroes* (London, 1948), p. 117.
7. Thomas North, *A Chronicle of the Church of S Martin in Leicester during the Reigns of Henry VIII, Edward VI, Mary and Elizabeth* (London, 1866), p. 238.
8. Toulmin Smith (ed.), *English Gilds*, Early English Text Society, Original Series 40 (1963), p. xl.

CHAPTER FIVE

1. Beryl Rowland, *Animals with Human Faces: A Guide to Animal Symbolism* (Knoxville, 1973), p. 69, citing John Brand, *Observations on Popular Antiquities* (Newcastle, 1777).
2. *Medieval Lore: an epitome of the science, geography, animal and plant folk-lore and myth of the Middle Ages: being classified gleanings from the encyclopaedia of Bartholomew Anglicus on the properties of things*, ed. Robert Steele (London, 1893), pp. 124–5.
3. R.W. Scribner, *For the Sake of Simple Folk: Popular Propaganda for the German Reformation* (Cambridge, 1981), p. 132.
4. Keith Thomas, *Man and the Natural World. Changing attitudes in England 1500–1800* (Harmondsworth, 1984), p. 38.

CHAPTER SIX

1. *Saint George and Saint Patrick: or, the rival Saintesses. An epic poem of the eighteenth century* (Dublin, 1800).
2. H.E. Luxmore, *The Guild of St George* (London, 1925), p. 5.
3. Anonymous pamphlet, *The Folk State. League of St George Policy Statement* (Enfield, 1995).
4. Anthony Cooney, *The Story of St George. The Life and Legend of England's Patron Saint* (Cheltenham, 1999), p. 51.

SELECT BIBLIOGRAPHY

There is a vast literature on the cult of St George in English, French, and, most notably, German, much of it concentrating on the genesis of the legend of the saint and the veracity of the different versions. As we have seen, there seems to have been a vogue for publishing more general studies of the cult in the early years of the twentieth century; many of these works are rather repetitive and poorly referenced, but they often provide an important source of information about 'traditional' views of the saint which are not recorded in more formal accounts. Some studies are narrowly focused on one aspect of the cult such as relics, folk tradition, or the links between the saint and the English monarchy, while other works, ostensibly focused on another topic, include important tangential references to the cult of St George. The most useful of these works include:

André, J.L. 'Saint George the Martyr, in Legend, Ceremonial, Art, etc.', *Archaeological Journal* LVII (1900), 204–23

Baring-Gould, S. *Curious Myths of the Middle Ages* (London, 1888)

Barnes, P. *St George, Ruskin and the Dragon* (Sheffield, 1992)

Bengtson, J. 'Saint George and the Formation of English Nationalism', *Journal of Medieval and Early Modern Studies* 27: 2 (Spring, 1997), 317–40

Blair, C. 'The Emperor Maximilian's gift of armour to King Henry VIII and silvered and engraved armour at the Tower of London', *Archaeologia*, 99 (1965), 1–56

Braunfels, S. 'Georg. Westen' in *Lexicon der Christlichen Iconographie*, Vol. 6 (Freiburg, 1974), 374–90

Braunfels-Esche, S. *Sankt Georg: Legende, Verehrung, Symbol* (Munich, 1976)

Budge, E.A.W. *The History of George of Lydda, The Patron Saint of England. A Study of the Cultus of St George of Ethiopia* (London, 1930)

Bulley, M.H. *St George for Merrie England* (London, 1908)

Chambers, E.K. *The Mediaeval Stage* (Oxford, 1903)

——. *The English Folk Play* (New York, 1966)

Clark, A. *Beasts and Bawdy* (London, 1975)

Cumont, F. 'La plus ancienne Legende de Saint Georges', *Revue de l'Histoire des religions* 114 (1936), 5–51

De Laborderie, O. 'Richard the Lionheart and the birth of a national cult of St George in England: origins and development of a legend', *Nottingham Medieval Studies* 39 (1995), 37–53

Delehaye, H. *Les Légendes Grecques des Saints Militaires* (Paris, 1909)

Didi-Huberman, G., *et al. St Georges et le Dragon* (Paris, 1994)

Erickson, P. '"God for Harry, England and Saint George" British National Identity and the Emergence of White Self-Fashioning' in P. Erickson and C. Hulse (eds), *Early Modern Visual Culture. Representation, Race and Empire in Renaissance England* (Philadelphia, 2000), 315–45

Fisher, J.A. 'Saint George the Martyr', *Reports of the Society of Friends of St George's* 4 (1960) part 1, 12–19

Fournée, J. 'Le Culte de Saint Georges en Normandie', *Annuaire des Cinq Départements de la Normandie* (Association Normande et les Assises de Caumont, Congres de Louviers, 1986), 105–27

Fox, D.S. *St George: the Saint with Three Faces* (Windsor Forest, 1983)
Frend, W.C.H. 'Martyrdom in East and West: the Saga of St George in Nobatia and England' in D. Wood (ed.), *Martyrs and Martyrologies* (Studies in Church History 30) (Oxford, 1993), 47–56
Girouard, M. *The Return to Camelot. Chivalry and the English Gentleman* (London, 1981)
Gordon, E.O. *Saint George, Champion of Christendom and Patron Saint of England* (London, 1907)
Grace, M. *Records of the Guild of St George in Norwich, 1389–1547*, Norfolk Record Society, 9 (1937)
Hanaeur, J.E. *Folk-lore of the Holy Land. Moslem, Christian and Jewish* (second edn, London, 1935)
Heath-Stubbs, J. 'The Hero as Saint: St George' in H.R.E. Davidson (ed.), *The Hero in Tradition and Folklore* (Folklore Society Mistletoe Series 19, 1984), 1–15
Hildburgh, W.L. 'Iconographical peculiarities in English medieval alabaster carvings', *Folk-Lore* 44 (1933) March, 32–56; June, 123–50
Hogarth, P., with Clery, V. *Dragons* (London, 1979)
Hole, C. *English Folk Heroes* (London, 1948)
——. *Saints in Folklore* (London, 1965)
Hoult, J. *Dragons, their History and Symbolism* (Glastonbury, 1987)
Hulst, C.S. *St George of Cappadocia in Legend and History* (London, 1909)
Lewis, S. *Reading Images. Narrative Discourse and Reception in the Thirteenth-Century Illuminated Apocalypse* (Cambridge, 1995)
Luxmore, H.E. *The Guild of St George* (London, 1925)
Marcus, G.J. *Saint George of England* (London, 1929)
Mode, H. *Fabulous Beasts and Demons* (London, 1975)
North, T. *A Chronicle of the Church of S Martin in Leicester during the Reigns of Henry VIII, Edward VI, Mary and Elizabeth* (London, 1866)
Ormrod, W.M. 'The Personal Religion of Edward III', *Speculum* 64 (1989), 849–77
Pegge, S. 'Observations on the History of St George . . .', *Archaeologia* 5 (1787), 1–32
Rowland, B. *Animals with Human Faces. A Guide to Animal Symbolism* (Knoxville, 1973)
Scribner, R.W. *For the Sake of Simple Folk: Popular Propaganda for the German Reformation* (Cambridge, 1981)
Setton, K.M. 'Saint George's Head', *Speculum* 48 no.1 (January 1973), 1–12
Seward, D. *Italy's Knights of St George – the Constantinian Order* (Gerrard's Cross, 1986)
Simpson, R. 'St George and the Pendragon" in R. Utz and T. Shippey (eds) *Medievalism in the Modern World* (Turnhout, 1998), 131–53
Stewart, R.J. *Where is St George?* (Bradford-on-Avon, 1977)
Wilson, T.H. 'Saint George in Tudor and Stuart England', Unpublished M.Phil dissertation, University of London (1976)

Given the huge number of extant images of the saint it is perhaps unsurprising that many of these publications are highly illustrated, although it should be observed that many authors use these images simply to decorate their work and do not make any real attempt to discuss the iconography of the cult. Even when writers have published specifically on visual images of St George there may be problems with completeness. For example, the most useful source of information on cycles of the legend of the saint is Klaus J. Dorsch, *Georgszyklen des Mittelalters*, Europäishe Hochschulschriften, 28 (Frankfurt-am-Main and New York, 1983), a PhD dissertation presented at the University of Erlangen-Nürnberg. The cycles, 102 in total, are organised chronologically, from a Passional at Stuttgart (dated to 1120–5) through to a decorated table at Colmar from the late seventeenth century, and a considerable amount of analysis of theme and narrative is presented. Despite this appearance of thoroughness, the author has contrived to omit at least four cycles in England and France, including the La Selle retable, the Bedford Hours roundels, and the woodwork at St George's Chapel, Windsor. A description of the Stamford cycle is included, but it is incomplete, with the first four subjects omitted.

Other important works on the visual material of the cult of St George are:

Fellows, J. 'On the iconography of a carving in King's College Chapel, Cambridge', *Journal of the Warburg and Courtauld Institutes* 39 (1976), 262

Gill, M.C. ' "Now help saynt George, oure ladye knyght . . . to strengthe our kyng and England ryght": rare scenes of St George in a wall painting in Astbury, Cheshire', *Lancashire and Cheshire Antiquarian Society* 91 (1995), 91–102

James, M.R. *The Sculptures in the Lady Chapel at Ely* (London, 1895)

——. *The Sculptured Bosses in the Cloisters of Norwich Cathedral* (Norwich, 1911)

——. *St George's Chapel, Windsor. The Woodwork of the Choir* (Windsor, 1933)

Kauffmann, C.M. 'The altar-piece of St George from Valencia', *Victoria and Albert Museum Yearbook* 2 (1970), 65–100

Lapeyre, A. 'Le Tympan de l'église du Heaulme (Seine-et-Oise) et la légende de Saint Georges', *Bulletin Monumental* 95 (1936), 317–32

Park, D. 'The "Lewes Group" of Wall Paintings in Sussex', *Anglo-Norman Studies* 6 (1984), 200–37

Riches, S.J.E. 'The lost St George cycle of St George's Church, Stamford: an examination of iconography and context' in *St George's Chapel, Windsor, in the late Middle Ages*, ed. C. Richmond and E. Scarff (Windsor, 2001), 135–50

—— 'The imagery of the Virgin Mary and St George in the Stalls of St George's Chapel, Windsor Castle' in *Windsor. Medieval Archaeology, Art and Architecture of the Thames Valley* (British Archaeological Association Conference Transactions XXV, 2002) ed. L. Keen and E. Scarff, 146–54

—— 'St George as a male virgin martyr' in Gender and Holiness: men, women and saints in late medieval Europe, ed. S.J.E. Riches and S. Salih (London, 2002), 65–85

Roosval, J. *Nya Sankt Gorans Studier* (Stockholm, 1924)

Rowe, B.J.H. 'Notes on the Clovis Miniature and the Bedford Portrait in the Bedford Book of Hours', *Journal of the Archaeological Association* 25 (1962), 56–65

Rushforth, G. McN. 'The Windows of the Church of St Neot, Cornwall', *Transactions of the Exeter Diocesan Architectural and Archaeological Society*, 3rd series, 4, part 3 (1937), 150–90

Studies of the literary versions of the life of St George are far fewer in number. The principal commentaries, both by J.E. Matzke, are: 'Contributions to the history of the legend of St George, with special reference to the sources of the French, German and Anglo-Saxon metrical versions', *Publications of the Modern Language Association of America* 17 (1902), 464–535; 18 (1903), 99–171; 'The legend of St George; its development into a Roman d'Aventure', *Publications of the Modern Language Association of America* 14 (1904), 449–78. However, the literary cycles discussed in this book, and summarised in Tables 1, 2 and 3 (pp. 218–21), are all published (although some are currently out of print):

(a) 'Saint George, martyr' in W.W. Skeat, *Ælfric's Lives of Saints* (Early English Text Society, Original Series 76, 1881), 307–19

(b) 'Saint George' in W. Granger Ryan (trans.), *The Golden Legend of Jacobus de Voragine* (Chichester,1993) volume I, 238–42

(c) 'George' in C. Horstmann, *The Early South English Legendary* (Early English Text Society, Original Series 87, 1887), 294–96. A second fragment that seems to be linked to the *South English Legendary* is published in R.E. Parker, 'A northern fragment of *The Life of St George*', *Modern Language Notes* 38 (1923), 97–101 (hence the appellations 'SELa' and 'SELb').

(d) 'George', in W.M. Metcalfe (ed.), *Legends of the Saints in the Scottish Dialect of the Fourteenth Century* (Scottish Text Society, 1891), 176–203

(e) 'The Legend of St George' in H.N. MacCracken (ed.), *The Minor Poems of John Lydgate* (Early English Text Society, Extra Series 107, 1910, reprinted 1962), 145–54

(f) 'De Festo Sancti Georgii, Martyris' in T. Erbe (ed.), *Mirk's Festial: a collection of homilies by John Mirk* (Early English Text Society, Extra Series 96, 1905), 132–5

(g) 'S. George' in E.H. Weatherly (ed.), *Speculum Sacerdotale* (Early English Text Society, Original Series 200, 1936), 129–33

The following three versions may be found in W. Nelson (ed.), *The Life of St George by Alexander Barclay* (Early English Text Society, Original Series 230, 1955):

(h) 'Georgius' by Baptista Spagnuoli 'the Mantuan'

(i) 'The life of St George' by Alexander Barclay

(j) 'The life of St George' from William Caxton (trans.), *The Golden Legend.*

Since this book was first published a modern edition of Richard Johnson's *The Most Famous History of the Seven Champions of Christendome* has appeared, ed. J. Fellowes (Aldershot, 2003),

PICTURE CREDITS

The author and publisher would like to thank the following for permission to reproduce illustrations. All efforts have been made to trace copyright. Any further information forwarded to the publisher will be included in any future edition:

Dr Jenny Alexander: 5.24; Alte Pinakothek, Munich/photo: AKG Photo: 4.9; © Artephot, Paris/photo A. Held: 1.4; © Artephot /Oronoz: 5.7; Author's collection: 1.3, 1.5, 2.6, 3. 22, 3.23, 4.7, 5.1, 5.6, 5.10 to 5.21, 5.23, 5.27, 5.29 ; St Bavo Cathedral, Ghent, Belgium/Bridgeman Art Library: 1.7; Steve Bell: 6.7; Bibliothèque Nationale, Paris, France/Bridgeman Art Library: 1.1; The Bodleian Library, University of Oxford: 4.2; By permission of the British Library: 2.8 to 2.14, 3.1 to 3.10, 4.15, 5.22, 6.5; British Library, London, UK/Bridgeman Art Library: 1.11; Castle Museum, Norwich: 4.17, 4.19; Sóren Brunn, The National Museum, Copenhagen: 3.11; The Governing Body of Christ Church, Oxford: 4.1; Cathedral, Clermont-Ferrand, France/Peter Willi/Bridgeman Art Library: 2.7; Conway Library, photo: Courtauld Institute of Art: 1.10, 4.12; Empics Ltd: 6.8; Dr Julian Eve: 4.11; Dr Duncan Givans: 1.9; Groeningemuseum, Bruges, Belgium: p. iii; 2.1; Groeningemuseum, Bruges, Belgium/Bridgeman Art Library: 4.16; Institut de France – Musée Jacquemart-André. Paris. France: 5.3; Kunsthistorisches Museum, Vienna, photo: AKG Photo/Erich Lessing: 5.28; Reproduced by permission of the Librarian, University of Leicester: page v, 5.26, 5.30; Liège Cathedral: 4.8; Phillip Lindley: 3.12, 3.13; Metropolitan Museum of Art, New York: 5.25; Musée Conde, Chantilly, France/Giraudon/Bridgeman Art Library: 5.4; Musées royaux d'Art et d'Histoire – Brussels: 2.5; © Museum of London: 4.13; National Gallery, London, UK/Bridgeman Art Library: 5.2; Newarke Houses Museum, Leicester: 5.9; Norfolk Museums Service: 4.18; © Crown Copyright. NMR: 3.14, 3.15; The Royal Collection © 2000, Her Majesty Queen Elizabeth II: neg. WC/SGC 1.5: 4.4; The Royal Collection © 2000, Her Majesty Queen Elizabeth II: RCIN 401228, OM 19 WC 2054: 4.6; © Salisbury & South Wiltshire Museum: 4.14; The Scout Association: 6.3, 6.4; The Shakespeare Birthplace Trust: 4.10; Société Nouvelle Adam Biro: 1.5; The Society of Antiquaries of London: 4.3, 5.5; Stadelsches Kunstinstitut, Frankfurt-am-Main, Germany/Bridgeman Art Library: 3.24; Sutton Publishing: 4.5; © Tate, London 2000: 6.2; The Master and Fellows of Trinity College Cambridge: TC classnumber VI.1.13: 5.31; © The Board of Trustees of the Victoria and Albert Museum: 1.2, 2.2, 2.3, 2.4, 5.8, 6.6; Victoria & Albert Museum, London, UK/Bridgeman Art Library: 6.1; By permission of the Dean and Canons of Windsor: 3.16 to 3.21.

INDEX